# BETWEEN THE HAMMER AND THE ANVIL? CHINESE AND RUSSIAN POLICIES IN OUTER MONGOLIA 1911-1921

Indiana University Uralic and Altaic Series
Volume 138

*Denis Sinor, Editor*

*Thomas E. Ewing*

# BETWEEN THE HAMMER AND THE ANVIL? CHINESE AND RUSSIAN POLICIES IN OUTER MONGOLIA 1911-1921

Research Institute for Inner Asian Studies
Indiana University, Bloomington
1980

ISBN No. 978-0-933070-06-6
Library of Congress Catalogue Number 80-52924

Other Volumes in the Uralic and Altaic Series

131. STUDIES IN FINNO-UGRIC LINGUISTICS IN HONOR OF ALO RAUN. Edited by Denis Sinor. Bloomington and Louvain, Edition Peeters, 1977, 440 pp., 2100.-FB., $70.

132. CHEREMIS LITERARY READER, WITH GLOSSARY, by Thomas A. Sebeok. Bloomington and Louvain, Edition Peeters, 1978, 120 pp. 500.-FB., $17.

133. THE POLITICAL ROLE OF MONGOL BUDDHISM, by Larry W. Moses. Bloomington, 1977, 299-x pp. 500.-FB., $14.95.

134. PROCEEDINGS OF THE EIGHTEENTH MEETING OF THE PERMANENT INTERNATIONAL ALTAISTIC CONFERENCE, BLOOMINGTON, JUNE 29-JULY 5, 1975. Edited by Larry V. Clark and Paul A. Draghi. Bloomington and Louvain, Edition Peeters, 1978, 212 pp. 1000.-FB., $34.

135. PRELIMINARY STUDIES IN TURKIC HISTORICAL PHONOLOGY by Vilhelm Grønbech, translated by John R. Krueger. Bloomington, 1979, 162 pp. $8.

136. THE STRUCTURE OF THE TURKIC LANGUAGES by Kaare Grønbech, translated by John R. Krueger. Bloomington, 1979, 188 pp. $8.

137. TANGUT (HSI HSIA) STUDIES: A BIBLIOGRAPHY, by Luc Kwanten and Susan Hesse. Bloomington, 1980, 125 pp. $8.

These volumes can be ordered in Europe from Edition Peeters, P.B. 41; B-3000 Leuven (Belgium), and in the United States from Uralic and Altaic Series, Research Institute for Inner Asian Studies, Goodbody Hall 101, Bloomington, Indiana 47405.

TO MY PARENTS

# PREFACE

The decade from 1911 to 1921 saw cataclysmic upheavals in the history of East Asia. The resistance of the Ch'ing and Romanov dynasties to the twin forces of nationalism and revolution was painfully futile. In both countries internal conflict--war-lordism in China and civil war in Russia--followed the collapse of the old orders. National interests came into collision with parochial concerns; an endless succession of sectarian wars, arising from either regional or political loyalties, resulted in appalling destruction; and many national minorities struck out boldly for independence. It was also in the latter years of this period, that is between 1917 and 1921, that both youthful regimes sought to take the full measure of the other--an awkward, often tiresome process which culminated finally in the Sino-Russian treaty of 1924.

For Outer Mongolia, the decade from 1911 to 1921 was surely the most crucial in its modern history. In 1911 the Mongols with Tsarist diplomatic support renounced two centuries of vassalage to China and declared their intention to create an independent, Westernized nation. Ten years later another group of Mongols, whose vision for Mongolia was similar in character if somewhat different in emphasis, established a revolutionary regime with the help of a Soviet expeditionary army. This state was in 1924 named the Mongolian People's Republic.

This book tells two stories. The first is the political maneuverings of Chinese and Russians over Mongolia during the closing years of the Tsarist and early years of the Soviet periods. Most Western and all Chinese historians, relying I think more on intuition than on analysis, have seen in the events of this decade the unfolding of a single, remorseless Russian strategy aimed at either dominating or absorbing Mongolia. Nor does the attachment of Communist historians, both Soviet and Mongolian, for spent clichés and Stalinist truths help us to understand the period.

A reexamination of this subject seems timely, not only because the ideas which have prevailed for so long need to be tested in a critical and nonpartisan way, but because a good deal of primary and secondary literature on this period in the Chinese, Russian, and Mongolian languages has become available since the 1960s. A careful study of this new scholarship, together with the valuable but relatively unused material published during the 1920s and early 1930s, reveals a rather different picture.

There is broad agreement among Western historians that territorial ambitions as well as anxiety over territorial security were two of the most important propelling forces behind both Tsarist and Soviet strategies in Asia. Published archival documents show beyond question that the Petersburg government supported Mongolian "autonomy" in 1911 wholly out of the conviction that a Mongolia under Russian tutelage was the surest, most economical, guarantee of Siberia's military security. Circumstantial evidence powerfully suggests that the Soviets supported Mongolian "autonomy" in 1921 for essentially the same reason.

But what is new, and what this book seeks to show, is that from 1917 to around February-March 1921 Russian policy toward Mongolia was indeed different from what it had been during the Tsarist era or what it was to be after 1921. It appears that the Soviets fully accepted China's claims to Mongolia and had no plans to recreate the kind of protectorate that the Tsarist government had succeeded in establishing over Mongolia. This policy was the product both of the high moral tone of early Bolshevik politics and, it must be stressed, of the indifference toward Mongolia of these Russians, who were after all absorbed in plotting world revolution. It was only after the invasion by von Ungern-Sternberg and the enormous threat this posed for the security of all Siberia that the Bolsheviks came to reapply Tsarist methods. Similar problems often invite similar solutions.

The second story which this book seeks to tell is the internal history of Mongolia between two revolutions, 1911 and 1921. It is a story which has never yet been adequately told, perhaps because of the inaccessibility of the sources and the difficulty of the languages in which they are written. But another equally important reason for this neglect by Western historians is the conviction, if expressed in its most extreme form, that the decisive political and economic events of this decade were determined principally by outside forces (that is, China and Russia). The need for studying the inner workings of Mongolian politics loses much of its urgency if such an argument is accepted, either explicitly or implicitly.

On the contrary, it is my belief that the decade cannot be properly understood without reference to the role and aspirations of the Mongols themselves. The Mongols, as the events of 1911 clearly showed, had discovered a new faith. It was a broader conception of national salvation than simply indepdence or Lamaist theocracy. It was a powerful vision of a twentieth-century nation-state governed by modern political, economic, and military institutions. This was the spirit that animated the revolutions of 1911 and 1921, indeed that shaped the character of the entire period.

This book differs from standard accounts not only in the interpretation of facts, but also in their presentation. Many names, dates, and figures have over the decades been used so selectively and carelessly that histories, be they Western or Communist, conflict often quite remarkably with one another in the kind of basic information which should have been corrected long ago. The question of dating is a useful case in point. During the period under discussion four different calendars were employed: the Gregorian, Julian, Mongolian lunar, and Chinese lunar. The Julian calendar, used by the Russians till early 1918, followed the Gregorian in this century by thirteen days; the Mongolian lunar usually agreed with or followed the Chinese lunar calendar by one day, but sometimes by as much as thirty. The problem is aggravated by the old practice of the Mongols to duplicate one or more days of the month if they were divined as "auspicious," or to omit them altogether if they were thought "inauspicious."

I have been able to correct most of these errors,

either by turning directly to the primary sources for the precise answers or, if this has been impossible, by deducing the probable answers based on my reading of the texts and knowledge of the period. In the interest of economy, however, I have avoided detailed explanations of the process by which any particular name, date, or figure was arrived at, except in those few instances when it is relevant to the general argument. I should also note that, again in the interest of economy, footnotes have been kept to the barest minimum. Specialists who are interested in such marginalia are advised to consult my dissertation. The transcription systems require little explanation, except to point out that I have followed the modern (Cyrillic) orthography currently used in the Mongolian People's Republic in preference to the old (Uighur) one. Thus, _khaghan_ (emperor) is spelled _khaan_, and _khan_ (king) remains unchanged.

And finally, I have the happy duty of recording my debts to the many people who have, in one way or the other, contributed to the successful completion of this book. To Prof. Denis Sinor, who first introduced me to Asian history and whose rare vision of Inner Asia has influenced so many young scholars in the field. To Owen Lattimore, who carefully read this manuscript in its earlier, dissertation form and suggested a number of valuable changes. To Charles Bawden, who very generously supplied me with items from his private library. I owe a great deal, moreover, to two well-known Inner Mongolian scholars: John Hangin, my _bagsh_ who taught me Mongolian, and Urgunge Onon, my friend and colleague at the University of Leeds. My thanks also to John Krueger, Larry Moses, and Philip West for reading the text of this book in its dissertation form and making many useful comments, and to Andrew Forbes and Philip Nugent for proof-reading the final manuscript. I also want to signal in a very special way the contributions of my wife Virginia, without whose counsel and support this book would probably not have been written at all.

But the greatest debt of all is owed to my parents, Col. Thomas P. Ewing and Evanelle Esson Ewing. It is to them that I dedicate this book.

Leeds

CONTENTS

# CHAPTER I

# OUTER MONGOLIA DURING THE CH'ING DYNASTY 1691-1911

By the early 1600s three potentially antagonistic forces were shaping up on the periphery of Khalkha Mongolia. To the east in Manchuria the Jurched, a Tungusic people who had once ruled part of north China under their dynastic name Chin, were growing to new power led by an energetic young nobleman, Nurhaci. At the other end of the continent small Cossack bands, attracted by the lure of adventure and wealth, began traversing northern Asia in the second half of the sixteenth century; in the course of their advance primitive forts were constructed at various strategic points along the way to ensure that the Russian presence was a durable one. And in the west, beyond the Altai mountains in the region known as Zungaria (northern Sinkiang), the Western Mongols (Oirats) were beginning to reassert themselves under the dynamic and visionary leadership of Baatar Khuntaij. It was the resolution of that conflict at the end of the seventeenth and middle of the eighteenth centuries which produced the basic political settlement of continental Asia until 1911.

## The Historical Setting

The years between 1368, when the Yuan dynasty collapsed and the Mongols were forced to retreat back into their ancestral lands, and 1600 in Khalkha had been far from uneventful. Wars with the Oirats and Chinese were punctuated by periods of relative calm, while the ascendancy of regional over national interests continued to prevail--indeed, it was integral to the customary pattern of Mongolian political life. Ligden Khan (1592-1634), ruler of the Chahars and the last titular king of all Mongolia, labored vigorously and ruthlessly to bring the various tribes (*aimag*) of Inner Mongolia under his unified rule. He met resistance, however, from these tribes which lacked Ligden's enthusiasm for centralization, and from the Manchus, who themselves had been courting the Inner Mongolians for several years. Ligden's efforts to subordinate the Inner Mongolians galvanized them into a union with the Manchus against the Chahars; Ligden was defeated by a Manchu army in 1632 and fled west with many of his subjects. He died two years later. The Inner Mongolian tribes were immediately reorganized into a banner system roughly similar to that which the Manchus had adopted for themselves. At an assembly in 1636, attended by the forty-nine princes of Inner Mongolia, fealty was sworn to the Manchu Emperor, who was declared to be the new khan of all Mongolia.

The capitulation of Inner Mongolia in 1636 and Korea in 1639 to the Manchus was an ominous warning for the future of Khalkha. The princes of northern Mongolia proceeded to maneuver evasively. On the one hand they sent an embassy to the Ch'ing court in Manchuria with the "Nine Whites" tribute (eight white horses and one white camel), and on the other sent representatives to an assembly in Zungaria called in 1640 by the Oirats to settle differences between the Eastern and Western Mongols in the face of the growing menace represented by the Manchus. Although the Khalkhas vainly sought some means to resist the Manchus, the pace of events was to exceed their capacity to deal with them. The overthrow of the Ming dynasty and the Manchu occupation of Peking in 1644, as well as a minor but politically decisive battle between a Ch'ing army and a combined force sent by the Tüsheet and Tsetsen Khans in 1646, demonstrated to the Mongols the futility of resistance. In 1655 the Khalkha princes agreed to send hostages to Peking, and in the winter of 1655-56 the Ch'ing Emperor reorganized Khalkha into eight banners. This was the first step in the eventual Ch'ing control of all Khalkha Mongolia.

Two succession struggles which occurred independently in the 1660s in Zungaria and the Zasagt Khan aimag were to have a profound impact on the history of both Eastern and Western Mongolia. The death of Baatar Khuntaij in 1665 had resulted in an internecine struggle during the next several years between his sons, who were dissatisfied with the inheritance arrangement. Eventually the youngest, Galdan, then studying in Lhasa under the Dalai Lama, returned and quickly consolidated his rule over Zungaria, extending it into other parts of Central Asia. Eastern Mongolia was the next object of Galdan's expansionist ambitions. The death of the Zasagt Khan Norov in 1661 and the resulting confusion presented Galdan with a pretext for invading Eastern Mongolia in 1688 and led directly to the Khalkha submission to the Manchus three years later.

The sequence of events is rather complicated, but, put briefly, after a succession struggle had broken out in the Zasagt Khan aimag following Norov's death, the Tüsheet Khan Chakhundorj intervened and installed his own candidate as khan. Friction soon developed, however, between the new Zasagt Khan who had fled to the Tüsheet Khan aimag during the troubled times earlier. This led to the intervention of Galdan, who stepped in on the side of the Zasagt Khan. Even the mediation of the Dalai Lama was without effect. Khalkha exploded in war when Chakhundorj led an army into the territory of the Zasagt Khan in 1687 and killed him. This provoked Galdan in the following year to invade Eastern Mongolia with an army of twenty to thirty thousand men, forcing Chakhundorj and the Jebtsundamba Khutukhtu Öndör Gegeen, along with other Khalkha princes and their subjects, to flee south into Inner Mongolia. Galdan now dominated Khalkha, and the Khalkhas were fugitives.

This extraordinary turn of events required careful deliberation, and a meeting of Khalkha princes was called on the Sino-Mongolian border to plot a course of action. Opinion among the princes and senior lamas was divided: some counseled an appeal for assistance to the Russians, while others recommended an approach to the Ch'ing government. Deadlocked, the assembly turned to Öndör Gegeen. The Khutukhtu is reported to have expressed himself in the following way:

> The Russians have never worshipped the Buddha, and their customs are not the same as ours; they are different in language and are different in clothing.

> This is really not a plan for ensuring a lasting peace. It is best that we all transfer (our allegiance) to China and submit to the Emperor. (Thus) we may find prosperity for ten thousand years.[1]

The assembly agreed. Emperor K'ang-hsi consented to the Mongolian request, less out of charity than an appreciation of the military threat to the frontier which Galdan could pose if allowed to continue his campaign unchecked.

In 1691 an assembly of Khalkha princes, headed by Öndör Gegeen and the Tüsheet and Tsetsen Khans, gathered at Dolonnor in Inner Mongolia to swear fealty to K'ang-hsi. The Emperor ordered the reorganization of Khalkha along feudal lines (just as had been done in Inner Mongolia previously) and added twenty-six more banners, making thirty-four in all (divided amongst three aimags). In a further move to bring the Khalkhas more in line with the Manchu system, some traditional Mongolian titles, such as khuntaij and jinon, were scrapped in favor of a new system of ranks: ch'in-wang, chün-wang, beile, beise, kung, and taij (four classes). And finally, the Jebtsundamba Khutukhtu was confirmed as the head of the Yellow Faith (Mongolian Lamaism).

With Ch'ing rule now unchallenged in China following the suppression of the Three Feudatories Rebellion in 1681, K'ang-hsi could devote more attention to Mongolia than had been possible before. Fortunately for the Manchus, Galdan's situation was exceptionally parlous: his troops were weakened by war; neither the Oirats in Zungaria nor those in Ch'ing-hai were willing to help him, and his approaches to the Russians, although received with interest, were finally rejected in favor of a more attractive offer from the Ch'ing government of a commercial treaty with China. In 1696 Galdan was decisively beaten by a Manchu army at Zuun mod, near present-day Ulan Bator; he died a year later.

It is not clear why the Mongols felt obliged to submit to the Ch'ing--or indeed whether they submitted at all. It must be remembered that we have only the authority of Chinese sources, which have naturally interpreted this event in the light of their own culture, to know how to define it. But if formal submission were the key to this arrangement, then the Khalkhas may have believed that only such an act would ensure Ch'ing intervention. This certainly was the pattern of Mongolian foreign relations during that and the following centuries. It is instructive that the Khalkha princes who in 1688 fled north, instead of south, declared to the Russians their readiness to submit--but these very princes who swore allegiance to the Tsar in 1688 promptly returned to Khalkha after peace had been restored, and just as promptly forgot their earlier pledge.[2]

Irrespective of the ceremonial trappings of the assembly at Dolonnor, the Mongols surely regarded this as a less complex arrangement than did the Manchus. As some historians have pointed out, the Mongols regarded the oath more as a treaty of friendship than as a binding act of loyalty or formal recognition of vassalage, and frequently accepted the oath in order to receive valuable presents from the tsars or in the hope of using Russian troops in their own domestic struggles.[3] This was a problem which continued to plague the relations of Russia and China with Mongolia right into the twentieth century. Although Russia and China had different diplomatic traditions, nonetheless both regarded the oath of allegiance as a solemn covenant out of which issued specific and binding responsibilities. The Mongols, on the other hand, perceived the oath in a distinctly pragmatic and tribal way; for them, such contracts were temporary and *ad hoc*, and in general practice were made only when military assistance was urgently required. The Mongols, therefore, regarded them as necessary and limited military alliances, while the other contracting party invariably claimed for them a broader and more political character. Military assistance was required urgently to repel Galdan, and the Mongols undoubtedly expected that, once they had returned to Khalkha, the pre-1688 situation would be restored unchanged. How could they have known that the Manchu grip, far from slackening, would endure for another two hundred years?

In 1636 Inner Mongolia and in 1691 Khalkha were brought within the orbit of China, but it would require another half-century to bring the Oirats to their knees. The Oirats continually disrupted the western frontier of the Ch'ing empire: their attempt to establish dominion over Tibet forced K'ang-hsi in 1719 to dispatch an army to expel them; and in 1732 and 1733 Oirat armies crossed the Altai into Khalkha, compelling the Ch'ing once again to muster a force against them. A succession struggle which broke out in Zungaria after 1745, however, brought relief to the frontier and was the beginning of the collapse of the Zungar state. The reigns of the next three khans were brief and violent; it was only when a certain Davaach, with the help of his ally Amursanaa, was able to seize the throne that Oirat troubles temporarily eased.

The Ch'ing government was following these events with keen interest. Since Ming times the Oirats, ensconced in the Zungarian depression in the distant northwestern frontier and sheltered by an imposing barricade of mountains and deserts, had been at liberty to range over the frontier from Tibet to the borders of Manchuria. The risks of sending an army against them were enormous, while the costs of maintaining a vigilant frontier defense were prohibitive. But this opportunity could not be missed. Emperor Ch'ien-lung immediately set about constructing a string of forts stretching from Hami in northern Sinkiang to Khara us in the northwestern part of Mongolia near the Russian border; a census of ablebodied men in Khalkha Mongolia was taken to prepare for conscription; and in 1753 the Ch'ing government began moving its troops closer to the frontier. Ch'ien-lung's foresight was rewarded when Amursanaa went over to the Ch'ing side after breaking with Davaach. A mobilization order was hurriedly issued in Khalkha, and in 1755 a combined force of Khalkhas, Inner Mongolians, Manchus, and Chinese invaded Zungaria from the east and south. Davaach was quickly overwhelmed, and Zungaria was reorganized into four khanates; Amursanaa was appointed one of the khans. But either out of caprice or for reasons of strategy Amursanaa soon turned against the Manchus, gathered an army, and declared himself ruler of all Zungaria. Determined to have done once and for all with these Oirats, Ch'ien-lung dispatched another army in 1756 and firmly put down the rebellion. Amursanaa fled to Russia, where he died in 1757.

Khalkha was not insulated from the rebellion in Zungaria. The Ch'ing court's insensitive treatment of the Khalkha nobility and a general weariness with the Ch'ing-Oirat war, the expenses of which were to a great extent borne by the Khalkha population, led to widespread disenchantment with the Manchus. One prince, Chingunjav, raised the standard of rebellion in 1756, while at the same time five Khalkha leaders, including the second Jebtsundamba Khutukhtu and the Tüsheet Khan, perhaps in the hope of Russian intervention turned to the commandant of Selenginsk with a request that they become subjects of Russia. It was too late. In January 1757 Chingunjav's revolt was suppressed by Ch'ing troops, and in the following year the Khutukhtu, the Tüsheet Khan, and the Commander of the Tüsheet Khan aimag all died under peculiar circumstances--probably assassinated at the orders of Ch'ien-lung.

## The Administrative and Social Organization of Mongolia

The administrative system devised by the Manchus was responsible in great measure for the long and relatively successful Ch'ing rule over Mongolia. This system was the product of evolutionary growth spanning the reigns of three emperors from the late seventeenth to the mid-eighteenth centuries; the changes in the Mongolian political and social organization imposed by the Manchus at Dolonnor in 1691 were only the first in a series of modifications that were ordered in response to special problems. Schematically the Ch'ing administrative system in Mongolia resembled a pyramid, the upper section of which was represented by the Ch'ing bureaucratic apparatus headed by the emperor and staffed with Manchus, Chinese, and Mongols. Many of its institutions, such as the imperial viceroys and the Bureau of Dependencies (*Li-fan yuan*), were totally unfamiliar to the Mongols. The lower part of the pyramid was represented by the Mongolian apparatus, which was responsible for the day-to-day management of local affairs and was staffed exclusively with Mongols. These institutions, such as the banners and leagues, were already well known in Mongolian institutional history.

It was this division which made the system such a practical instrument of government. Ch'ing officials, who were primarily responsible for ensuring the smooth and proper operation of the system, seldom interfered in local affairs; the Mongolian herdsman continued to be governed by his hereditary prince and was rarely affected by the presence of Manchu representatives in his country. Ultimately the success of the entire system turned on the principle of autonomy. Two hundred years later, when the Ch'ing abandoned this principle, there was revolution.

The Bureau of Dependencies in Peking was the most important agency for the management of the affairs of the entire northern and western frontier (including relations with China's new and unwelcome neighbor, Russia). Immediately under the Bureau of Dependencies were the resident officials (amban) in Outer Mongolia: the Uliastai military governor (in theory the senior Ch'ing official in Mongolia), set up in 1732 in connection with the Zungar wars, was responsible for the affairs of the two western aimags (Zasagt Khan and Sain Noyon Khan); the Urga viceroy, organized in 1762, was responsible for the two eastern aimags (Tüsheet Khan and Tsetsen Khan), as well as the Sino-Russian frontier, commercial and other affairs; and the Khovd deputy military governor, formally established in 1762, was in charge of the Oirat tribes residing in the Khovd region.

If the ordinary Mongol seldom came into contact with the ambans or their assistants, his life was profoundly influenced by the league, banner, and sumun administrations. Because the native administrators were a vital bridge between the Ch'ing state and the Mongolian population and were the main executors of Ch'ing policy, an elaborate set of regulations evolved over the years to define their powers and guide their activities.

By the time the reorganization of Outer Mongolia was completed, that is, by the end of the eighteenth century, the country was divided into two regions: Khalkha Mongolia and the Khovd region. The Khalkhas, who today account for 75% of the entire population of the Mongolian People's Republic, were divided into four aimags and eighty-six banners. The Khovd region was inhabited by Oirats (comprising today 6.4% of the population)--Dörvöd (the largest), Bait, Torguud, Ööld, Mingat, Zakhchin--

divided among nineteen banners. The largest territorial-administrative unit was the league (league and aimag boundaries were coterminous, the league being only an official designation for an aimag), headed by a league chairman, who together with his staff supervised the activities of all the banners within his area. Despite the formal authority of the league government, however, the banner was in fact the most important administrative unit in Mongolia. The banner system itself was conceived by Nurhaci, who sought to replace traditional Jurched loyalty to the tribe with loyalty to a centralized state. To this end he organized banners out of several different tribes and made them both civil and military units which regulated the entire life of their members. When the Manchus introduced the system to the Mongols they were not concerned about breaking down tribal loyalty (as evidenced by their willingness to follow traditional tribal boundaries when demarcating the new banners in Inner Mongolia for example): the banner system was a practical form of government for a nomadic people with a feudal social structure, and its military character enabled the Manchus to draw levies quickly. The banners were divided into sumun, which functioned essentially as military units and were in theory composed of a hundred fifty men and their families. These banners were ruled by hereditary princes, who were assisted by various rotating officials.

Under the Manchus there were no fundamental changes in the Mongolian social system; indeed, the Manchus sought to buttress and crystallize social stratification by lifting it out of the opaque world of customary law into the realm of written statutes. The Manchus were the champions of the status quo, both in Mongolia and in China. They produced an elaborate feudal code (the similarities to European feudalism are close enough to warrant, in my opinion, the use of the term "feudal") which bound the ruling princes to the emperor, and the banner subjects to their princes. As one historian has noted, the "crown and key" of the Manchus' Mongolian policy lay in the success which they had in establishing a personal relationship with every noble in the country.[4] The emperor dispensed titles, ranks, fiefs, and stipends; conversely, he could expropriate, demote, imprison, and execute. The Mongolian aristocracy inevitably came to identify their own fortunes with those of the dynasty. In the final analysis this was the most powerful link of all. The non-ruling nobles (that is, aristocrats who did not govern banners), generally speaking, were treated with a certain benign indifference by the Ch'ing government. Instead, it was the ruling nobles (banner princes) who were the objects of Manchu interest--sometimes affectionate, sometimes implacable, but never impassive. Descended from Chinggis Khan, they claimed to be the lawful and hereditary rulers of Mongolian society, and the Ch'ing did all it could to reinforce this claim. Ultimately, the success of Manchu rule hinged on the support which it could draw from the princes, and the institutional history of the Ch'ing administration of Mongolia testifies to how profoundly the Manchus understood this.

The system in its maturity was a curious amalgam of the classic ingredients of feudalism--service and privilege--and of the tributary system familiar to students of Chinese foreign relations. Mongolian princes ruled by hereditary succession, which required confirmation from the emperor. In return for this confirmation the princes were expected to perform a variety of duties, including attendance at the court in Peking on a rotating basis (the _nien-pan_), providing military assistance when required, and rendering tribute to the emperor. The Ch'ing government paid each banner prince an annual salary, which was a particularly important source of their income; its suspension during the late Ch'ing created a great deal of discontent among them.

The male non-noble population may be divided roughly into three social categories: state arats, whose labor service (such as serving on the postal relays, the frontier pickets or in the military, and tending the imperial herds) was owed to the banners (that is, to the state); the khamjlaga, who were bound for life either to ruling or non-ruling nobles, performed a variety of personal services for them and their families (the shav' nar, or church serfs, were the equivalent of the khamjlaga and owed precisely the same services to the khutukhtus and monasteries); and the lamas.

No discussion of the Ch'ing period is complete

without an analysis of the material extension of Mongolian Buddhism--Lamaist ecclesiasticism. The Lamaist church was the most powerful and cohesive institution in Mongolia, possessing enormous wealth and representing an ideology to which the entire population subscribed. It was fragmented into hundreds of monastic communities, varying greatly in size, most of which were subject to nineteen senior church princes (the "seal-bearing" khutukhtus) or to other lesser reincarnations who were merely local figures and not registered in Peking. The most prominent of the senior khutukhtus was, of course, the Jebtsundamba Khutukhtu of Urga. Although commonly referred to as the patriarch of the Buddhist church in Mongolia by Western writers, his authority was based on consent rather than on canonical authority, and it was by vastly eclipsing the other khutukhtus in wealth, subjects, and religious prestige that he was able to enforce, to an extent, his will over the rest of the church. The aggregate human and material wealth of the Urga Khutukhtu was called the Ikh Shav' ("Great Disciple"), administered by the Shav' Yamen under an erdene shanzudba. At its peak in the mid-nineteenth century the Ikh Shav' included over a hundred thousand persons, over a hundred monasteries, and several hundred monastic herds (_jas_).

Predictably, the Ch'ing government was sensitive to the importance of the Lamaist church and to the obedience it commanded among all Mongolian and Tibetan Buddhists. In the same way as the Manchus courted the lay aristocracy, they ingratiated themselves with the ecclesiastical leadership by extending many courtesies and privileges and favoring the church with a variety of endowments, particularly for the translation of Tibetan scriptural texts and the construction of monasteries. By promoting the physical growth of the church and enlarging the influence of its leaders, however, the Ch'ing government was creating its own Frankenstein monster which someday might be powerful enough to defy China. After a time, therefore, the Manchus sought to regulate the church by a variety of measures, such as discouraging the growth of the number of lamas, encouraging the structural devolution of the church through the development of regional primates (the Dalai Lama and Panchen Lama in Tibet, the

Jebtsundamba Khutukhtu in Outer Mongolia, and the Janjya Khutukhtu in Inner Mongolia, for example), and supporting the autonomy of local khutukhtus and monasteries against the authority of those primates. Surely the most famous example of this policy was the imperial edict of 1761 which directed that all future Jebtsundamba Khutukhtus be discovered in Tibet, thereby severing their political and family ties with important aristocratic families in Mongolia and preventing the creation of a powerful theocracy (as happened with the first two khutukhtus of Urga).

The Mongolian policy of the Manchus was not based on any blueprint, but evolved out of the changing conditions in both Mongolia and China and the limited resources available to the Ch'ing government. The Manchus ruled an immense and diverse empire, and if they lacked the manpower to oversee it all, they could at least keep fingers pressed on its several pulses--in the case of Mongolia this meant the Jebtsundamba Khutukhtu and the banner princes. Ch'ing officials maintained an inconspicuous presence, intervening rarely in Mongolian affairs and then only to make relatively minor adjustments. They sought to ensure that power was distributed evenly between the two major spheres of Mongolian society, the secular and ecclesiastical, and to achieve this they occasionally created new, artificial institutions or modified existing ones in order to maintain the political balance. This was very effective in neutralizing the ruling strata of the Mongols. Toward the rest of Mongolian society the Manchus adopted a *laissez-faire* attitude.

## Breakdown of the Ch'ing Order in Mongolia

By the mid-eighteenth century the Ch'ing administrative system with its elaborate organization of checks and balances was for the most part perfected, and for the next hundred years there was peace in Mongolia. By the middle of the nineteenth century, however, the Ch'ing began experiencing enormous political and financial presures: there was humiliation and defeat at the hands of the British and the French, and the Taiping

Rebellion, which broke out in 1850 and continued into the following decade, threw China into a massive convulsion. These events hastened the disintegration of the central government and underlined the urgency of modernization in the face of Western intrusion and domestic rebellion. By the year 1900 a vast range of abuses, which had accumulated over many decades and especially in the latter part of the nineteenth century, and which the Ch'ing government was powerless to curb, was radically to disturb the social balance of the Mongols and to alter the nature of privilege and service among the classes.

The nineteenth century saw a general deterioration in the quality of Ch'ing administrators, especially those appointed to manage frontier affairs. As the Ch'ing became less careful in its selection and supervision of its frontier officials, corruption not surprisingly had unprecedented opportunities to flourish. Just as administrative posts were being sold throughout the empire to relieve the desperate financial condition of the government, Ch'ing offices in Mongolia, especially that of the Urga viceroy, were being sold for large sums of money; their occupants however could expect to extort even larger amounts during their period of service. The Russian traveller Przheval'skii noted that bribery and graft had developed to such an extreme degree that with it everything was possible, but without it nothing.[5]

As Mongolian princes found themselves squeezed by Ch'ing officials, they were also hurt by the austerity measures of the Peking government. Loss of tax revenue resulting from the economic dislocation of the Taiping and Nien Rebellions in the interior of China, as well as the tremendous expenses required for their repression, exhausted the Ch'ing treasury and obliged it to cease paying salaries to the banner princes. The chronic indigence of the Ch'ing government, aggravated by the "silver drain," led the Manchus to seek additional revenue, and beginning toward the end of the nineteenth century Mongolian banners were increasingly being taxed in silver rather than in kind as had been the custom. Since the Mongolian economy was based on barter and not on money, the Mongols had to turn to Chinese moneylenders, from whom they borrowed silver at burdensome rates of interest.

One could continue almost indefinitely cataloguing the grievances of the Mongols, but arguably the single most important catalyst of discontent was Chinese commerce, or more precisely the usurious credit system that lubricated it. The penetration of Chinese merchants into Mongolia during the early Ch'ing was to have an immense impact on Mongolia, not only economically but socially and politically. Chinese, and to a lesser extent Russian, commerce bore a heavy responsibility for the impoverishment of Mongolia and eventually created tremendous disruptions in Mongolian society during the second half of the nineteenth and the early twentieth centuries. The Mongolian economy was a natural economy, in which the Mongols traded the products of their livestock-raising, such as meat, lard, wool, hair (horse, camel, and sarlyk), hides, and animals on the hoof, for Chinese goods, in particular green (brick) tea, textiles, processed hides, and metalware. Even into the twentieth century the overwhelming bulk of the trade was conducted by barter.

The unfortunate although unavoidable consequence of the natural economy of the Mongols was the widespread credit system. Because of the seasonal character of pastoralism, which limits the productive part of the year--lambing, sheepshearing, livestock-fattening--to the months from spring to autumn, domestic articles required at other times had to be purchased from the Chinese on credit. As European travellers unanimously testified, credit purchasing led to a number of abuses in these transactions, especially the imposition of crippling interest rates. On top of the private obligations of the herdsmen were the "official debts" of the banners, which according to 1917-19 estimates amounted to something between eleven million and thirty million taels.[6] These debts were generally incurred by the banner princes, whose financial needs were almost insatiable. Monumental sums were required for such things as periodic trips to Peking and bribes to Ch'ing officials, money which was obtained from Chinese banking firms. Mongolia was held in economic bondage to the Chinese.

Growing debts, diminishing number of livestock, and rising Ch'ing taxation inevitably led to the impoverishment of the country. In recent years Mongolian historians have been publishing archival documents, primarily appeals from league chairmen and banner princes to Ch'ing representatives, which attest to the extreme poverty throughout the country. Many Westerners in the late nineteenth century were also struck by the horrible destitution which they saw in Mongolia. James Gilmour wrote that "one of the saddest pictures to be seen anywhere is in the market place of Urga, where human beings lie night and day on the stony ground, covered with a few scraps of filthy skins and cast-off felts." Przheval'skii also remarked on the crowds of hungry beggars swarming in the marketplace, and Piassetsky was appalled by the number of Mongols dressed in rags living between Urga and Kyakhta.[7] The growth of the number of beggars reflected a general breakdown in the social order; people were increasingly fleeing their banners, in spite of attempts by banner authorities to apprehend them, for the illusory havens of the towns and monastic settlements.

Mongolian dissatisfaction with the Manchus, which had lain dormant since the mid-1700s, rose to the surface and occasionally flared up in different parts of the country during the second half of the nineteenth century. With increasing frequency arats were organizing into groups (_duguilan_) and submitting petitions of grievances to their banner or, failing satisfaction, league governments. These petitions generally expressed a whole range of complaints, including protests against certain banner taxes, exactions of princes, and frauds of Chinese merchants; the mix of these elements depended on local conditions, although protests against princes shifting their private debts on to the banner populations were a feature common to almost all of them. While it would be too much to infer, at least from the material published so far, that the system of hereditary rule was under attack, these incidents do reflect an increasing dissatisfaction with individual banner princes. Foreign observers certainly remarked on the tyranny of banner rulers, and the remark made by a clerk of

Amur Bayasqulantu monastery to one Russian traveller at the end of the nineteenth century, that the people were becoming discontented with their own princes, suggests that at least a part of the native bureaucracy was beginning to generalize about their behavior.[8] It is surely a modest step from this sort of criticism to a more fundamental questioning of the entire autocratic system. It is important to note, moreover, that men such as Bodoo, Danzan, Sükhbaatar and others who were to play vital roles during the 1921 revolution came from this very bureaucracy.

There were other more palpable symptoms of eroding Manchu influence in Mongolia and of the very collapse of Ch'ing authority. When the Chinese Muslims (Dungans) invaded western Mongolia in the late 1860s, many banners refused to supply Ch'ing troops with foodstuffs or deliver their quota of banner troops, and many of those Mongolian soldiers who were called up for service, soon thinking better of it, returned home. Troops which had been assembled in Urga to await the expected Dungan assault were so unreliable that the Russians had to stiffen the defenses with six hundred of their own Cossacks. Mutinies and riots began occurring with alarming regularity: in 1880 there was an insurrection of Mongolian troops at Uliastai; in 1881 about three or four hundred Mongols (lay and lamas) beat up some Chinese merchants; in 1887 a group of Ch'ing soldiers in Urga was attacked; in 1900 there was another mutiny of Mongolian troops at Uliastai; in 1905 several Chinese shops in Urga were destroyed; in 1907 more Ch'ing troops were assaulted in Urga.

## Russian Relations with Mongolia

During the eastward advance of the Russians and in their search for routes to China, they encountered the Mongols, with whom animated diplomatic and commercial exchanges were maintained throughout most of the seventeenth century. The first Russian mission to contact the Mongols, sent in 1616, visited the Altyn khanate in the northwestern part of the Mongolian People's Republic and the Tuva A.S.S.R. of the Soviet Union; the Russians next made contact with the Oirats, with whom Russian contacts were far more frequent and regular, especially during the reign of Baatar Khuntaij (nine missions were sent to the Oirats during the years 1636 and 1652 alone); and in 1647 the first mission was sent to Khalkha, although its envoys were denied an audience with the Tsetsen Khan because of their refusal to kneel at the sight of his yurt.

Relations were on the whole, however, inconclusive and occasionally hostile. The question of the oath of allegiance to the tsar, which Russian emissaries were invariably instructed to obtain in return for military protection, stipends, and unrestricted trading rights in Siberia, frequently complicated the diplomatic atmosphere. The Mongols, and the Altyn khans in particular, occasionally agreed to or even suggested accepting Russian suzerainty when threatened with military invasion from one of their neighbors; but their interest invariably cooled once the threat had passed (apparently only the Altyn Khan Ombo Erdene in the 1630s actually did swear fealty to the Tsar). More vexatious was the question of Mongolian subjects who had nomadized into Russia. Both their former Mongolian princes and the Russian administrative authorities in Siberia claimed them as subjects and continued to exact fur tribute from them; armed clashes between Mongols and Russians over this problem were not rare. During the second half of the seventeenth century relations between the Mongols and Russia were particularly abrasive. The Khalkhas became increasingly apprehensive about the growing Russian strength in the Transbaikal region, and tensions culminated in a series of border clashes, especially during the 1680s; the Altyn khanate also disturbed the peace of the Siberian frontier by its repeated raids on Russian settlements. With the invasion of Galdan Khan in 1688, the flight of Khalkhas south and their submission to the Ch'ing, and the Sino-Russian treaty at Nerchinsk in 1689 and later at Kyakhta in 1727, the Russians quickly lost interest in the Mongols. There was little further contact between the two for another century and a half.

Despite occasional problems in relations between Russia and China, the treaties of Nerchinsk and Kyakhta inaugurated a period of peace and laid the basis for the growth of a mutually profitable trading activity centering at Kyakhta; but beyond this, there was little communication between the two governments. During the mid-nineteenth century, however, at a time when the Ch'ing was so totally absorbed in its own internal troubles, the Russians began showing new signs of life on the northern frontier. From this time onward the Russian presence in the north would become a central element in the Ch'ing frontier strategy. This was also a formative period in Russo-Mongolian relations when the basic pattern of Russian interests and policies was established for the next century.

In the 1850s the young governor of Tula, Nikolai Muraviev, dispatched several expeditions down the Amur river which were to result in the annexation of that region. The Sino-Russian treaties of Aigun and Tientsin in 1858 and Peking in 1860 established Russian dominion over the Amur, Priamur, and Ussuri regions, and a large tract of Central Asia--these agreements, which vastly enlarged Russia's empire in Asia, continue to irritate Sino-Soviet relations to this day. But Muraviev's vision extended beyond the regions of northeastern Asia to Mongolia as well. During the 1850s it seemed to many European and Chinese observers that the Taipings would as surely overthrow the Ch'ing dynasty as peasant rebellions had destroyed so many dynasties in China's past. In 1854 Muraviev proposed to his government that, in this event, there was no reason why Russia should permit China's next government to reassert its control over Mongolia. Muraviev's proposal generated the first serious discussion of a Russian policy toward Mongolia, and the principles set down between 1854 and 1862 remained unchanged until well into the twentieth century.

In 1854 a Special Committee reviewed Muraviev's suggestion but resolved on a more moderate course: "The plan of action of the Russian government with respect to Mongolia, where the aspiration to separate from China has already been observed, must consist in maintaining peaceful and the most friendly relations with the Mongols and by all means (excluding force) in trying to subordinate them to our rule."[9] The Amur Committee again took up the question in 1861 and in the presence of the Tsar came to the following conclusion:

> ...in the opinion of the Committee any unnecessary participation in this matter, and in particular the placing of these two provinces (Manchuria and Mongolia) under our protection, will on the contrary arouse the opposition of the European powers and could force them moreover to occupy any part of China, Korea for example, and thereby put us in contact witha neighbor far more dangerous than the territory of China.

This, incidentally, is one of the clearest statements of an important historical constraint which inhibited Russia's freedom of action in Mongolia: the concern for Western reaction. In 1862 the Amur Committee issued a second and final declaration on Mongolia which has been the spirit of Russian policy ever since:

> The political and commercial interests of Russia, even the security of our extensive land frontier, compel us to hope that these regions will return to their former independence...in the event of the fall of the Empire of the Manchus our activities must be so aimed as to enable the formation of an independent domain (*vladenie*) in Mongolia and Manchuria.

In short, the Tsarist government desired the full restoration of Mongolian independence provided that it occurred naturally, that is, as a consequence of the overthrow of the Ch'ing dynasty. Mongolia was of considerable geopolitical importance to Russia, sharing a border stretching about seventeen hundred miles. The security of the Russian Far East required that Mongolia be independent--the reality of independence was more important than its form--of any potentially hostile power, Chinese or European. On the other hand, the Russians worked tirelessly to prevent the Mongols from declaring formal independence from China. There was intense competition among

Western powers for commercial or political advantages in China; reverberations from an attempt by one to secure special privileges in China not shared by the other powers would be felt in every major capital of the West. As long as Russia continued to regard itself as part of the European community, it had to act with restraint. The Russians recognized, moreover, that a certain amount of good will with China was important: the two countries shared an extensive border, and China was one of Russia's most important trading partners; there was also the problem of Manchuria, a delicate and often contentious issue in Sino-Russian relations. Thus, while the Russians were prepared to encourage Mongolian claims of autonomy, as they did during the early part of the twentieth century, they could support the Mongols in a bid for complete and formal independence only by irreparably damaging their relations with China. This the Russians would not do.

Although the Russian government was loath to intervene politically or militarily in Mongolia, it was nevertheless eager to establish wide commercial privileges in the country. Beginning with the Treaty of Peking in 1861 a series of agreements were signed, steadily enlarging Russia's commercial rights in Mongolia and culminating in the Sino-Russian Treaty of 1881, which permitted unrestricted Russian trade and movement throughout Mongolia. Following the Chinese pattern Russian firms were located in the major urban centers and traded both in the towns and in the steppe, supplying their agents (many of whom were Chinese peddlers) who lived and worked in the countryside. The dramatic growth of Russian industry in the 1880s, however, which created an enormous appetite for raw materials of all kinds, and the opening of the Trans-Siberian Railroad in the 1890s, which made factories in European Russia accessible for the first time, shaped the special character of Russian commerce in Mongolia. It was now more profitable for Russian merchants to purchase Mongolian livestock and livestock products with ready silver and then ship them west. The cumbersome barter trade was consequently abandoned. But even by 1911 the proportions of Russian commerce in Outer Mongolia and the number of its citizens remained modest in comparison with the Chinese: trade fluctuated between eight and ten million rubles per year, and there were probably around only eight hundred Russians in the entire country.[10]

Russian political interest in Mongolia faded after the policy debate in the Petersburg government between 1854 and 1862. Indeed, the tide of Tsarist activity in the Far East ebbed measurably following the suppression of the Taipings and the demonstration that the Manchus were once again securely in the saddle, and for the next quarter of a century the recently acquired eastern domains of Russia were virtually ignored. During the 1880s, however, new political and economic forces emerged in Russia calling for more positive action in East Asia: the Vostochniki ("Easterners") were championing an ideology of eastward expansion; the opening of a sea link with the Pacific seaboard in the 1880s gave a modest boost to the colonization of the Amur region; and in 1891 construction work began on the Trans-Siberian Railroad, which would connect Russia with the Chinese market. The defeat of China in the war with Japan in 1895 and the subsequent retrocession of Liaotung penninsula generated a new purposefulness and energy in Russia's eastern policies. The Russo-Chinese Bank (later the Russo-Asiatic Bank) was formed to promote Russian economic enterprises in China, and in 1896 this bank, which unknown to the Chinese was operating under the direction of the Russian Ministry of Internal Affairs, won a concession to construct a railroad (the Chinese Eastern Railway) across Manchuria. Northern Manchuria was now virtually under a Russian administration. With the acquisition in 1898 of another concession for a railway line south into Liaotung and the introduction of Russian armed forces into Manchuria in 1900 at the time of the Boxer Rebellion, the occupation seemed complete.

But the Russians had overreached themselves. Japan, already embittered by the forced retrocession of Liaotung, to which Russia had been a party, and by Russia's seizure of Liaotung, was even more alarmed by what appeared to be a permanent military presence in Manchuria. War broke out in 1904, ending in Russia's defeat and the transferrence of its leased territory in southern Manchuria to Japan. The Japanese victory did bring an unexpected benefit to

Russia. Between 1907 and 1916 four treaties were signed with Japan defining their respective spheres of interest: Russia recognized Japan's special interests in southern Manchuria and Korea, while northern Manchuria and Mongolia were recognized as the special interests of Russia.

The conventional wisdom, that Russia, deflected from its imperialistic drive into Manchuria by the war with Japan, rechannelled its energies into Mongolia, is not supported by the facts. Russian interest in Mongolia, far from beginning suddenly in 1905, had been growing steadily since the last decade of the nineteenth century. The Russians viewed Mongolia and Manchuria as a single territorial unit over which they wanted to establish a protectorate. In 1897 they sought China's agreement to exclusive railroad construction, mining, and other rights in both Manchuria and Mongolia; in 1899 the Scott-Muraviev agreement recognized the Yangtze as England's sphere of influence, while the territory north of the Great Wall fell to Russia. In that same year China agreed to an exclusive Sino-Russian condominium over railroad construction in the northern region. And in 1903, when the "seven demands" which would have ensured predominant Russian influence in Manchuria were presented to China, an eighth demand, withdrawn at the last minute for unknown reasons, called for the retention of the present form of administration in Mongolia.

For several decades before the war with Japan, therefore, the Russians had tried, albeit with some diffidence, to secure world recognition that Mongolia lay within their own sphere of influence. It must be emphasized, however, that distortion inevitably comes with magnification, and that by focusing on Russia's activities in Mongolia there is the danger of exaggerating their proportions. Russian diplomatic activity regarding Mongolia in fact was almost invariably linked with, and very subordinate to, its interests in Manchuria. Indeed, Mongolia was relatively ignored throughout this period, at least until 1911. To be sure, a few expeditions financed either by the government or by private organizations were dispatched to Mongolia, but this hardly compares with the diverse projects feverishly pursued by Russia in Manchuria and other parts of Asia.

Although there is no milestone to be found which marks a new appreciation by the Petersburg government of Mongolia's importance to Russia, certainly after 1905 the Russians did begin showing a very modest growth of interest in the country. This appears to have been primarily the result of increased Chinese activity there, growing Mongolian discontent with Ch'ing frontier policies (a point regularly stressed by Russian pamphleteers), and the defeat by Japan in 1905, which alerted many Russians to the "Yellow Peril" and the vulnerability of their Far Eastern interests. During the decade before 1911 the Russian state was represented, rather ineffectively, by only two semi-official agencies in Mongolia: the first was the Russo-Chinese Bank, which opened branches in Urga and Uliastai in 1900 but was forced to close down a few years later because of the unprofitability of its operations; the second and perhaps better known was the joint-stock gold mining company, Mongolor, which was formed in 1900 but did not actually begin operating until 1906. The Russian government was also making modest efforts to acquire more precise and reliable information about the Mongolian market, and several individuals and commercial expeditions visited the country and published valuable information on the economic and social conditions there.

## The Mongolian Revolution of 1911

Political developments in China during the first decade of the twentieth century were to have a profound importance for Mongolia. The growing internal reform movement generated by China's humiliating defeat in 1895 at the hands of its former tributary, Japan, and in particular by Japan's victory over Russia in 1904-05 made a special impression on the Chinese and stimulated a great deal of self-analysis and debate among Chinese intellectuals, who sought an explanation for Japan's achievements (and conversely, for China's failures). The answer favored by most was that Japan, unlike China and Russia, had successfully reconstructed itself into a constitutional monarchy and that if the Chinese were to be masters of their own fate, a constitutional form of government was vital. Beginning from 1901 a host of reforms, collectively referred to as the New

Administration (*Hsin-cheng*), were introduced; in 1906 the court was induced to order the reorganization of the central government and in 1908 a nine-year program of preparation for constitutional government was ordered.

Hand in hand with the internal stocktaking, the Ch'ing government was also in the process of redefining its frontier policy. Unlike the Western powers, which were essentially interested in wringing commercial concessions from China, the Russians and Japanese were preoccupied with territorial acquisitions or regional domination and were therefore far more dangerous. If the entire northern frontier were not to be lost, the traditional Ch'ing policy of exclusion had to be abandoned in favor of a more aggressive effort to tie this region firmly to the center. Between 1901 and 1910 the old proscriptions dating back to the seventeenth century which had been the backbone of its policy of exclusion were officially abolished: intermarriage between Manchus, Chinese, and Mongols was permitted; Manchuria and Mongolia were opened to large-scale colonization; Chinese were permitted to bring their families into the frontier; the government considered dividing Mongolia into a number of provinces; the prohibition against Mongols using the Chinese language was lifted; and officials were sent to Mongolia to conduct various surveys.

The new Ministry of Dependencies, replacing in 1906 the Bureau of Dependencies, organized two agencies to investigate such matters as land reclamation, mining, timber and fishing, and education in Mongolia. It was decided that the planned reforms should be implemented gradually and that the costs were to be shouldered by the Mongols themselves. In 1909 the court announced that the New Administration would be extended to Outer Mongolia.[11]

In March 1910 San-to, a Manchu bannerman and former deputy lieutenant governor of Kuei-hua (in Inner Mongolia), arrived in Urga to supervise implementation of the New Administration. He organized around twenty offices and bureaus similar in purpose and design to those formed a few years earlier in China as part of the general effort to prepare for constitutional government. Preparations for the colonization of Mongolia were naturally an important part of San-to's work, although by the outbreak of the revolution in late 1911 they had not advanced beyond the stage of demarcating land for future cultivation.[12]

The Mongols could hardly be expected to share San-to's enthusiasm for sinification. As far back as 1905 the Russian Consul-General in Urga V. Lyuba reported to his government that Ch'ing plans for the reorganization of the native administration and the colonization of Mongolia with Chinese farmers had led to a surge of national consciousness among the Mongols and a growing dissatisfaction with Ch'ing rule.[13] Tempers flared in 1910 when a group of lamas attacked some Chinese at a carpentry shop in Urga. The fracas quickly got out of hand, and when San-to arrived with some soldiers to restore order, a mob of several hundred lamas stoned him and destroyed the shop. The refusal of both the Jebtsundamba Khutukhtu and the Erdene Shanzudba Badamdorj to surrender the ringleaders so angered San-to that he induced the Ch'ing court to remove Badamdorj from office and fine the Shav' Yamen.

The Mongols were even more disquieted by the arrival of T'ang Tsai-li, the chief military officer in Mongolia, especially when he announced that Mongolian youths would be conscripted for military training and that a tax of 160,000 taels would be levied on the population for the construction of barracks, reportedly intended for occupancy by Chinese troops soon to arrive in Urga. In a letter from the League Chairmen of the two eastern aimags and the Erdene Shanzudba, San-to was warned of the consequences of posting a Chinese regiment in Urga.[14]

By 1911 the Ch'ing had governed Mongolia for over two hundred years with relatively little opposition. Its policy of careful attention to the ruling lay and church princes and studied non-intervention in the local affairs of the Mongols (and perhaps the sobering experience of 1757, when the Khalkhas learned the consequences of armed opposition) had been largely responsible for this remarkable record. But the circumstances of 1911 were very different--Mongolia's parlous economic situation, which touched the princes as directly as it did the arats, and the broad challenge laid down by the Ch'ing court to their traditional culture fortified the will of every

Mongol, irrespective of class, to resist. In July 1911 the inchoate anti-Ch'ing movement in Mongolia was given new impetus and direction when a secret meeting of Mongolian princes was held in the Shav' Yamen to discuss a united response to the New Administration. Because the assembly was locked in stalemate--some argued for opposition to the entire New Administration while others urged selective resistance--a second meeting was convened in the neighboring Bogd uul mountains, attended by eighteen men, which decided that the Mongols must declare independence in order to save their religion and country. It was believed that to win independence, foreign assistance would be necessary, for which purpose Ch'in-wang Khanddorj, Da Lama Tserenchimed, and the Inner Mongolian Khaisan were selected as envoys to Russia. This recommendation was passed on to the Khutukhtu, who gave his approval.[15]

The Russians were thrown into confusion by the Mongolian approach, a move which they had never expected and which at least some members of the government preferred to ignore. In a letter on July 30 to the Chairman of the Council of Ministers Vladimir N. Kokovstov, Acting Minister of Foreign Affairs Neratov wrote: "Whatever may be the decision of the Imperial Government regarding its attitude toward the agitation arising among the Mongols, the appearance of the deputation (of Khanddorj) at the present moment, when we have not prepared the grounds to exploit this agitation in our interest, is in my opinion untimely." Neratov believed that the delegation should be headed off before it reached Petersburg with the excuse that preliminary discussions with the Mongols were necessary in view of the seriousness of the mission.[16]

But Kokovtsov's reply on August 3 was rather more calculating and set the tone of government policy toward Mongolia. Kokovtsov, believing that to halt the mission en route would create disagreeable complications with the Mongols, advised that the delegation be received in Petersburg, where the Imperial Government could "try to give this matter (of Mongolian independence) a character desirable for us. It could then perhaps even take on a useful importance in our approaching negotiations with China."[17]

On August 9 the Russian Minister in Peking, I. Korostovetz, was informed of the government's attitude in this matter: "The internal situation in Khalkha does not touch upon our vital interests. For us, the Mongolian question is important as a means, and it must be used by us for the resolution of our other political problems in China." Neratov went on to explain that the unrest in Khalkha and the appearance of the Mongolian delegation did offer Russia an excuse to intervene and an opportunity to influence the Mongolian policy of the Ch'ing government.[18]

The Mongolian delegation arrived in Petersburg on August 15 bringing with it a letter, addressed to the Russian Tsar and signed by the Jebtsundamba Khutukhtu and the four Khans of Khalkha, requesting help against the Ch'ing government. On August 16 the delegation was received by Neratov, and on the following day the Special Conference on Far Eastern Affairs met to determine the position of the Russian government toward the Mongolian request. It was the opinion of the Special Conference that active intervention of the Imperial Government in the Mongolian question would result only in diminishing Russian influence with the Western powers and in deflecting attention from the more pressing Near and Middle Eastern questions. On the other hand, the colonization of a zone along the Russian border with Chinese farmers, the linking of this region with China by a railroad (the planned Kalgan-Urga line), and especially the concentration of Chinese troops near Russian territory were very disturbing. Therefore:

> ...it would best correspond to our political tasks as well as to the present political situation, if the Imperial Government, without taking the responsibility upon itself of giving armed support to the separation of China planned by the Mongols, would step forward as a mediator between them and, through diplomacy, support the aspiration of the Mongols to preserve their distinctiveness without breaking with their suzerain, the Emperor of the Ta Ch'ing dynasty.

The Special Conference further recommended that Khanddorj be made to understand clearly that, for the moment, Mongolian plans to secede from China were not feasible, although the Mongols could expect Russian support in their struggle to maintan a "distinct" Khalkha regime. Finally, in order to protect the returning delegation from Ch'ing reprisals and to ensure the success of the Khalkhas' efforts to achieve that "distinct" regime, the Conference urged the immediate reinforcement of the consular guard in Urga with two Cossack squadrons in accordance with a request made by the Khutukhtu to the Russian Consul in Urga in late July.[19]

Neither the Special Conference nor senior ministerial officials seemed aware that their efforts to plot a course for Russian policy regarding Mongolia had been anticipated during the years 1854-62, when very similar recommendations were made for very similar problems. The security of the Russian border demanded only that Tsarism support the Mongols in a bid for autonomy, not independence. There could be no question, moreover, of large-scale military intervention--the Russians would have to seek a political solution to the Mongolian question through negotiations with China.

The exchanges with the Ch'ing government that followed were on the part of the Russians a calculated mix of bluff and bombast. On August 19 Neratov wired the decision of the Special Conference to Korostovetz in Peking and instructed him to explain that the implementation of its military and administrative reforms in Khalkha "would be viewed by us as a hostile act against Russia." Some ten days later Korostovetz personally handed a note to the Ch'ing Foreign Minister stating that its measures in Mongolia--immigration, training of troops, and administrative reorganization--had produced considerable fear among the Mongols and had compelled them to send special officials "one after the other" with complaints to the Russian government. The Foreign Minister's response was cautious. He explained that these measures were designed to promote the cultural and economic development of the country; the obstinate character of the Mongols accounted for their opposition. Korostovetz was impressed only with the Minister's equivocation and advised Petersburg that more pressure would have to be brought to bear on Peking before there could be a serious exchange of views.[20]

Korostovetz's assessment of Peking's attitude was accurate--a few days later he was told by the Chinese Foreign Minister that the Mongolian question was an internal affair of China and of no concern to the Russian government. The negotiations which followed established a pattern that was to be repeated over and over again during the next few years, whereby Chinese refusals to accept Russian demands regarding Mongolia invariably led the Tsarist government to escalate discussions into a diplomatic war of nerves. In accordance with instructions from his government on September 9, Korostovetz informed the Ch'ing government that while Russia did not deny that the Mongolian question was an internal issue of China, it could not but be concerned because of the contiguous border which Russia shared with Khalkha. Korostovetz's ominous remark, that the Ch'ing would have to take responsibility for the consequences if it failed to accept Russian advice, was trenchantly underscored by his comment that the situation in Khalkha had forced the Russians to strengthen their consular guard in Urga.

A few days passed during which Ch'ing officials evidently pondered the full weight of Korostovetz's message. The Ministry of Foreign Affairs suddenly reversed its earlier position and innocently claimed that San-to had been ordered simply to study the situation in Mongolia and to explain the goals of the reforms to the Mongols, and that some of these measures had even now been suspended to please the Mongolian people. The ministers had known nothing of San-to's harsh measures until informed by the Russians.[21]

It is not impossible that Peking authorities had not grasped the depth of Mongolian resentment against the New Administration--Chinese governments, like governments of many multi-racial countries, have never been particularly sensitive to the aspirations of their national minorities--or this may have been an unworthy effort to shift responsibility on to San-to. In either case the Russians were not satisfied with vague Chinese assurances that the tempo of the New Administration would be reduced. On

October 13, therefore, just three days after the outbreak of revolution in China, Neratov instructed Korostovetz that he should take advantage of the Ch'ing preoccupation with the revolutionary movement in the south to force Peking into confirming, in writing, the legitimacy of Russian rights insofar as they affected the fate of Mongolia. The device used by Korostovetz was an artfully worded aide-memoire, dated October 19, which noted the decision of the Ch'ing government to suspend all reform measures in Mongolia and added that the Tsarist government must be informed in advance should the Ch'ing contemplate altering this decision. To circumvent the need for a reply, a sensible precaution in view of the dynasty's uncertain future, the note concluded with a statement that the Russian Legation in Peking regarded this communication as unconditionally settling the question unless the government of China raised immediate objections.[22] This document established Russia as a guarantor of the status quo in Mongolia and was the foundation of the future Sino-Russian condominium over Mongolia.

On September 3 the Ch'ing Ministry of Foreign Affairs had informed San-to that, according to the Russian Minister in Peking, a letter had been delivered to the Petersburg government by several Mongolian nobles and lamas expressing serious discontent with the New Administration; San-to was instructed to look into this and to take any measures of accomodation he felt were necessary. San-to undoubtedly realized that the Mongols were unhappy with him and his work, but there had been no hint until now that they had taken such a drastic course. The shaken Viceroy immediately summoned Badamdorj and interrogated him closely; Badamdorj submissively related the entire plot. San-to quickly ordered the Jebtsundamba Khutukhtu to send a telegram withdrawing the request for Russian troops and directing the Khanddorj delegation to return home. The Khutukhtu agreed, but demanded that the New Administration be revoked and all members of the delegation amnestied. San-to transmitted these terms to Peking; he soon received a reply permitting him to suspend any feature of the New Administration to which the Mongols objected.[23]

On October 10 revolution broke out in China; by

the end of that month five provinces had declared their independence and by the end of November nine more had joined them. The impact of these events was immediately felt in Mongolia. Khanddorj and his companions, after their secret return to Urga, reported the results of their trip to an assembly of nobles and lamas; the Khutukhtu, whose advice was sought on this matter, issued a decree stating that the time had now arrived for the Mongolian peoples (ovogton) to unite and form an independent state. Emboldened by the promise of Russian aid--not to mention the arrival of Russian troops--by the paralysis of the Peking government, and by the benediction of the Khutukhtu himself, a provisional government of seven men, including Khanddorj and Tserenchimed, was formed. On November 28 the Provisional Government issued instructions for each of the four aimags to send a thousand troops to Urga; within a day or two there were around five hundred soldiers, drawn from the neighboring banners, camped in the vicinity of the city. On November 30 San-to received a perplexing communication, signed in the name of the nobles and and lamas of the four aimags of Khalkha, stating that four thousand troops had been mobilized to protect the Emperor from rebel forces in Peking; San-to was asked to provision and equip these men and was given three hours in which to answer. San-to did not reply; a reply in any event would have been pointless. That evening he received a second letter stating that the oppression suffered by the Mongols in recent years at Chinese hands had convinced them that Mongolia must become independent; consequently there was no longer any need for Chinese troops or officials. The Viceroy was invited to leave the country within three days.[24]

San-to was outflanked and outgunned. With only one hundred fifty poorly armed and mutinous troops (angered by arrears in their pay) there was no choice but to capitulate. His soldiers were disarmed by Mongolian militamen and Russian Cossacks, and he along with his staff moved into the compound of the Tsarist Consulate after the Consul had expressed fears for the Viceroy's safety; on December 5 San-to was escorted to the border by Russian troops. On December 1 the Provisional Government issued a general proclamation declaring the end of Ch'ing rule and announcing the establishment of a theocracy under the Jebtsundamba Khutukhtu.

---

The intervention of the Russians on behalf of the Mongols, both on this occasion and in 1921, has preoccupied a number of scholars and is one of the central problems of this study. Chinese historians in particular have been active in developing the theme of Russian provocation and manipulation to explain the 1911 revolution in Mongolia. But this explanation is unsatisfactory because it ignores the complexity of Russian policy in the Far East and minimizes the important role of the Mongols in the playing out of their own history. This revolution was the logical culmination of a growing nationalistic consciousness of the Mongols and of the Ch'ing mismanagement of Mongolia in the final decade of its existence--aggravated to no little degree by the misrule of Mongolian princes and a deteriorating economy. The Russians had been quite unprepared for Mongolia's split with China, and only at the eleventh hour, after the Mongols had already decided to appeal to Russia, did the Petersburg government hurriedly work out a position regarding its neighbor. The appearance of Russia as a land power in East Asia in the second half of the seventeenth century had altered the old pattern of China's relations with the Mongols and created new opportunities for the latter. The Mongols used Russia--not always with a great deal of success--as a political and military counterweight to China. They tried to do it in the early 1600s and in 1757; they succeeded in 1911.

## CHAPTER II

## THE RUSSIAN YEARS, 1912-14

On December 29, 1911 the Jebtsundamba Khutukhtu was ceremoniously installed on the "Bejewelled Throne" as bogd khaan ("holy emperor") of Mongolia, and a new government of lamas and princes was formed. During the early years of the Bogd Khaan period (1911-1919) this government looked eagerly to its patron Imperial Russia for material aid and diplomatic support in the creation of an independent theocratic state embracing all the Mongolian peoples (excluding the Buryats but including the Tuvins, or Uryankhais). The Mongols were soon keenly disappointed, however, by Russia's inflexible opposition to these aims and by its determination to see Mongolia remain a part of China. The efforts of the Tsarist government to steer a middle course between Mongolian expectations and Chinese demands seemed faithless to the Mongols, predatory to the Chinese, and irresolute to contemporary Rusian observers.

Russian policy from the last half of the nineteenth century to the revolution of 1917, however, had been perfectly consistent: Mongolia must remain an autonomous member of the Chinese state. The Russians naturally preferred that their influence be preeminent in the country, although this was not absolutely essential. But what was necessary was that no potentially hostile nation--China, Japan, or one of the Western powers--should have more than a nominal presence in the country. This continued to be the core of Soviet thinking regarding Mongolia, although it was never stated so precisely, either publicly or privately. This policy was the product of certain irresistible forces: concern for the security of the Russian border, treaty obligations with Japan, pressure from Western powers, the importance of some measure of Chinese good will, and the belief that the Mongols were incapable of governing themselves.

## Formation of the Bogd Khaan State

From the moment their state was formed, the Khalkha Mongols envisaged a country which would embrace all of the land and peoples living on the ancient territory of the Mongols, rather than one simply confined to their own four aimags and the Khovd region. In December 1911 emissaries had been dispatched to Inner Mongolia and the Barguts of Hulunbuir (northwestern Manchuria) with an invitation to join this new independent state. Among the first to respond were the Barguts, who in January 1912 expelled their Ch'ing superintendent and requested that their region be annexed to Mongolia. In the summer of 1912 the five banners of Tannu-Uryankhai, a Turkic-speaking people living in the present-day Tuva A.S.S.R., also petitioned Urga for inclusion in the new Mongolian state, as did the seven banners of the Altai-Uryankhai, a Mongolian-speaking people who lived on both sides of the Altai mountains. Reaction from Inner Mongolia, while not unequivocal, was nevertheless encouraging: thirty-five of the forty-nine banners asked to join, as did the eight Chahar banners. The Bogd Khaan approved these petitions, rewarded the princes with ranks and titles, and confirmed their right to administer their lands.

But even while the Bogd Khaan was receiving the homage of the Mongolian tribes, the western part of Outer Mongolia had not yet been completely liberated from the Chinese. In Uliastai, where the Manchu Military Governor resided, a crowd of angry Mongols had gathered outside the Governor's yamen and forced him to seek refuge in the Russian Consulate. Seeing that resistance was useless, the Governor and his staff left the city with a Cossack escort in either December 1911 or the first part of 1912.

The boldness of the Khovd Deputy Military Governor P'u-jun, however, forced events there to take a very different course. An assembly of Oirat princes, convened in the summer of 1912 and attended by the notorious Dambiijantsan (Ja Lama) among others, decided to send a petition to the Khutukhtu requesting that the district be included in the Bogd Khaan state and that assistance be rendered in the liberation of Khovd. An army of five thousand poorly armed Oirats, Khalkhas, and Tuvins, commanded by Dambiijantsan and two officers sent from Urga, Damdinsüren and Magsarjav, besieged the heavily outnumbered garrison. Although P'u-jun's resistance was at least partly bolstered by the knowledge that relief units could be expected from Sinkiang (in July reinforcements of between three and five hundred men had indeed been sent from Shara sume, but were routed by the Mongols near Khovd), in early August the Khovd stronghold was attacked and overrun. The amban and remnants of his garrison (two hundred to three hundred fifty Chinese, including soldiers and merchants, were killed), were conducted to the Russian border by Cossacks; Chinese shops were looted, debt records were burned, and Chinese merchants were murdered.[25]

Before discussing the new relationship between Russia and Mongolia, it may be useful to explore the philosophy and machinery of the Bogd Khaan state, especially in view of the little attention which this subject has received in Western literature. The new government of Mongolia was a curious and ultimately unworkable amalgam of the political and administrative traditions, both Chinese and Mongolian, inherited from the Ch'ing and earlier periods, and of modern ideas and institutions borrowed from Imperial Russia and late Ch'ing China. In the countryside the overthrow of the Manchus had brought few changes: the principles of hereditary privilege and class rule continued to be the fulcrum of Mongolian society, although this system was just beginning to be challenged by an embryonic meritocracy which developed during the Bogd Khaan years. The prince governed his banner as he always had, the khamjlaga continued to serve his master, and the state arat now owed his labor service to the government in Urga rather than to Peking; Ch'ing law endured as the guide for political and social administration. It was only in Urga where one could discover any changes wrought by the revolution. The ceremony and declarations of December 29 reflected the ambivalence of the Mongolian rulers toward both tradition and modernity, and they were to discover that bridging the chasm between the old, familiar ways of the past and the new, unfamiliar ones of the present was far more difficult than they could have imagined.

The choice of the Urga Khutukhtu as the new khaan of Mongolia was natural and logical. He was the revered symbol of Mongolian Lamaism and was famed throughout the country for his special oracular and supernatural powers. There was, moreover, the example of Tibet with its highly developed theocracy under the Dalai Lama. One very significant feature was the elevation of the Khutukhtu as emperor in the traditional Chinese manner. All the symbols and regalia of imperial China were adopted and the customary tributary rites continued to be enforced (the lay and church princes of Mongolia now owed tribute to the Urga Khutukhtu). The Bogd Khaan also assumed the power, jealously guarded by past Ch'ing emperors, of conferring ranks and seals and of confirming the ruling rights of all Mongolian princes. This, parenthetically, was a clear assertion that the mandate of the new Khaan was not limited to Khalkha alone but ran throughout the Mongolian territory of the old Ch'ing empire. The ceremony reflected other, perhaps less important but nevertheless instructive, signs of how tightly the Mongols were bound to their past. Following Chinese practice at the accession of a new emperor, the Bogd Khaan adopted a reign title, "Elevated by the Multitudes," a style which according to tradition was used by the ancient kings of Tibet; and again, following Chinese practice, the Khaan promoted all the lay and church ruling princes of Mongolia by one grade.

But surely the real importance of December 29 is that the Mongols, having on this day irrevocably set a new course which would guide them into the modern age, began a struggle, continuing even now, to obtain recognition as a full and sovereign member of the Asian and world community. The decrees of December 29 reflected an awareness that this goal could be achieved only through modernization. The various reforms instituted during the Bogd Khaan years and aimed at promoting modernization, however, were generally superficial and ineffective, and were more important for their intent. Nevertheless, the very recognition that reforms were needed generated interest, concern, and debate among Mongolian intellectuals over the path and pace of modernization. The parochialism of the Mongols, as these and other innovations showed, was quietly eroding in the face of a growing awareness of the modern world.

There were several measures announced on December 29 and in the following two or three years which illustrated the new Mongolian interest in the symbols of modernity and in reshaping their country into a twentieth-century nation-state. December 29, for example, was declared to be independence day and a national holiday. It was also felt that another name must be found for Urga (_Ikh khüree_ or _Da khüree_, "Great Monastery") which would reflect its new national role. In 1912 the Ministry of Internal Affairs sent a circular letter to the other ministries, aimag and shav' governments stating: "Because of the custom to name the cities in which the emperors of the nations of the world reside as the 'capital,' henceforth in all official documents (the name Urga) will be written as 'Capital Monastery' (_Niislel khüree_)."[26] The first national flag of Mongolia was devised (decorated with the traditional _soembo_ design), and it was ordered that the birthdays of the Bogd Khaan and his consort, the Ekh Dagina, were to be commemorated nationally with special services. Other more important signs of statehood were the formation of a central government organized along Western lines with five ministries: internal affairs, foreign affairs, finance, justice, and the army; the opening of a national parliament (_ulsyn khural_) in the first half of 1914, consisting of an upper and lower house (this "parliament" functioned only as a consultative body); and the formation of a national army.

Perhaps the most important reform measure of 1911-1912 was the creation of a Western-style government, staffed with a permanent professional bureaucracy instead of the rotating service which was the normal pattern for Mongolian officials. This government during its eight-year existence, however, was a generally ineffective instrument of administration and was headed, for the most part, by colorless men who lacked the vision and skills which were so urgently needed. Russian diplomats were alternately amused, frustrated, and appalled by their Mongolian counterparts. Korostovetz believed that they had "very little understanding of the business of state" and merely played a passive role in government.[27]

The judgement of the Russian Diplomatic Agent A. Miller was rather more harsh: he charged them with refusing to take account of the long-term future of their country, the welfare of its people, or any reforms, and reported that they were interested solely in advancing their own material well-being.[28] Although Miller's sentiment was possibly exaggerated, colored perhaps by his usually abrasive relationship with the Mongols during his years in Urga, the conduct of the government on the whole seems to confirm these impressions. But at the same time we must recall that the bureaucratic experience of the Mongols was limited to the administration of aimag, banner, and shav' units: the Ch'ing had never prepared them for governing an entire state.

The first ministerial appointees were a rather motley group with sharply contrasting backgrounds and abilities. Appointments seemed to have been made casually and arbitrarily, the single indispensable qualification was apparently an early commitment to independence (all of the ministers had served in the short-lived Provisional Government of Urga). Until he died in 1914 the Minister of Internal Affairs Da Lama Tserenchimed, the only commoner in the cabinet, was in the opinion of his arch-antagonist Korostovetz the most competent. (It is interesting that, with the exception of the Sain Noyon Khan and possibly Khanddorj, it was primarily men of more humble origin, such as Tserenchimed, Tserendorj, Magsarjav, and Damdinsüren, who won the respect of foreign diplomats in Mongolia.) Tserenchimed, who had distinguished himself at an early age during his service in the Ikh Shav' administration, was an indefatigable champion of a sovereign and pan-Mongolian state, and regularly challenged or frustrated the efforts of the Tsarist government to deny the Mongols both. Ch'in-wang Khanddorj, Minister of Foreign Affairs until 1915 when he was assassinated at the orders of the Bogd Khaan's court, was well known for his pro-Russian sympathies, which suggests that his selection to this post was grounded in the hope or belief that he had some particular influence with the Russians.

If there were logical reasons for choosing Tserenchimed and Khanddorj to serve in the first cabinet in Mongolian history, the other three

Ministers had less obvious credentials. The Minister of Finance Tüsheet Wang Chagdarjav was a sickly individual but with a reputation for probity--in a society like that of pre-revolutionary Mongolia this was possibly the supreme recommendation--although in the opinion of one contemporary Mongolian observer he was indecisive, excessively cautious, and pusillanimous. If Chagdarjav's qualifications were tenuous, the skills of the Minister of Justice Namsrai Wang and Minister of the Army Dalai Ch'in-wang Gombosüren were even more suspect. Namsrai was illiterate, although he had served in the Shav' Yamen like Tserenchimed; he was a drinking companion of the Jebtsundamba Khutukhtu, which may have had no little influence on his selection, and together with Khanddorj was widely regarded as one of the most pro-Russian of all the influential nobles in Urga. Gombosüren was the youngest of the five, poorly educated and with no experience in military affairs.[29]

## Theocracy Under the Jebtsundamba Khutukhtu

Ultimately it was neither the inexperience of the Mongolian government nor the eclectic character of its institutions which can be blamed for the failure of the Bogd Khaan years. The Bogd Khaan government eventually foundered because its fundamental proposition, the principle of theocratic government, proved unworkable and divisive. Lamaism since its arrival in Mongolia in the sixteenth century had been favored by devout aristocrats with many donations and franchises, not the least of which were the exemption of lamas and shav' nar from certain corvée and the right to nomadize on all banner land. Pious nobles often transferred many of their own arats and livestock to the registers of the khutukhtus and monasteries, and by the nineteenth century the church had prospered so enormously that it was indisputably the richest and most powerful institution in Mongolia. But the unforeseen result of this growth was that the church came increasingly to compete with the lay princes for people, livestock, and pastures. Until 1911 this antagonism was moderated by Ch'ing law and Ch'ing officials, who were particularly careful to check the encroachment of the church on to the secular arena. As long as the Manchus ruled, a manageable if uneasy balance was consciously maintained between them.

This equilibrium was radically disturbed in 1911 when the primate of Mongolian Lamaism, the Jebtsundamba Khutukhtu, became the supreme temporal authority in the land. The church quickly discovered new opportunities for growth and maximized them. When the Khutukhtu took the reins of state, ecclesiastical politics were permitted to develop without restraint and to intrude on the economic and political interests of the lay princes. Although nominally the senior executive officers of state during the Bogd Khaan period, cabinet ministers (excepting its lama members) were rarely included as full partners in the formulation of government policy and were effectively isolated from the real seat of power during these years: the entourage of the Jebtsundamba Khutukhtu.

The government was in a real sense a creature of the court, and to ensure that it remained so the Ministry of Internal Affairs under Da Lama Tserenchimed was raised to the unofficial status of a prime ministry. But this immediately aroused objections from other princes, especially Khanddorj. The court reluctantly conceded, and in the fall of 1912 the thirty-four year-old Sain Noyon Khan Namnansüren was appointed prime minister while leaving Tserenchimed as minister of internal affairs.

The choice of the Sain Noyon Khan was an intelligent one. He struck contemporary observers as a man of some ability and integrity, an impression supported by his conduct in office. The court may have yielded but it certainly had not surrendered: an extra-governmental Office of Religion and State was soon formed under Badamdorj (serving concurrently as erdene shanzudba). Although this office operated very discreetly during the Bogd Khaan period (it is not mentioned in any of the Russian or Chinese sources) it nevertheless wielded more influence and power than any of the ministries.[30]

Not only did the church exhaust its political credit among the princes but it seemed bent on destroying the already unhealthy Mongolian economy. Between 1890 and 1920 the Khutukhtu's treasury borrowed over five million silver taels from Chinese merchants, a loan and its interest which could be repaid only by taxing the church serfs. The Shanzudba Badamdorj, therefore, began transferring large numbers of wealthy banner arats to the rolls of the Ikh Shav', an effort which not only antagonized banner officialdom but meant that a decreasing proportion of the population (and the one least financially able to bear it) was forced to shoulder an increasingly heavier tax burden.[31]

The intense conviction of every class of Mongolian society that Heaven could be moved by sacrifices led to the proliferation of a whole range of prodigal offerings, which took an enormous toll on the economy. There is no better illustration of this than the numerous and expensive attempts to restore the eyesight of the Khutukhtu. In 1912 ten thousand statuettes of the Buddha, manufactured in Poland and Dolonnor, were purchased. At about the same time a cast-iron statue of the Maidari Buddha, eighty-four feet tall, was brought to Urga from Inner Mongolia and housed in a temple specially constructed to receive it. This colossus cost 100,000 taels and the temple another 230,000.[32]

The Shav' Yamen did not expect to bear such devotional expenses by itself--the aimag and banner populations often were asked (they had little choice but to agree) to make contributions as demonstrations of piety. During the Bogd Khaan period the national government was also obliged to divert part of its meagre income to the church treasury. In 1914, for example, the Shav' Yamen asked the government to defray the costs of the *Khailan* religious ceremony, amounting to over 778,000 bricks of tea (brick tea was a common medium of currency), a gigantic sum in those days.[33]

One of the most important and at the same time obscure questions of the Bogd Khaan period is the problem of identifying the person or persons who were actually responsible for the policy decisions of the government. Except for the daily administration of public business, there is nothing in the sources to indicate that the ministers or their deputies played decisive political roles. Indeed, the available evidence suggests that they were little more than figureheads acting for more shadowy figures whose existence is merely alluded to in the contemporary sources. By culling information from a wide range of documents, however, it is possible to reconstuct in broad outline the process by which decisions were made. Because decrees and other state pronouncements were issued in the name of the Bogd Khaan, it has been commonly assumed that it was he who personally presided over the councils of government. It appears, however, that there were other individuals, close to the Khutukhtu, who were actually manipulating the strings of power.

The Khutukhtu was an extraordinary character who deserves a fuller study than is possible here. He was an intelligent man, somewhat infantile and capriciously brutal. He had an uncommon fascination with Western mechanical devices, which after tiring of them he would periodically throw out his palace window to eager crowds below. An alcoholic, he was known to indulge in week-long drinking bouts which rendered him partially comatose. His "cabinet" meetings were said to be little more than drunken reveries lasting until long after midnight. Foreigners who met the Khutukhtu generally described him as bloated and sickly looking, appearing much older than his forty-two years would indicate. In 1910 he went blind. His interest in and command over government affairs surely languished as a result of his dissipated lifestyle and chronic ill-health.[34]

If the Khutukhtu were as a rule incapable of making decisions, then we must search elsewhere for the power behind the throne. The Mongolian government, like all governments with a regular bureaucracy, to a great extent ran itself--this was certainly easier in a country such as Mongolia, where the requirements of state were less urgent and complex. When some kind of direction was required, however, it was his court advisers and his consort, the Ekh Dagina, in particular who were either making the key decisions themselves or at least influencing the Khutukhtu to an extraordinary degree.

While the evidence for this is circumstantial, it is nevertheless compelling. The Bogd Khaan's powers were partially withered by sickness, alcohol, and blindness, and it would have been natural, perhaps unavoidable, that his physical vulnerability forced him to depend emotionally on the people around him for counsel and support. The person closest to him was his consort. While several Westerners remarked on the exceptional influence of the Ekh Dagina on her "husband," the testimony of the Russian diplomat Korostovetz, who spent a year and a half in Urga and was friendly with all the leaders of the Urga administration, is the most persuasive. He wrote that she had an enormous amount of power over the Khutukhtu and had become his first counselor in matters of church and state. After his blindness, he reported, her influence deepened still more, and she worked relentlessly to secure the throne for their adopted son.[35]

It is an unfortunate although inevitable corollary of court politics, where power is more personal than contractual, and where regular procedures for reaching decisions are often vague or non-existent, that intrigues not only exist but flourish. Rumors circulated in abundance throughout Urga telling of political leaders who had been poisoned by the Ekh Dagina at palace banquets. Among those generally throught to have been murdered were the Tüsheet Khan Dashnyam (1912), the Zasagt Khan Sonomravdan (1912), Bint Wang Gonchigsüren (1913?), Da Lama Tserenchimed (1914), Khanddorj (1915), and the Sain Noyon Khan (1919).

## Chinese Reaction to Mongolian Independence

After the fall of the Ch'ing a new Republican government, under the brief presidency of Sun Yat-sen and then Yuan Shih-k'ai, endeavored to recapture the loyalty of the Mongols. Sun sent a telegram to Urga assuring the Mongols that in this new republican order all nationalities of China would be treated impartially. A five-colored flag, representing the five nationalities, was adopted for the Republic and a bill of rights was promulgated by the Nanking government guaranteeing equality for all minorities and freedom of religion. The offensive term "dependency" was dropped, and the Ministry of Dependencies was replaced in April 1912 by the Office of Mongolian and Tibetan Affairs (in 1914 renamed the Bureau of Mongolian and Tibetan Affairs and placed under the direction of the Kharchin Mongolian prince, Gungsannorov).

The Chinese government continued to go through the motions of administering frontier affairs, never conceding publicly that anything had happened to change its relationship with Mongolia. The Provisional Constitution of the Republic, issued in March 1912, included a clear and uncompromising affirmation of the territorial integrity of China; and in August a law dealing with the election of the National Assembly was promulgated, providing for delegates from each of the Outer Mongolian leagues and from Uryankhai. Between 1912 and 1916 the Peking government continued to appoint representatives to Khovd and Uliastai (but rather oddly not to Urga).

Right from the first the new Peking government realized that there could be no hope of restoring the old ties between the frontier and China unless the policy of upholding the interests of the princely class, so successful for the Ch'ing, was followed with similar care. Thus, the system of hereditary and theocratic rule among the Mongols, Tibetans, and Moslems was left intact. The anomaly of a republican government endorsing imperial practices was reflected most clearly in the "Regulations for *Nien-pan* Affairs," issued in January 1913. The document, prescribing procedures for the yearly tributary missions to Peking, was remarkable for its faithfulness to Ch'ing regulations, differing mainly in detail: nobles were required to come to Peking at the time of the solar instead of the lunar New Year, and audiences were to be held with the president of China rather than with the emperor.

The refusal of the Republic to break with traditional policies regarding the minorities in general, and the Mongols in particular, was the distinguishing feature of its strategy toward the frontier. Throughout the Bogd Khaan period until 1921 the Chinese government consistently and incessantly sought to restore all of the trappings of the tributary relationship as they had existed during the Ch'ing. The only changes were terminological, when names were condescending or smacked too baldly of the old imperial order.

But the Mongols were not tempted by these seductions. A telegram was sent by the Urga government to Peking congratulating the Chinese on taking power but politely refusing to renew old bonds: "...the mores (surtal) of Mongolia and China are different, religions are different, and languages and scripts are mutually unintelligible. For over two hundred years we Mongols have been oppressed by the Ch'ing state and up to the present have still not absorbed the wisdom and mores of China. Therefore, we cannot join."[36]

What followed was a remarkable exchange of telegrams between the Bogd Khaan and Yuan Shih-k'ai, which certainly proved that the Mongols were the equal of the Chinese in the use of allusion and rarified speech. In the first telegram Yuan pointed out the inability of the Mongols to govern themselves, the dangers of seeking help from the Russians, and the necessity for the Chinese and Mongols to remain united: "The regions of Mongolia and China are, in their mutual relationship, like the lips and the teeth, or like the entrance door and the innermost recesses of a home. Together they can profit, while separated both can only suffer." The Khutukhtu's reply was masterful in its subtlety and effacement. He agreed with the President, but pointed out that if China were to aid Mongolia in the building of a new state, this would certainly redound to China's benefit. In the final exchanges Yuan proposed that he send envoys for further discussions, but the Khutukhtu replied that the course of the Mongols was set and that further talks would be profitless.[37]

Since Yuan had failed to persuade the Mongols, he tried to cow them. In July he telegraphed the Khutukhtu demanding that the Peking government be compensated for the imperial livestock in Mongolia which had been seized at the time of independence. If the Mongols refused, Yuan warned, either the five ministers of the Urga government must come to Peking, or Chinese troops would go to Urga. Yuan's government, however, was in such a wretched financial state that a military expedition to Outer Mongolia was for the moment inconceivable. It was, incidentally, the enduring financial exhaustion of the Peking government, which became even more chronic after Yuan's death, that prevented China from acting more forcefully in Mongolia throughout the Republican period.

Russia was not happy about Mongolian independence either and was determined to reach an understanding with Peking whereby Mongolia would be autonomous but remain part of China. Foreign Minister Sazonov was particularly exercised by the way in which the Mongolian question was developing. China had refused to countenance autonomy for Mongolia and he feared that the inability of the Mongols to govern themselves might eventually compel Russia either to establish a protectorate over Mongolia or even to annex it. Sazonov was irrevocably opposed to either step, however, which would "have an adventurist character, alienate us from China, be followed by enormous expenses, and, finally, weaken our position in Europe."[38]

In June 1912 V.K. Krupenskii, the new Minister in Peking, presented a note to the Chinese Ministry of Foreign Affairs proposing joint discussions based on China's agreement to three principles of autonomy which forbade the presence of Chinese troops, colonization, or interference in the internal administration of Mongolia. Although opinion within the Peking cabinet was divided, the reasoning of the Minister of Foreign Affairs Lu Cheng-hsiang eventually satisfied the other members. He warned that to accept these three conditions would mean that China had in effect relinquished any claim to sovereignty over Mongolia. This surrender, he predicted, might lead to other Russian importunities. The government decided not to negotiate.[39]

## Mongolian Diplomatic Initiatives

With the Chinese unwilling to come to terms, the Russians proceeded to take matters into their own hands. In 1912 a secret convention was concluded with the Japanese, according to which their respective zones of influence were delimited by the Peking meridian (Outer Mongolia fell to the Russians). The Russian government also decided to sign a separate agreement with the Mongols recognizing its autonomy, a matter of some urgency because of reports that China was in the midst of negotiating a foreign loan (the so-called "Reorganization Loan"). It was feared that this money might provide Peking with the means to finance a military expedition against Urga.

Korostovetz was appointed plenipotentiary for negotiations with the Mongolian government and he secretly left St. Petersburg in September carrying a draft of a political agreement and commercial protocol worked out in the Ministry of Foreign Affairs. But as soon as negotiations between Korostovetz and the Mongols began, the latter raised vigorous objections to the Russian draft. The Sain Noyon Khan complained that the Russian government had ignored its promise to Khanddorj in late 1911 that it would support the complete independence of a pan-Mongolian state. Tserenchimed argued that the Russian draft offered no concrete advantages to Mongolia, and that it was better for the Khalkhas to perish than to accept freedom at the expense of their brothers in Inner Mongolia.[40]

Korostovetz could see that Russian prestige among the Mongols was falling at the same meteoric velocity it had risen a few months earlier. The Mongols were beginning to vacillate in their partiality to Russia, and even the Sain Noyon Khan now favored direct discussions with China. Korostovetz also learned that Tserenchimed was intriguing against him and exciting his colleagues with the spectre of Russian imperialism.

The Mongols countered with their own draft treaty which, although incorporating the Russian text unchanged, included some articles that modified it substantially: there was, for instance, a more emphatic statement of Mongolian independence; the Russians were to agree to the appointment of a diplomatic representative in Urga with a higher status than the present consul-general; the Mongols were given the right to appoint their own representatives to Petersburg; and finally, Inner Mongolia, Barga, and other Mongolian regions were recognized as part of the new state.

The main stumbling block to agreement, however, continued to be Urga's pan-Mongolian scheme to which the Russians could not possibly agree because of their secret treaties with Japan. Realizing that further discussion was pointless and that a more spectacular gesture was necessary, Korostovetz at one of the sessions dramatically flung his draft treaty on the floor and declared that negotiations were broken off. Tserenchimed and some others were happy to see the talks end, for Russia was obviously not prepared to yield on the pan-Mongolian issue, but the Khutukhtu ordered (according to rumor, on the advice of his consort) that discussions continue. To ensure that there were no further interruptions Korostovetz demanded that Tserenchimed be excluded from future meetings.

Without a great deal of happiness the Mongols finally resigned themselves to a treaty which made no provision for either full independence or pan-Mongolia. But, as subsequent events were to show, the Khalkhas were far from ready to abandon these goals. The Russian government did make some minor concessions of form: "Outer Mongolia" was replaced with the more imprecise "Mongolia," and Russia agreed to raise the status of its chief representative in Urga to that of a diplomatic agent, although it refused to accept a permanent Mongolian representative in Petersburg.

Despite the frantic efforts of the Chinese government at the last minute to dissuade the Mongols, the agreement was signed on November 3, 1912. In brief, the agreement provided for Russian recognition of Mongolian autonomy and for assistance in the training of any army (on February 16, 1913 Korostovetz signed a military agreement with the Sain Noyon Khan for the formation of a Mongolian brigade of nineteen hundred men--two cavalry regiments, a machine-gun company, and an artillery detachment--to be trained by Russian instructors at an estimated cost of 600,000 rubles). The second part of the document, the Commercial Protocol, enumerated Russian trading privileges in Mongolia, including duty-free commerce and the right to establish extra-territorial "factories" of Russian subjects.

Although the Mongols were hardly satisfied with the 1912 agreement, there was some compensation: if nothing else it was an international treaty by which a major world power had recognized the existence of the Mongolian state. The Mongols may have thought that Russian recognition would prepare the ground for recognition by other foreign states, and that their strengthened diplomatic position would eventually enable them to achieve full sovereignty and the unification of all Mongolian peoples, despite

Russian objections. For the Mongols, the Russian treaty was simply the opening volley in a general diplomatic offensive to obtain world recognition for their new state.

In November 1912 they tried to widen their circle of diplomatic contacts by sending notes to the foreign consuls in Hailar. None responded. In January 1913 the Mongols signed a treaty with Tibet, whose own history during the early years of the Republic bore a striking resemblance to that of Mongolia. The two countries recognized one another as independent states and promised to assist each other in times of danger and to support Lamaism. The treaty was, however, irrelevant and was never taken seriously by the powers. Any importance which the Mongols may have attached to it quickly died in the face of foreign indifference.

A more serious effort to retrieve Mongolia's position was a second mission to Russia, headed by Khanddorj and Deputy Prime Minister Shirnindamdin Beise, to "thank" the Tsar for the 1912 agreement. In reality, the Mongolian court hoped that Khanddorj might be able to prod the Tsarist government into agreeing to a pan-Mongolian state. The delegation was also directed to negotiate a loan, arrange for the arming of the Mongolian brigade, and contact diplomatic representatives accredited to Petersburg letters announcing the formation of a Mongolian state and expressing the desire for diplomatic relations had been prepared for the governments of such countries as Great Britain, France, and Germany).

Although the members of the mission were treated to full diplomatic courtesies, including an audience with the Tsar, the actual results of the trip fell far short of expectations. The Russians were at that moment in the midst of negotiating with the Chinese over Mongolia and were anxious that nothing should happen to prejudice the success of those talks. The movements of the delegation were supervised carefully, making contact with foreign ambassadors impossible, and the Russians refused to discuss Pan-Mongolia.

The delegation nevertheless did not return to Urga empty-handed: an arms agreement was signed, although it provided for significantly fewer weapons than the Mongols had requested, and the Russians agreed to a vital two-million-ruble loan, secured on the mining tax paid by the Russian company Mongolor. The Khutukhtu's court, however, was extremely disappointed by the results of the delegation. It had failed to win Russian recognition of an independent pan-Mongolia; it had failed to meet with any foreign ambassadors; and it had failed to obtain the desired quantity of arms. The loan was inadequate consolation. The court was so angry at Khanddorj that some of its members, according to reports, even accused him of treason. Later in the year the Minister of Religion and State reduced Khanddorj's salary and rebuked the Sain Noyon Khan for being slow to bring charges against him.[41]

While Khanddorj was negotiating with the Russians in Petersburg, Tserenchimed and the Inner Mongolian Bint Ch'in-wang Gonchigsüren departed for Tokyo with a letter to the Japanese Emperor proposing the establishment of relations. When Korostovetz learned of this delegation he moved immediately to head it off. He demanded an explanation from the Sain Noyon Khan, who replied somewhat impatiently that the Urga government considered it desirable to enter into direct relations with Japan because of its geographical proximity and common religion. Korostovetz then met with Tserenchimed, probably the prime mover behind this initiative, whose explanation illustrates the tunnel-vision of the Mongols with regard to the question of pan-Mongolia and their very imperfect understanding of the realities of international politics in Asia.

According to Tserenchimed's scheme, the Japanese would establish a protectorate over Inner Mongolia while simultaneously recognizing Outer Mongolia and the sovereignty of Outer Mongolia over Inner Mongolia. The Da Lama was visibly irritated by Korostovetz's reply that neither Russia nor Japan would consent to such a plan. In spite of Korostovetz's objections the delegation proceeded to Harbin, where it was told by the Japanese Consul that because Russia was opposed to this trip, he could only advise them to avoid unpleasantness and return to Urga. Tserenchimed was incensed and reported to the court that it was the Russian government which had obstructed his trip.[42]

"War" Between China and Mongolia

When news reached China that a Russo-Mongolian agreement had been signed, the Chinese were outraged and were now convinced of what many had suspected all along: Mongolian "independence" was a sham contrived by the Russians to camouflage their aggresive plans toward Chinese territory. There were public demonstrations throughout the country demanding that the government, now coming under strong criticism for its anaemic handling of frontier problems, should send an expedition against Urga. The seriousness of these demands was emphasized by an anti-Russian boycott in Peking and Tsingtao. Krupenskii wired his government that money was being openly collected to finance a punitive expedition against Urga, and that the Peking government was busying itself with war preparations, including the concentration of troops and supplies in various areas bordering Mongolia.

While Krupenskii may have overstated the seriousness of this threatened invasion of Khalkha--the expenses and logistical problems of sending a Chinese army deep into Mongolia were numbing--a military expedition to Khovd, because of its proximity to Sinkiang, was more plausible. Too late to save the beleaguered garrison at Khovd, the Sinkiang Governor Yang Tseng-hsin had ordered troops into winter quarters at Tsagaan dünkhen (on the southern slope of the Altai mountains, about one hundred fifty miles south of Khovd), apparently with the intention of moving them across the Altai passes when the spring thaws permitted movement.

At roughly the same time the Khalkhas had decided to intervene in Inner Mongolia after reports had reached them of Chinese troops pillaging and killing throughout the region. Mongolian princes, concerned by these reports, met with Korostovetz and explained that the eastern region could be defended by themselves against a Chinese attack, but that help was needed in western Mongolia where the Chinese were stronger; they urged that rifles, artillery guns, and Russian officers be sent to Khovd and Uliastai.[43]

Appreciating, or perhaps exaggerating, the seriousness of this Chinese threat in the west (the Chinese Foreign Minister had informed Krupenskii that there were only two detachments at Tsagaan dünkhen and, under pressure from the Russian Minister, promised to withdraw these units[44]), a conference chaired by the Tsar himself met in mid-February 1913 and decided that Khalkha and the Khovd region must be defended. Two squadrons of Verkhneudinsk Cossacks which had arrived in Uliastai a month earlier were immediately transferred westward, and units were soon ordered from Biisk to shore up the defenses in western Mongolia (the Biisk reinforcements, numbering about three thousand, did not arrive in Khovd until the summer of 1913).[45]

The appearance of this large Russian force produced an immediate military stalemate, which was not broken until December 21, 1913 when the Russian Consul at Share sume (Altai) and the Altai High Commissioner Prince Palta concluded a provisional agreement ending hostilities between China and Mongolia in that region. It was not until the spring of 1914, however, that most of these troops returned to Russia.

At the same time as the Mongols asked Korostovetz for Russian military assistance in the west, they informed the Russian diplomat of their decision to intervene in Inner Mongolia. Korostovetz was told that the Khalkhas planned to aid the rebellion in Inner Mongolia, and that another hundred-thousand rifles, together with machine-guns and cannon, were required for a military campaign. Though one must not minimize the genuine determination of the Khalkhas to defend their fellow Mongols, they may have regarded the events in Inner Mongolia as a stroke of luck which would force the Russians to see the error of limiting the geographical scope of the Mongolian state. The decision to send troops into Inner Mongolia, as Korostovetz himself suspected, may have also been a gamble calculated to provoke dissension between China and Russia. To Korostovetz's objection, that Russia could not support the Khalkhas in an expedition against Inner Mongolia, an act which would be tantamount to war, the Sain Noyon Khan reminded him that the Russians had no alternative in view of the responsibility they had undertaken to protect Mongolia.

In February a Mongolian army rode out of Urga under the command of the Bargut Mongol Manlai baatar

Damdinsüren. The history of the "war," the first between Chinese and Khalkhas in over two and a half centuries, is known in only the roughest outline. Fighting, episodic and small-scale (skirmishing may be more precise), continued for several months. Mongolian forces were generally victorious despite the Chinese advantage in men and material. The role of the Inner Mongolians in this "war" was probably considerable--the Mongolian army included many Inner Mongolian officers and doubtlessly a large number of troops, who must have contributed substantially to the campaign.

In spite of the remarkable victories of the Mongols, the Urga court by the summer of 1913 was facing problems so formidable that further prosecution of the "war" seemed impossible. Food and clothing for the army were increasingly in short supply, while guns and ammunition, inadequate to begin with, were running out. The Russians refused to replenish these material losses, the Urga government lacked the wherewithal to purchase new arms (the cost of the campaign had made devastating claims on the national purse), and the early enthusiasm among the Khalkhas for this war was waning as the banners were asked to bear more and more of its expenses. In December 1913 the Urga government finally promised the Russians to withdraw its units.[46]

## The Sino-Russian Declaration

The Russians had never taken the 1912 agreement with the Mongols very seriously. For them it was something of a diplomatic fiction, a political lever with which to demonstrate their determination to secure their minimum program in Mongolia--preferably with Chinese participation but without it if necessary. At the same time the Imperial Government appreciated that without Chinese recognition of Mongolian autonomy, Russian rights there would always be vulnerable. It had concluded an agreement with the Mongols in the first instance only because the Chinese refused to accept the minimum conditions imposed by Russia, but even as Korostovetz was negotiating with the Mongols in Urga, Krupenskii was pressing the Chinese Foreign Ministry for separate discussions in Peking. The priority which the

Russians placed on their relations with China over Mongolia is an enduring theme of this period and continued well into the Soviet era.

On November 6, 1912 Krupenskii was instructed to inform Peking that an agreement and protocol had been signed with the Mongols and to remind the Chinese that it was only their decision to ignore earlier warnings from Petersburg regarding the importance of the Russian position in Khalkha which had forced it to enter into direct relations with Mongolia. For the time being Russia had refrained from recognizing the complete separation of Mongolia from China and simply promised to help the Mongols preserve their autonomy. But if they refused to recognize this agreement, Russia would be forced to strengthen the Mongolian government.[47]

The Chinese were still unwilling to negotiate and replied that Mongolia was an integral part of China and had no right to conclude foreign treaties. Nevertheless, however much the Chinese detested the idea of parleying over land which they believed was incontestably theirs, they were quickly running out of other options. An attempt to enlist the support of the great powers against the Russo-Mongolian Agreement was met only with gestures of sympathy.

The Peking government was perhaps more impressed by public opinion in China itself, which had been so incensed over the agreement that Liang Ju-hao, Foreign Minister for only two months, was forced to resign. There was every likelihood that other careers in the cabinet would be similarly shortlived unless the Mongolian question were settled. Lu Cheng-hsiang, reappointed Foreign Minister, proposed to Krupenskii on November 19 that his government would be happy to discuss the Mongolian problem if the Russians repudiated their agreement with the Mongols. The Russian Minister, replying that this was impossible, suggested instead that the two governments conclude a new treaty based on the November agreement with Urga. The Chinese agreed, but insisted that such a treaty automatically invalidate the Russo-Mongolian Agreement. The Russians refused.[48]

Although the decision to conclude a new treaty had been reached, the two parties were pursuing entirely different and contradictory aims. The Chinese government realized that public opinion would not be assuaged until the Russians had abrogated their agreement with the Mongols. The Chinese moreover wanted their sovereignty over Mongolia recognized, without any curbs on troops, administration, or colonization. In return, they were prepared to promise the restoration of the old order as it had existed under the Ch'ing--an implicit, but not binding, acceptance of autonomy for the Mongols.

The Russian position, presented on November 27, forbade China to alter the historic system of government of Mongolia, permitted the Mongols the right to defend and police themselves, prohibited colonization, and obliged Peking to accept the "good offices" of Russia in resolving basic questions concerning Mongolia; finally, because the Russians believed that the right to conclude commercial contracts issued from autonomous powers, they wished the Russo-Chinese treaty to confirm the 1912 Commercial Protocol with the Mongols.

Negotiations continued sluggishly for the next several months, its progress impeded by the Chinese, who in desperation lingered over every article, every word, trying constantly to win any concession they could. They wanted, for example, the name "Mongolia" replaced for "Urga," which would have reduced Outer Mongolia to the two eastern aimags, and the word "suzerainty" substituted for "sovereignty." A tedious pattern developed in which the Russians invariably replied to each Chinese effort to moderate Tsarist conditions with the threat of negotiating directly with the Mongols. Such a threat, in its turn, brought the next Chinese draft a little closer to Russian demands.

On May 7 a weary Krupenskii informed the Chinese Foreign Minister that his continued delays evidenced Peking's unwillingness to reach an agreement on the Mongolian question, and that Petersburg would simply prefer China to declare openly that talks had failed. In this event, Russia would continue to shape its relationship with Mongolia by direct consultations with the Urga government. The Chinese reacted quickly. They agreed to a draft treaty identical almost word for word to the Russian proposal of November 17, 1912. But when the Peking government presented this treaty to the National Assembly in June for ratification, the House of Representatives, dominated by the opposition party the Kuomintang, fulminated against its terms. Changes were demanded which would have altered the agreement beyond recognition: Mongolian troops were to be placed under the command of Chinese officers; colonization was forbidden to all except Chinese and Mongols; and Russian commercial rights were to be limited to ten years.[49]

On July 11 Krupenskii received new instructions ordering him to inform the Peking government that because of the serious disagreements which had occurred on the Chinese side at the moment of signing, there should be a simple exchange of declarations merely defining their points of view. These declarations were to serve as the basis for later tripartite negotiations which would include the Mongols. Krupenskii then presented a new set of conditions which, although largely similar in substance, were phrased rather more bluntly than the draft treaty submitted to the National Assembly.

This time it was Lu Cheng-hsiang who was sacrificed to Chinese public opinion, and it was not until mid-September that the new Foreign Minister, Sun Pao-ch'i, took up once again the threads of the negotiations. Progress was briefly held up by Sun's insistence that the declarations include a statement that Mongolia was part of China. While the Chinese regarded this more as a question of form, intended to mollify the unavoidable public protest against the declaration, the Russians feared that such an assertion would make it unacceptable to the Mongols as a basis for tripartite discussions. It was finally agreed to include this statement in an exchange of notes.[50]

Throughout the talks with Sun Pao-ch'i, Krupenskii had held the whip-hand, particularly during the "Second Revolution" in the south of China when it became more necessary than ever for the Peking government to resolve the Mongolian problem. Sun reminded Yuan Shih-k'ai that the history of negotiations over Mongolia had demonstrated Russia's readiness to act independently if China were unwilling or unable to come to an acceptable arrangement. He warned the President that if the matter were not soon resolved, "in the end this will become China's northern sorrow."[51] Yuan agreed, and on November 5,

1913, just one year and two months after the Russo-Mongolian Agreement, texts of the declaration were simultaneously released in Peking and St.Petersburg. A day before, for reasons only partially related to the Sino-Russian Declaration, the Kuomintang party was outlawed, helping to distract public attention from the Declaration.

The Sino-Russian Declaration and Exchange of Notes were a complete victory for the Russians. China recognized Mongolia's autonomy in its internal administration, agreed to refrain from sending troops or officials or to permit colonization (Russia took a similar pledge), accepted the "good offices" of Russia in Chinese-Mongolian affairs, and consented to attend a tripartite conference in which the "authorities" of Outer Mongolia would participate. Mongolia was free to dispose of commercial and industrial questions without interference, although matters of a political or territorial nature were subject to the Chinese government (with Russian and Mongolian advice). The pan-Mongolian aspirations of the Khalkhas were dealt a blow by the definition of "Autonomous Outer Mongolia" as including the administrative regions of the Urga viceroy, the Uliastai military governor, and the Khovd deputy military governor during the Ch'ing dynasty, that is, Khalkha and the Khovd region.

The vital difference between the Sino-Russian Declaration and the Russo-Mongolian Agreement was that the latter did not endeavor to place any limits on Mongolia's size and by implication recognized Mongolia as a sovereign state, whereas the declaration reduced Mongolia to a quasi-independent (autonomous) state with powers confined strictly to its internal affairs. The term "internal administration," a very ambiguous one, was to cause a multitude of problems later, for the Mongols and Russians tended to interpret it broadly while the Chinese preferred to interpret it more narrowly.

## The Sain Noyon Khan Mission to Russia

The Mongols had known as early as November 1912 that discussions were taking place in Peking and were distressed and angered to be excluded from talks on which their own future rested. The fact that they did not have a very clear understanding of the substance and progress of these negotiations only aggravated their fears. Korostovetz arranged an audience with the Khutukhtu in May to clear up these misapprehensions and to explain the purpose of the current negotiations. The Bogd Khaan said he understood the benefits of the treaty, but suggested that it should not include any article recognizing Chinese suzerainty over Mongolia. The Khutukhtu had evidently understood nothing.

Mongolian nerves were slowly fraying from uncertainty and fear, and the future of the Mongolian state seemed to balance on the outcome of the talks in Peking. With an eye to influencing those talks a second mission, more influential than the Khanddorj delegation, was sent to Petersburg headed by the Prime Minister, the Sain Noyon Khan. The objectives of this embassy were almost precisely identical to those of the 1912-13 Khanddorj mission: enlist Russian support for pan-Mongolia, meet with foreign ambassadors in Petersburg, and obtain another loan and additional weapons.

The Sain Noyon Khan left Urga in November 1913, a few days before the announcement of the Sino-Russian Declaration, and remained in Russia until early January 1914. In Petersburg he was shown the text of the declaration by the head of the Far Eastern Department of the Foreign Ministry, Kazakov, who emphasized that although this agreement recognized Chinese suzerainty over Mongolia, the Urga government was in fact independent in all matters excluding those of a political or territorial nature. It was impressed upon him in several conversations which followed, however, that full independence and a pan-Mongolian state were out of the question: the Western powers would oppose the dismemberment of China, and Japan and England would become troublesome if they believed that their interests in Inner Mongolia and its contiguous regions might be jeopardized. The Sain Noyon Khan nevertheless continued to insist that the Khalkhas would not relinquish Inner Mongolia.

Once the Bogd Khaan Government had a chance to study the declaration, it was furious. In Petersburg the Sain Noyon Khan told Korostovetz that the Mongols were "enraged" at the duplicity of Russian policy which contravened all responsibilities undertaken by the Tsarist government toward Mongolia since 1911. The "pro-China" faction at court was gaining influence, he warned, and was accusing those known for their pro-Russian sentiments of high treason. The Mongolian Ministry of Foreign Affairs delivered a note to the new Diplomatic Agent and Consul-General in Urga, Alexander Miller, refusing to recognize the declaration. On December 16 the Sain Noyon Khan sent a letter to Sazonov stating that Mongolia had once and for all broken with China and would not recognize a subordinate relationship with it. The letter did express Urga's willingness to participate in the proposed tripartite talks, but once more emphasized its hope that Russia would support the aspirations of the Barguts and Inner Mongolians to join the Mongolian state.[52]

Like Khanddorj before him, the Sain Noyon Khan made a futile attempt to contact Western ambassadors in Petersburg and to recruit their support. Notes were sent to the embassies of the United States, Great Britain, France, Germany, and Japan announcing the independence of Mongolia and the formation of a pan-Mongolian state. There were no answers. Rather naively, the Sain Noyon Khan asked the Russian Foreign Ministry to help him meet with the foreign ambassadors and visit Western Europe. The Ministry demurred with the excuse that such contacts would be "inappropriate."[53]

A rather interesting footnote to Urga's efforts to break into foreign diplomatic circles was its approach to Japan and the curious Kodama affair. Kodama (a pseudonym), a retired naval captain employed by the South Manchurian Railway Company, visited Urga apparently at his own initiative in the latter part of 1913 and met with several Mongolian leaders. Although it is unclear what he told the Mongols, the latter interpreted his presence and remarks as an official demonstration of Japanese support for pan-Mongolia. A letter was then written to the Japanese Emperor proposing that a permanent and close friendship be established between the two countries, for which purpose the Mongols invited the Japanese government to assign a representative to Urga. The Emperor was also asked to help in the unification of Inner and Outer Mongolia. The Sain

Noyon Khan took the letter to Petersburg, where he asked the Russians to transmit it to the Japanese. The Foreign Ministry did decide to pass the letter on, but only in order to impress upon the Mongols the hopelessness of looking for help elsewhere than Russia. As expected, the Japanese refused to accept the missive, and the Russians returned it to the Sain Noyon Khan, chiding him that this incident should be a lesson to the Mongols.[54]

One of the more pressing objectives of the mission was the purchase of weapons, then in especially short supply. The Sain Noyon Khan submitted a request for a hundred thousand rifles, ten cannon, and forty machine-guns, which he averred were to be used only for the maintenance of internal order. The Russians refused, suspecting (probably correctly) that they were intended for use in the Inner Mongolian campaign. They explained that the Mongolian treasury was incapable of shouldering such a debt, and that the presence of the Mongolian brigade and, more importantly, a sensible administrative and financial system would be far more effective in ensuring peace in the country. Later, however, the Russian ministers reconsidered this refusal, fearing that the Sain Noyon Khan's influence at home would be undermined if this request were rejected out of hand. They agreed in the end to sell twenty thousand rifles, six cannon, and four machine-guns.

The final item on the Mongolian shopping list was a loan, made necessary by the extravagant southern expedition, the fiscal irresponsibility of the Urga government and the Khutukhtu's court, and by the obsolete and inadequate tax system of the Bogd Khaan state inherited from the Ch'ing. Although the original request for five million rubles was rejected, the Russians realized that the Urga government could not possibly continue functioning without financial aid. They agreed to a loan of three million rubles secured on the income of the Mongolian government itself.

Tsarism had a stake in this fledgling government and wished to see it develop the economic resources and cultivate the political skills that would allow it to operate without constant underpinning. Since the Petersburg government was determined that this money was to be used for productive activities which would benefit the country as a whole, it stipulated that the loan was to be employed for the "cultural improvement and enrichment of Mongolia." To ensure that the money was spent sensibly and properly, they demanded that the Sain Noyon Khan sign a contract with an official of the Ministry of Finance, S.A. Kozin, who was to serve as financial adviser to the Mongolian government for a period of three years. The contract authorized Kozin to reorganize the Mongolian treasury, to draw up a national budget, and to fix taxes. The Urga government refused to accept these conditions and ordered the Sain Noyon Khan to return home immediately. But when he informed the Russian Foreign Ministry of these instructions and of his refusal to sign the contract, the Russians applied rather crude pressure: the Mongolian Prime Minister was warned that unless he signed, the Imperial Government could only assume that he lacked plenipotentiary powers and would be forced therefore to invalidate all of the other agreements made with the Khan. The contract was signed.[55]

Although the Sain Noyon Khan's mission should have been regarded as a qualifed success, the Bogd Khaan's court characteristically saw a glass that was half-empty instead of one half-full. He had not obtained the desired quantity of arms, although he had secured a promise for more than the Mongols could themselves use; he had obtained a smaller loan than was wanted, not to mention the undesirable conditions attached to it; but most important, he had wholly failed to win either Russian or Japanese support for Mongolian unification. The court was deeply disappointed and not a little angry at him.

## Further Agreements between Russia and Mongolia

Before 1914 was to close there were yet other agreements signed with Russia which were designed to foster economic prosperity in Mongolia and to expand Russian influence at the same time (it is important to remember that the Russians regarded both propositions as indivisibly linked). The penury of the state treasury had obliged the Mongols to find additional sources of revenue quickly. While the Sain Noyon Khan was being sent to Petersburg to negotiate a new loan, there was renewed interest in the almost forgotten national bank concession extended to the Russian State-Councillor Yuferov in 1912, which Mongolian ministers, who never did succeed in grasping the political and economic realities of the modern age, expected could keep the government magically solvent through continual loans. The Russian government, fearing that the Mongols would transfer the concession to a foreign national, decided in July 1914 that the concession would be taken up by the Siberian Commercial Bank, which agreed to form an independent bank rather than simply open a branch in the belief that only an independent institution (managed by Russians of course) could convincingly serve as a national bank of Mongolia. It was agreed to call it the Mongolian National Bank, to capitalize it with one million rubles, and that it would conduct normal banking functions, including the printing of paper money. The statutes of the bank, incidentally, gave the Imperial Government control over its entire activity through appointed representatives.

Both the Russians and the Mongols were excited by the possibilities of the bank. For Russian merchants in Mongolia, it would extend much needed credit, which, it was hoped, would improve their competitive position vis-a-vis the Chinese. The Russian government regarded the bank as an instrument to force greater financial responsibility on the Urga government and as a political lever against the Mongols if necessary. And the Mongols, whose hopes for the bank were monumental, believed that it would be an inexhaustible source of credit. There was something for everyone.

By the opening of the Tripartite Conference at Kyakhta in the autumn of 1914 several additional agreements--weapons, military instructors, loan, and telegraph and railroad--were concluded or on the verge of being concluded between Russia and the Mongols. These agreements laid the finishing touches to the first, "Russian" episode of the Bogd Khaan years.

Discussions in Urga between the Diplomatic Agent and the Mongolian government over the weapons agreement, the army brigade, and the three million-ruble loan, while occasionally somewhat turbulent, were concluded without extraordinary difficulty. The Russians had misgivings about the wisdom of selling weapons worth two million rubles, precisely two-thirds the entire value of the loan. But Mongolian insistence that the railroad agreement (vital to the Russians) was contingent upon the delivery of the agreed weapons speedily removed their doubts. The sale went ahead.

Regarding the brigade agreement, the Mongols complained that they did not have the financial means to support such a unit and wanted its size reduced from nineteen hundred to three hundred men and a much smaller staff of Russian instructors. While the Russians were convinced that the brigade was necessary for the preservation of Russian influence and was the only reliable means available to the Urga government to discourage the separatist inclinations of certain princes, Mongolian tenacity eventually wore the Russians down. A one-year agreement was signed at the end of May 1914 providing for a brigade of four hundred soldiers and twenty-two instructors.

And while the Mongols were dissatisfied with the amount of the loan and its supervision by Kozin, the Mongolian treasury was so exhausted that they simply had no choice but to accept Russian terms.

Although by the end of July 1914 the weapons and loan agreements were ready for signing, they were not officially concluded until late September. The explanation for the delay was the difficult, protracted, and sometimes acrimonious discussions over the railroad question. The Petersburg government wanted to acquire exclusive right to build railroads in Mongolia (which eventually would be linked up with the Siberian railway system) in order both to supply Mongolia more easily with Russian goods and to advance Tsarist influence. Although the volume of commerce with Mongolia at that time did not warrant the construction of a line, the Russians believed that an agreement was necessary which at least excluded foreigners from obtaining the concession. Although initially receptive to the proposal, the Mongols changed their minds, in part because of opposition to the monopolistic character of the railroad agreement but primarily because of their exaggerated hopes for the huge sums which they believed could be obtained from granting a railroad concession. All of Miller's persuasion and threats could not change their minds.

By mid-July, however, a new realism seemed to be evident among the Mongolian leaders, who probably were very sobered by the prospect of bankruptcy and, in the opinion of the Diplomatic Agent, by their consistent failure to generate interest in their country among the European powers or Japan. This, combined with Miller's ultimatum that the Petersburg government would repudiate the loan and weapons agreement unless the Mongols acquiesced, forced them to concede. On September 30 the railroad, telegraph (Mondy-Uliastai), loan, and arms agreements were signed.[56]

---

By October 1914, when the Tripartite Conference was just getting underway, the Russians appeared to have finally tamed the Mongols. They had secured a number of agreements which collectively gave the appearance of undisputed Russian domination over Mongolia. The 1912 Commercial Protocol, Mongolian acceptance of a financial adviser, plans for a national bank under Russian supervision, and the railroad agreement, to mention only a few, were the signs and instruments of Russia's future in Mongolia. But these were merely paper arrangements and, as I shall show in the following chapter, never repaid in benefits the time invested to obtain them: Russian merchants failed to exploit their favored position and advantages; Kozin was ignored; the Mongolian National Bank operated briefly and ineffectively; and no railroads were built.

Western and Chinese accounts of this period, indeed of modern Mongolian history generally, often portray the Mongols as obliging marionettes responding obediently to their Russian puppeteers. But after a careful study of the sources, a different story emerges. The Mongols, although untutored in diplomatic finesse, were nonetheless tenacious and scrappy negotiators, who frequently drove their Russian opposite numbers into paroxysms of frustration and anger. They met Tsarist bullying with procrastination, and Tsarist threats with evasions.

When the Mongols conceded, they expected compensation; when dissatisfied, they looked elsewhere.

One must equally remember, however, that there was a broad range of mutual interests which linked the Russians and Mongols, and attempts to characterize Russian policies as predatory obscure the complexity of Tsarist activities in Mongolia. Of course, the Russians were moved more by self-interest than by charity in their foreign policy. This is no more than a truism of international politics. But the various agreements which Russia concluded with Mongolia from 1912 to 1914 were all designed not only to promote Russian interests but to build a prosperous and modern state under a strong, responsible government. Ironically, one of the principal sources of irritation between Urga and Petersburg was that the Russians showed greater resolve in pushing Mongolia into the twentieth century than did the Mongols.

# CHAPTER III

## REVIVAL OF CHINESE INFLUENCE, 1915-17

By the fall of 1914 the Russian Ministry of Foreign Affairs could feel very satisfied with the results of its labors in Mongolia. Separate agreements concluded with the Chinese, Mongols, and Japanese had recognized Mongolia as a semi-sovereign state, formally part of China but under the political and economic influence of Tsarist Russia. This arrangement was not the product of a single battle--it was the result of innumerable diplomatic skirmishes with the Chinese, and especially the Mongols, who bitterly contested every inch of ground they were forced to yield. For several decades the Chinese had watched Western politics being played out on their very doorstep and were therefore initiated into its usages and artifices. But the Mongols, who played by an altogether different set of rules, continually exasperated the Russians by their unconventional behavior.

This was, nevertheless, a counterfeit settlement. With the exception of the secret treaties signed with Japan between 1906 and 1912, the agreements with China and Mongolia between 1912 and 1914 neither had the force of international law nor were even honored by all parties concerned: the Chinese repudiated the 1912 Russo-Mongolian Agreement and the Mongols refused to acknowledge the 1913 Declaration and Exchange of Notes. The latter in reality was no more than a statement of principles by which neither of the contracting parties was bound. It was important to the Russians that all the participants come to a common and binding agreement on a definition of Mongolia. They consequently invited Mongolia and China to send delegations to Kyakhta, where such an agreement would be hammered out.

## Tripartite Conference

The conference was scheduled for the spring of 1914, and already by early 1914 both Russian and Chinese delegations had been appointed and were preparing for departure to Kyakhta. The Russians had no little difficulty, however, in persuading the Mongols to attend this conference and to ratify an agreement which denied the very *raison d'etre* of their new state.

Despite their earlier consent, the Mongols in mid-March suddenly asked that the conference be postponed until the beginning of autumn because, as Miller suspected, of their hopes of seeking better terms from the Chinese. There may have been some basis for this suspicion. Somewhat earlier the Diplomatic Agent had learned that the Chinese government was trying to inveigle the Mongolian princes back into the Republic with promises of renewing the salaries paid during the Ch'ing, of redeeming their old debts to the Ch'ing state bank, and of granting a loan to the Urga government. In response, the Petersburg government warned the Mongols that Russia and China might proceed without them, and simultaneously warned the Chinese that if they persisted in ignoring the Russo-Mongolian Agreement and the Sino-Russian Declaration by trying to reach an independent understanding with Urga which excluded the Russians, Russia would stop exercising a "moderating influence" on the Mongols.

But the Mongols persevered. In June they threatened not to attend the conference unless Chinese persecutions in Inner Mongolia were ended. The timing and choice of this issue may have been designed to wreck the chances of the conference meeting at all. And in July they went further by demanding that the Peking government repeal its recent annexation of Inner Mongolia--between November 1913 and June 1914 Inner Mongolia had been carved into three "special regions": Suiyuan, Jehol, and Chahar--and repudiate its suzerainty over Outer Mongolia before the conference began.

Just when the future of the conference, at least with Mongolian participation, looked so bleak, Miller was told in a private audience with the Khutukhtu on July 29 that Mongolian delegates would be present after all for the opening session of the negotiations.

We can only surmise the reasons for this spirit of accommodation, but it was probably related to the new "realism" which Miller himself had observered earlier. After three years of almost heroic efforts the Khalkhas were no nearer to winning Mongolian unification or full independence than they had been in 1911. Their approaches to the Western powers had been ignored; when diplomacy failed they tried war, but the southern expedition was equally unproductive. The need for a quick settlement of the Inner Mongolian question may have been impressed on the Mongols by the recent Chinese administrative absorption of that region and by the fear that Miller's threat to convene the conference, with or without Mongolian participation, was not an idle one.

This did not imply, however, that the Mongols had abandoned either goal. The Russian Foreign Ministry had decided that its position could be more effectively presented if a united front were formed with the Mongols at Kyakhta, and Miller was instructed to work out a joint program in advance. But this proved to be another unhappy and frustrating experience for the Diplomatic Agent, as one can sense from his telegram to Petersburg on August 1, 1914:

> ...the Mongols are in no hurry. At our joint discussions most of the time is taken up with debates over the questions of annexing Inner Mongolia to Khalkha and abolishing Chinese suzerainty. For the hundredth time the question will be put to me: why is Mongolian territory considered part of China? They will always hear the same explanation, and they will then pronounce on the misfortune which will befall them because of this and which has led Russia to refuse to support the annexation of Inner Mongolia. Then they will return to a methodical discussion of my draft. The same thing will be repeated at the beginning or the conclusion of the next meeting.[57]

Miller never did succeed in composing a common Russian-Mongolian program.

In spite of these hurdles, the first session of the conference opened on September 8 in the Russian Chamber of Commerce at Kyakhta.[58] The Chinese delegation, which with around fifteen members was by far the largest, was headed by two very competent and talented men, Pi Kuei-fang (chief of the delegation) and Ch'en Lu. Pi was a former Chinese bannerman from Hopei, who had studied at the Peking College of Languages (T'ung-wen kuan) and then in Russia; he had just been recalled from a troubled tour as military and civilian governor of Heilungkiang. Ch'en Lu, a southerner from Fukien province, was to become China's first high commissioner in Outer Mongolia and then later to play a prominent role in the foreign affairs of the Chinese Republic until his assassination about 1938. Like many other Chinese leaders who emerged during the Republican period, he had received a Western education in China and then went abroad to Europe for further study.

The Russian delegation was headed by the Diplomatic Agent and Consul-General A. Miller, and included the Frontier Commissioner of Kyakhta A.D. Khitrovo and an agent of the Ministry of Industry and Commerce attached to the Urga Consulate, A.P. Boloban.

And finally, the Mongolian delegation was headed by Minister of Internal Affairs and concurrently deputy head of the Ministry of Religion and State Da Lama Dashjav (he was replaced in November 1914 by Deputy Minister of Justice Shirnindamdin Beise) and Minister of Finance Ch'in-wang Chagdarjav. They were assisted by Deputy Minister of Justice Ch'in-wang Udai, First Councillor of the Ministry of the Army Manlai baatar Damdinsüren (both of these men, significantly, were Inner Mongolians), Deputy Minister of Foreign Affairs Jigjidjav Kung, and Tserendorj Kung who was also Deputy Minister of Foreign Affiars. The Buryats Ts. Zhamtsarano and Ts. Badmazhapov served as translators.

The conference throughout was an acrimonious affair. The constant references in Ch'en Lu's diary to "stubborn" Mongolian objections and "stern" Chinese rebukes reflects the bitterness of the exchanges between the Chinese and Mongolian representatives. The conference would certainly have broken up at the first session had it not been for the skill of the Russian representative, who was tireless in forging compromises between the contradictory postions of the Chinese and Mongolian delegates and then forcing them into accepting more modest arrangements when normal discussions failed.

In reality, however, the only meaningful talks went on between the Russian and Chinese delegations, despite the very voluble role played by the Mongols, and these constructive and serious exchanges occurred either over the conference table or (more commonly) behind closed doors, or at ministerial level in Petrograd (after the beginning of the First World War in August 1914, Petersburg was renamed Petrograd) and Peking. To be sure, the Mongols were needed to ratify whatever agreement issued from the conference, but they were regarded as somewhat irrelevant by the other two parties and were excluded from the closed meetings of Miller, Pi Kuei-fang, and Ch'en Lu, where many of the most thorny questions were worked out.

It was the very clarity and simplicity of the Chinese and Mongolian positions that made compromise so difficult. The Chinese sought to minimize, ideally to abrogate altogether, Mongolian autonomy and to maximize Chinese rights and powers in that country. The Mongols were determined at the very least to stretch autonomy into de facto independence and to deny the Chinese more than vaguely worded, ineffectual suzerain powers. The Russian position lay somewhere in the boundless tract separating the two. There seemed to be no obvious compromise between the two extreme positions. The Russians, therefore, had to manufacture one and then cajole or coerce the principals into accepting it.

Although Russia was ultimately successful in forcing the other parties to subscribe to its program, this was done at the cost of thoroughly exhausting its limited reserves of good will with both the Chinese and Mongols. It must also be said that the Russians, in acting out their role as mediators, did observe a certain formal impartiality, although in practice they generally, but by no means invariably, supported the Mongolian representatives.

During the first two months of the conference the delegates were absorbed in the problem of defining the precise nature of Mongolia's "autonomous" relationship with China. At the first meeting the Chinese delegation demanded that the Mongols formally renounce independence, revoke the titles of "bogd khaan" and "bogd ezen" and the reign-title "Elevated by the Multitudes," and adopt the Chinese Republican (solar) calendar. In the context of their imperial tradition, of course, the Chinese were right to insist that the Mongols renounce the word "state" (Ch. kuo, Mg. uls), the title "holy emperor" (Ch. huang-ti, Mg. bogd khaan), and other symbolic but vital paraphernalia of sovereignty historically reserved for the Middle Kingdom in its relations with the "barbarians." The Mongols, supported by Miller, rejected these demands.

Later in the month the Chinese delegates presented two documents which detailed Peking's interpretation of autonomy. The first restored to the central government those suzerain rights previously enjoyed by the Ch'ing dynasty (investiture, appointments, and so on). The second was much more contentious, inasmuch as it sought to prune autonomy to the status of a special region of China: the Mongols were denied the use of the term "government" (Ch. cheng-fu); Mongolian officials were to regard themselves as officials of the Chinese government; all rights acquired by Mongolia through international treaty were to revert to the Peking government; the "autonomous ministry" of Outer Mongolia, that is, the Urga government, was denied the right to negotiate with foreign powers; and the Peking government was empowered to send troops into Mongolia in the event of internal disturbance.

The Mongols, in a rather uninformative document of six points purporting to set forth their position, merely agreed to recognize Chinese suzerainty. The debate which followed became so heated that the Chinese delegates wired Peking requesting that they be recalled and the conference boycotted.

The diplomatic position of the Chinese Republic, however, was never so weak as it was at this time. In addition to the problems of the Peking government with indigence, incipient warlordism, and a fractious south, the Japanese had just seized Shantung following their declaration of war against Germany, and on January 18, 1915 presented China with the notorious "Twenty-one Demands." Tense discussions with Japan continued until May 25. The Chinese government, as it frequently advised its plenipotentiaries in Kyakhta, wanted the northern problem settled as quickly as possible, and the delegates were urged to continue the talks. Krupenskii moreover had informed the Chinese Foreign Minister of the unacceptable way in which their delegates were behaving and warned that discussions would end prematurely unless a fundamental change occurred.

Working by these anarchic procedures the conference could not hope to make any progress. Therefore, a more systematic method of conducting discussions was devised. Each delegation was to submit a draft treaty; those articles to which all parties agreed were to be considered first, leaving the more contentious issues (railroad construction, postal and telegraph service, commercial tariffs, and Inner Mongolia) for later examination. The adoption of these new procedures resulted in infinitely greater efficiency.

The Russian draft differed only in relatively minor respects from the final treaty. The Russians had the clearest understanding of the terms under which the conference met (set forth in the agreements with China and Mongolia), and the most realistic appreciation of the possibilities and limitations of a tripartite settlement. But perhaps most important of all, they were in the strongest position politically to dominate the conference.

The next Chinese draft still contained all of the objectionable articles which had been presented earlier, while the Mongolian draft of them all bore the least relation to reality or to the eventual treaty: it recognized the "sovereign independence" of Mongolia, albeit under Chinese "limited rule;" it defined the Mongolian state as including Barga, Inner Mongolia, and Uryankhai; and it permitted the Mongolian government to post diplomatic representatives to China and Russia.

In the latter part of November Pi Kuei-fang and Ch'en Lu met privately with Miller over the question of railroad construction and postal and telegraph service in Mongolia. They endeavored to persuade Miller that these were matters which fell under the suzerain powers of China. Miller rejected the argument, insisting that they were part of the Mongolian internal administration, and added that the question was by then academic because Russia and Mongolia had just concluded railroad and telegraph agreements.

The Chinese delegates, who had been angered earlier on learning of these agreements, did not believe that there was any profit for China in continuing the talks and advised Peking that, in the hope of "retrieving the situation," discussions should be suspended and a different venue chosen for future negotiations. This suggestion was not accepted. The Chinese also wanted a statement included in the treaty about their right to establish a postal service in Mongolia, arguing that this was an essential prerogative of suzerainty. The Russians and Mongols refused. The subject was dropped.

Not long afterwards, the question of tariffs on Chinese commerce was brought up for discussion. This proved to be the most vexatious issue of all and was to absorb the representatives from late January to the first part of Arpil 1915. The Russians and Mongols insisted that Chinese merchants pay some kind of commercial duty; the Chinese rejected this on the grounds that taxation was one of the fundamental components of suzerainty. The reason for the protracted debate is not difficult to understand. By the Russo-Mongolian Commercial Protocol of 1912 Russians were given the right of duty-free trade in Mongolia, a privilege they were not eager to surrender because of the belief that their merchants could not compete with the Chinese without special tariff protection. The Mongols were also keen to control such a tax as the income would help relieve their financial problems. And finally, the tariff issue was important politically since it was regarded as a touchstone by which Mongolia's autonomous powers could be tested.

The Chinese delegates in the days following did agree to a 2.5% _ad valorem_ internal transit duty (likin), provided that it was levied only once per trip. This was a major concession on the part of the Chinese, as it recognized the taxation rights of the Mongolian government. Miller, however, insisted on leaving the amount of duty undefined. Frustrated, the Chinese delegates for a third time urged their government to recall them; Peking refused once again. In mid-March, after Miller's warning that the obstinacy of the Chinese was making further negotiations useless, the Chinese delegates agreed to a 5% ad valorem transit duty but on conditions that Miller thought unacceptable.

The unwillingness of Pi Kuei-fang and Ch'en Lu to accept the Russian article in toto led the Russian Foreign Ministry on March 23 to order the suspension of negotiations. The Chinese delegates notified Peking of this development and for the fourth and last time urged the government to abandon the talks until the Sino-Japanese negotiations were concluded. The Peking government, however, was evidently in a hurry to resolve its nagging "northern problem" and decided to accept the Russian draft of the tariff article.

During April and May the delegates were occupied with the last major question of the conference, Inner Mongolia. This issue was in fact composed of three separate problems: Chinese colonization in Inner Mongolia, amnesty for Inner Mongolian refugees to Urga (according to one estimate, over a thousand Inner Mongolians fled to Khalkha as a result of the 1912 disturbances[59]), and freedom of pilgrimage for Inner Mongolian Lamaists to worship in Urga. This matter actually proved to be much easier to settle than one would have anticipated in view of the bitter controversy which it had generated in earlier years, for the Chinese delegates, who without support from Peking proved to be very ineffective negotiators, were unable to bring much resistance to bear.

It was hypocritical of the Russians, however, who until now had meticulously observed the principle that the scope of the conference was limited to questions arising from Mongolian autonomy, to introduce a topic so completely unrelated and obviously outside the conference's province. The Russians probably hoped to exploit China's negotiating weakness by raising a question which, if resolved in their favor, would strengthen and geographically enlarge Mongolia's buffer role, while at least partly assuaging the disappointment of the Khalkhas at losing Inner Mongolia. The Chinese delegates did protest to Miller that this subject exceeded the scope of the conference. The Russian, without even troubling himself to argue, merely warned that he would be obliged to ask his government when it wanted to end the conference. The Sino-Japanese negotiations had at that very moment reached an exceptionally critical stage, and the wounded Chinese government had no alternative but to submit. Yuan Shih-k'ai rather pathetically asked the Russian Minister in Peking to "demand no more from China in its present difficulties."[60]

It was decided that the Inner Mongolian problem would be treated in a special note, and that the precise breadth of the zone in which Chinese colonization was forbidden would await the demarcation of the Inner and Outer Mongolian border as provided for in article eleven.

The Kyakhta treaty, composed of twenty-two articles and signed on June 7, 1915, did not make any substantial changes in the status of Outer Mongolia which did not already exist, either in fact or by previous diplomatic arrangement. The Chinese and Mongols were now contractually bound to a form of autonomy fashioned by the 1912 agreement and the 1913 declaration, which had long been the goal of the Russians. The treaty was therefore an unqualified victory for Russian diplomacy, although its successful outcome was not so much the product of Miller's diplomatic skills as China's preoccupation with Japanese aggression and the desire of the Peking government to finish with the conference as quickly as possible. Among Chinese observers only the most unrepentent optimist could have found any satisfaction in the treaty--the clause conceding Chinese suzerainty gave small solace. And yet, by permitting Peking to appoint a high commissioner to Urga and deputy high commissioners to Uliastai, Khovd, and Kyakhta, the Chinese did gain one vital advantage wholly unappreciated at the time. With an official presence in Mongolia, the Chinese were given an instrument through which they could realize the political goals they had been unable to secure by other means.

Although the Kyakhta treaty should not have contained any surprises for the Mongols--on the contrary, they made some unexpected gains, such as the right to impose a tariff on Chinese commerce and ownership of that part of the Kyakhta-Urga-Kalgan telegraph line which ran across Mongolian territory --it was nonetheless regarded by the Khutukhtu's court as an unmitigated disaster because it still denied full independence to Outer Mongolia and a pan-Mongolian state.

## Russian Influence in Decline

In June 1915 the Chinese and Mongols had finally consented to a new autonomous order for Mongolia which the Russians had doggedly sought since 1911. The various settlements with China, Japan and Mongolia gave Russia impressive rights in the country which have been seen by many contemporary and later observers as amounting to political and economic rule. There has been rare unanimity among Western and Communist historians who have described Mongolia as under Tsarist "domination" or as a Russian "colony."

It is instructive to note, however, that Tsarist diplomats themselves, such as Sazonov, Korostovetz, Miller, and others, invariably commented on the willfulness of the Mongols and on their efforts--sometimes successful, sometimes not--to impede or sabotage Russian policy. The assertion of one historian, that "the Mongols owed many things to Russia--for instance, money and arms--but one should be on one's guard against over-emphasizing the effectiveness of her influence," I believe is correct.[61]

The cause of this error is to be found in the conclusion, drawn all too quickly, that Russian paper privileges in Mongolia were translated into material benefits. They seldom were. From the Tsarist point of view, its record in Mongolia from 1911 to 1917 was mix. On the one hand, it was successful in forcing China to limit its claim over Outer Mongolia, but attempts to exact obedience from the Mongols or to establish effective agencies of political and economic control had very disappointing results. The Mongolian nomad may have been unlettered, but he was not ignorant, nor was he ever the dormant, pliable creature the Russians initially took him to be.

Historians have generally placed the decline of Russian influence either at 1915 following the Kyakhta conference, or at 1917 when the Russian revolution broke out. I. Korostovetz, however, the Russian diplomat who negotiated the 1912 agreement with the Mongols and who was in a unique position to observe and assess the attitudes of the Urga government, wrote that shortly after the agreement the "honeymoon of our friendship was over." From this point on, he remarked, the Mongols became more intractable in negotiations and even expressed mistrust of Russian motives.[62]

This rapid change of heart was primarily the result of Russia's insistence that the Mongols accept autonomy rather than independence, and the exclusion of Inner Mongolia, Barga, and Uryankhai from the Bogd Khaan state. But the decline of the Russian star over Mongolia was the consequence of a variety of other circumstances, the cumulative effect of which was thoroughly to estrange Mongolian leaders from Tsarism. In the next few pages these disappointments will be isolated and analyzed, while at the same time discussing in more detail Russian activities in Mongolia after 1911.

As Korostovetz noted, the Russo-Mongolian "honeymoon" ended very quickly, perhaps by the early part of 1913. The Mongols did not completely abandon hope in Russia after this, but as time went on the stamina and influence of the Russian partisans in the Khutukhtu's court and government progressively weakened with each new reverse. When the Mongols went to Kyakhta in September 1914 they were determined to present their case with all possible vigor, perhaps realizing that this was their last opportunity to rescue something from the political wreckage of the last three years. This undoubtedly made their failure at Kyakhta especially bitter.

After the Kyakhta treaty the issue of pan-Mongolia quietly dropped from sight for the rest of the Bogd Khaan period, except for a brief period in 1918-19 when it was revived by the Buryats and Semenov. It is interesting that the Chinese and Russian sources of the Kyakhta conference do not show the Mongols pressing for pan-Mongolia with the same purposeful energy which they had shown only a few months earlier. Perhaps the Khutukhtu's court had finally bowed to the inevitable, or perhaps the court may have yielded because of friction with the Inner Mongolian refugees in Urga after 1912, who had been angered by the arrogance and neglect with which they were treated by the Urga government. For whatever reason, after 1915 the dream of pan-Mongolia never again figured so large and obsessively in Khalkha thinking as it had between 1911 and 1915. The return of the Inner Mongolians to their homeland in the south after the signing of the treaty removed the last physical reminder of this vision.

If the Mongols were rankled by the merely passive Russian resistance to Urga's claim to Inner Mongolia, Russian territorial designs on Barga and Uryankhai surely embittered them. Support for Urga's claim to Barga was clearly out of the question. It was an indisputable part of a Chinese province (Heilungkiang), contained two international treaty ports (Hailar and Manchouli), and was traversed by the strategic Chinese Eastern Railway under joint Russian and Chinese ownership. After the 1913 declaration the Russians approached Peking directly and suggested that they mediate between the Barguts and Chinese for the restoration of China's sovereignty over this region, and proposed that Barga be transformed into a special district with broad autonomous rights. In return for these services, the Tsarist government expected to be granted certain economic privileges. A treaty incorporating most of these conditions was signed on November 6, 1915.

Although Uryankhai was never such a visceral issue with the Khalkhas as was Inner Mongolia or Barga, the establishment of a Russian protectorate over the region in 1914 was perceived as another Russian ploy to undermine the Mongolian state. After the 1912 Russo-Mongolian Agreement had been signed, Korostovetz was visited by a few Khalkha officials who demanded that Uryankhai be returned to Outer Mongolia. Da Lama Tserenchimed, surely reflecting the general mood of the Urga government, noted sarcastically during the meeting that the Russians apparently understood what constituted Mongolian territory better than did the Mongols themselves.

In addition to the territorial issues of Inner Mongolia, Barga, and Uryankhai, which troubled relations between the two countries, there was a variety of other forces at work that progressively eroded Russian influence in Mongolia. One of the most important was the First World War. While the Far East generally speaking never exercised the Tsarist government to the same degree as did other parts of the world, notably Europe, the outbreak of war in August 1914 meant that all of the military, economic, and human resources of Russia were concentrated on the European conflict. By mid-1915 when the Russian military position on the front had deteriorated so badly, the Petrograd government had no alternative but to abandon its Asian interests altogether, which were now allowed to drift aimlessly. News of the February Revolution simply accelerated this decline. The spiraling inflation of Russian currency after the outbreak of war (by 1919 paper rubles were no longer accepted in Mongolia) did little to restore confidence in Russia among the Mongols.

If the Mongols strongly resented what they regarded as crass insensitivity to their political aspirations, Russian attempts to introduce certain social reforms also generated deep resentment and fear amongst a large number of influential nobles and lamas and did nothing to allay Urga's misgivings about Russia.

Surely the most controversial of these reforms, and parenthetically one which illustrates the growing secularization of at least a part of Urga society during this period, was the beginning of journalism in the country. The first Mongolian-language paper, <u>News of Mongolia</u> (<u>Mongolyn sonin bichig</u>), began publishing in 1909 under the sponsorship of the Chinese Eastern Railway. Korostovetz, believing that this paper was written in too sophisticated a language, organized in 1913 a new journal, <u>New Mirror</u> (<u>Shine tol'</u>), edited by the Buryat intellectual Ts. Zhamtsarano and published by the Russian Consulate in Urga. Korostovetz felt that the Mongols lacked reliable information about world events and were compelled to rely on either Chinese newspapers or rumor, neither of which could be counted on to present a very satisfactory image of Russia. He therefore set up this newsmagazine "in order to be better able to advance Russian influence by means of the printed word."[63]

Under the editorship of Zhamtsarano and with the assistance of other progressive Buryats and Khalkhas (including Bodoo), however, this periodical was immediately transformed into a platform for advocating fundamental political and social change. In addition to articles on political affairs, both domestic and foreign, the magazine provided elementary lessons on social and natural sciences and endeavored to correct misapprehensions about the world, many of which were cherished beliefs of the church. The lamas were incensed, for example,by one article in the first issue which denied that the world was flat. In the same issue was another article describing the major political systems of the world (autocracy, democracy, and constitutional monarchy). Other articles could be more blunt:

> Beyond the fact that the ministers and princes enjoy luminous reputations, favors, and excessive salaries bestowed on them by the Bogd Ezen...they continue to exploit the enslaved masses by collecting offerings and taxes. Not only do they not work to advance (Mongolia's) future strength and fame, to promote a just system for the present, or to spread the good name and firm principles of our ancestors, they do not (strive) sincerely to advance the fame of our state but always elevate their own persons.[64]

When Zhamtsarano translated and published Leo Tolstoy's Buddha on the New Mirror press, the volumes were quickly bought up, but the reaction of the lamas was so hostile that Korostovetz had to dampen the reforming enthusiasm of Zhamtsarano. He forbade all future traffic in matters relating to public beliefs or prejudices.

Medical and especially veterinary service was another area of Russian-sponsored reforms which met resistance from the lamas, especially since ministering to the ill was traditionally a lucrative sideline of the priestly craft. In 1913 the Russian Red Cross and the Office to Aid the Blind began operating in the country. The ophthalmologists Levitskaya and Borodin, who treated a total of seventeen thousand patients, and the Consulate doctor Tsibiktarov, a Buryat Mongol himself who opened a clinic for Russians and Mongols in 1913 and soon had a practice numbering up to seven thousand patients a year, were especially popular.[65]

There was also a certain amount of veterinary work, particularly the inoculation of livestock purchased by Russian merchants for export to Russia. But many lamas opposed inoculation because of a religious proscription against introducing foreign bodies into the blood. As Korostovetz noted, "They resisted anything which could in any way shake their privileged position and which could contribute to the enlightenment of the people."[66]

One other factor which helped to reduce the good will of the Urga court toward Russia was the personality of the Diplomatic Agent Alexander Miller. He was accredited to the Mongolian government in October 1913 with "extraordinary ceremony, unprecedented even in Urga," and was awarded the rank of chün-wang and the Order of the Vachir, recognitions probably intended to win Miller's sympathy and testifying to the hopes of the Mongols for his tour of service in Urga. The Mongols were soon disabused of their illusions whey they saw how conscientiously Miller worked to execute the policies of his government and to keep a tight rein on them. Moreover, the Mongols found him autocratic and complained of his partiality to the Chinese. Judging from his correspondence with Petrograd, Miller returned their dislike. He had little respect for most Mongolian officials, whom he regarded as incompetent in the extreme, and did little to disguise this contempt.

One of the grossest misconceptions about the Russian "domination" of Mongolia during the Bogd Khaan period is the belief in a free-wheeling Russian control over the Mongolian economy from 1912 to the 1917 revolution. After 1911 many, but far from all, Chinese merchants in Mongolia had fled either back to China or deep into the countryside (although the evidence is thin on this point, the majority of Chinese who did leave their shops probably did the latter). The Russians were suddenly left with a clear field in Mongolia. They secured moreover a number of commercial advantages by the 1912 commercial protocol (especially duty-free trade). There were other auspicious signs of the future of Russian commerce with the formation of the Russo-Mongolian Company and the Russian Export Company, and later the acquisition of concession areas (similar to those in Chinese treaty ports) in Urga and Khovd.

Although figures vary somewhat, the different sources do point emphatically to increased Russian trade with Mongolia beginning in 1912, particularly Russian exports to Mongolia which increased by two or more times, although imports from Mongolia remained roughly at their pre-1912 level.[67]

Nevertheless during the two or three years following the Mongolian revolution, Russian merchants were unable to take full advantage of the unusual commercial opportunities offered them or to caputre the Mongolian market as they had so confidently expected. Two years was an impossibly short period in which to build the necessary commercial organization of inventory, warehouses, employees, vehicles and so forth to serve adequately a country as large as Mongolia. The Russians were neither prepared nor equipped to replace the Chinese in 1912. With the Russian entry into the World War, moreover, Russian factories were converted to military production and manufactured goods were badly needed at home. As a consequence the entire country, and western Mongolia it seems in particular, was hit by a severe "goods famine," aggravated to no little degree by the practice of Russian merchants selling their goods at inflated prices (according to one estimate Russian commerce was able to satisfy only thirty to thirty-five percent of the market demand).[68]

By 1914, when Chinese traders began drifting back to their former businesses, the severity of the "goods famine" had abated. At the same time the Chinese-Mongolian "war" in Inner Mongolia had ended, thereby reopening the major trading routes between the two countries, and Chinese goods began appearing once again in considerable quantities to restore life to the economy. It would be more accurate to say, therefore, that the Chinese had abandoned the Mongolian market during the years from 1912 to 1914 than that the Russians controlled it--as soon as the Chinese returned in 1914 they immediately restored their commercial supremacy in most areas of the country.

Another treasured stereotype of this period represents the Russian Financial Adviser S.A. Kozin as the _éminence grise_ of the Urga government. According to one observer he became the "de facto master of the country."[69] The truth is much less colorful. Petersburg had always lacked confidence in the ability of the Urga administration to govern sensibly, and these reservations were confirmed in their eyes when they saw how recklessly and profligately the 1912 loan had been spent. When the Sain Noyon Khan came to Petersburg in 1913 seeking more money, the Russians made the approval of a loan conditional on the Mongols hiring a financial adviser to reorganize their chaotic national finances and to administer certain reforms which, it was hoped, would help to modernize and stabilize the country. The contract, signed in January 1914, gave Kozin supervision over the disbursement of all state revenues, the largest single item of which was the Russian loans. Despite his far-reaching economic powers, however, Kozin's work was handicapped by the inertia of the Mongolian government and the cupidity of Mongolian rulers. His proposed reforms frequently met with suspicion and in the end were either actively sabotaged or allowed to languish through inattention.

Kozin arrived in Urga in May 1914 and immediately set up the Office of the Russian Adviser. His first task was to reorganize and centralize state finances, which meant depriving the banners and aimags of their financial independence and completely reforming the irregular and primitive banner tax system. The irreconcilable opposition of the lay and church princes ultimately forced Kozin to abandon this work, although he was successful in introducing a certain rationality into the state finances of the central government and in balancing the state budget. Kozin was also expected to locate new sources of revenue for the Mongolian treasury, to which end he outfitted a large and expensive expedition in 1915-16 to make a geographical and statistical investigation of the country, but the data were never used for this purpose. In 1916 a Special Office of State Property was organized with broad powers to promote the exploitation of Mongolian natural resources. Here again the results were disappointing because of opposition he encountered, particularly from the church.

Kozin's work, however, was not entirely unsuccessful. He composed the first budget in Mongolian history and laid the groundwork for the 1918 census. He also established a "reform fund" which was used for a variety of useful state enterprises: coal mining at Nalaikh, setting up a printing press, building an electric power station, and organizing a modest telephone system in Urga. Nevertheless, in 1918 the Office of the Russian Adviser was liquidated by the Urga government. The court, which had always regarded this office as a nuisance, tolerated its presence because it appeared to be a precondition for additional Russian loans; but with the end of Tsarism its continued existence could no longer be justified.[70]

Another agency which many Russians had expected would serve as a vehicle for the insinuation of Tsarist economic and political influence into Mongolia was the Mongolian National Bank, opening in Urga in May 1915 with branches in Uliastai, Khovd, and other commercial centers. The bank was given the exclusive right to issue bank notes and was empowered to extend credit to the Mongolian government and lay and church princes. But this institution proved to be another major disappointment. It failed to print a single note, possibly because of the growing political and economic troubles of Russia after 1915. More importantly, it refused to extend loans to the Mongolian government, while loans to individual Mongols, if made at all, were granted only at very high rates of interest. In 1918 the Mongols formed their own national credit agency empowered to issue loans to the government, banners, and individuals, and simultaneously revoked the Russian bank concession.[71]

The Mongolian brigade suffered the same fate as other Russian projects. The first chief instructor, who had been sent to Mongolia in 1912, recognized that Mongolian nomads were already experienced horse- and riflemen and believed that they could be turned into effective cavalry troops with minimum training. The Petersburg government, on the other hand, thought that this amateurish instruction was inappropriate to the new Mongolian state and pressured the Mongols into signing an agreement in 1913 for the formation of a proper European-style brigade. The new instructor, Colonel Nadezhnyi, was an unhappy choice. He had a disdainful and abrasive manner and regarded the Mongols as a lower race unfit for military service, a preconception which he helped to realize by demanding that Mongolian recruits adopt Western standards of discipline and learn formation marching drills instead of the more practical cavalry maneuvres which were so natural to them.[72]

The Mongols resented this brigade agreement and argued that the organization of a military force along the lines contemplated by the Russians was an unnecessary luxury. Nor did they understand why they had to pay such large salaries to these Russian officers when the efforts of the first instructor and his much smaller staff had been perfectly adequate. The Mongols agreed, albeit very reluctantly, to renew the brigade agreement in 1914 but on substantially more limited terms.

The Mongolian government must also accept a certain share of the blame for the failure of this brigade to become an effective military unit. As early as 1912 Russian instructors were complaining that recruits sent by the banners for training were either too old or too young, and were generally suffering from disease (syphilis and rheumatism in particular). Soldiers were unpaid, nor were they furnished with accomodations (except for the barracks at Khujirbulan) or with clothing, and the food was frequently inedible. Desertion became a serious problem and there were a number of mutinies, for example in 1913 and 1914 at Khujirbulan (the young Sükhbaatar was involved in the second), in 1914 among the units on the western border, in 1915 at Urga, and in 1919 on the eastern border. According to the Diplomatic Agent, the average size of the brigade in 1913 never exceeded six hundred men, let along nineteen hundred as originally planned, because of desertions, sickness, and lack of qualified recruits; by the spring of 1914 most of the brigade horses had perished for lack of fodder.[73]

Russian influence in Mongolia was thus in irretrievable decline. The Mongols had been forced to abjure independence and pan-Mongolia, and unpopular reforms imposed by the Russians, inadequate financial backing, and a diminishing presence in the Far East disposed the Khutukhtu's court to regard their association with Russia as an encumbrance for which it received far too little compensation. The echoes of this new thinking reverberated from the court to the ministries of the Urga government, which in 1915 experienced a major reshuffling of senior officers. The evidence suggests that the reorganization of the government was closely linked with the eclipse of Russian influence in Mongolia. To what extent it was also the consequence of rancorous court politics must await the release of more archival material.

In the middle of February 1915 Minister of Foreign Affairs Khanddorj was murdered by agents of the Khutukhtu's court after attending a palace banquet.[74] While explanations for his assassination differ, his well-known Russian sympathies made him a particularly vulnerable target at a time when Russian policy was coming under greater criticism. He was replaced by the Deputy Minister of Foreign Affairs Tserendorj Kung, half-Chinese himself and one of the most able and interesting members of the Khutukhtu's government. Although Tserendorj's political orientation at this time is unknown, he later came to favor the return of Mongolia to China and was one of the principal Mongolian negotiators in the abolition of autonomy from 1918 to 1919.

Later in the year the Ministry of Religion and State and the post of prime minister were abolished (the Ministry of Religion and State had been organized only as a counterweight to the Office of the Prime Minister; the elimination of one necessarily affected the existence of the other). The Sain Noyon Khan, another man closely linked with the so-called "pro-Russian party," was appointed to the relatively powerless position of minister of the army, although he was left with the title "prime minister without portfolio." The lama Dashjav, then minister of internal affairs, replaced Badamdorj as erdene shanzudba, and Badamdorj was appointed minister of internal affairs. It is instructive that Badamdorj, a man described by Ch'en Lu as "fervently pro-Chinese," was brought back into the government and appointed to the important office of minister of internal affairs--a position which regained the preeminence it had enjoyed in the early part of 1912.

While the evidence is indeed equivocal on this question, the murder of Khanddorj and the demotion of the Sain Noyon Khan, together with the rising fortunes of Badamdorj and Tserendorj, surely do reflect the end of Russian influence with the Urga establishment. The only certain conclusion we can draw from these events is that by the close of 1915 the forces of Russian partisanship were in disarray, and the tables had been cleared for a new gamé with different players.

## The Ch'en Lu Period, 1915-17

The Kyakhta treaty made an important and unappreciated concession to Chinese suzerainty over Mongolia by allowing the Peking government to appoint a high commissioner to Urga and deputy high commissioners to Uliastai, Khovd, and Kyakhta "to exercise general control lest the acts of the Autonomous Government of Outer Mongolia and its subordinate authorities may impair the suzerain rights and the interests of China and her subjects in Autonomous Mongolia." These officials were forbidden, however, to interfere in the internal administration of Outer Mongolia. In June 1915 the Peking government appointed Ch'en Lu as high commissioner, a selection wisely made in view of his intelligence, ability and the valuable experiencc he had obtained at the Tripartite Conference.

The arrival of Ch'en Lu in Mongolia in late October 1915 and the deputy high commissioners a month or so later marks the resurgence of Chinese influence in Outer Mongolia. Dissatisfaction with Russian policies, as well as the receding Russian presence in northern Asia generally, made the Chinese appearance more conspicuous by contrast and probably welcome in certain quarters of the Mongolian nobility. The reality of China's "return" was underlined by the arrival of armed Chinese soldiers who were attached to the Commissions (according to the Tripartite Treaty, the High Commission in Urga was allowed one hundred fifty guards, while each of the Deputy High Commissions was allowed fifty). But no sooner had Ch'en settled into his new residence than his considerable abilities were tested by some difficult problems, the most serious and potentially explosive of which was the Bavuujav affair.

Bavuujav, an Eastern Tümed Mongol from Inner Mongolia, had joined the Japanese army during the war with Russia in 1904-05 and served in its reserve force. He later became chief of police in the district of Chang-wu in Liaoning province. In 1912 like many other Inner Mongolians he decided to cast in his lot with the new Mongolian state and went to Urga, where he was appointed battalion commander and awarded the rank of kung; he 1913 he was one of the senior officers in the army which advanced from Khalkha into Inner Mongolia. Despite the recall of these troops in 1914, Bavuujav remained with about a thousand men in the area of Khuuchit banner in Silingol league (along the southeast border of Outer Mongolia) to await the results of the forthcoming Tripartite Conference and its decision regarding pan-Mongolia. In the meantime he wrote to the Urga Khutukhtu several times urging him not to abandon Inner Mongolia to China.[75]

Deeply disappointed by the treaty, Bavuujav declared to the Urga government in July 1915 that he would never accept its terms. According to a report of the Russian Minister in Peking in late 1915, Bavuujav decided to create a principality for himself out of the Silingol league and demanded that the Chinese government exempt this region from all taxes and imposts and cede to him the lucrative salt excise of the territory; in return for this Bavuujav allegedly promised to submit to the government and disband his men. This offer was refused, and Bavuujav made preparations for a winter military campaign.[76]

In late October 1915, three days after arriving in Urga, Ch'en Lu received a telegram from the regional military authorities in Kalgan stating that disturbances caused by Bavuujav had necessitated the dispatch of a "bandit-suppression commander" a few days earlier to deal with him. Ch'en was asked to invite the Mongols to interdict the border and prevent Bavuujav's escape into Khalkha. On November 10 Ch'en received another telegram informing him that troops of Mi Chen-pao had defeated Bavuujav five days earlier and forced him to flee to the Yegüzer monastery (in the southeast corner of Outer Mongolia at or near present-day Erdenetsagaan, about thirty miles north of the present border).

The Mongols interpreted these events differently. Ch'en received a protest from the Bogd Khaan Government regarding the unprovoked assault on Bavuujav, whose troops, it was claimed, were returning to their original banners in Inner Mongolia at the instructions of the Urga government and were therefore under the protection of the Kyakhta amnesty for Inner Mongolians who had fled to Khalkha in 1912.

Ch'en Lu nevertheless urged the Kalgan military administration to instruct its officers that everything in their power must be done to destroy Bavuujav: "...if you can succeed in your present attack against the Mongolian bandit, it will be sufficient to instill fear into the hearts of the Mongols." Ch'en then replied to the Mongolian protest in a most uncompromising way. He accused Bavuujav of pillaging merchants and daring to take up arms against Chinese troops, forcing the dispatch of soldiers to protect the commercial routes between Inner and Outer Mongolia. The wisest course for the Urga government, Ch'en advised, was to send troops to the border in order to prevent Bavuujav's escape into Khalkha; the next best course was for it to persuade Bavuujav to lay down his arms. Ch'en concluded with a warning that any attempt to shelter him could only complicate Chinese and Mongolian relations. The Mongols seemed daunted by the High Commissioner's tough line and replied that they thought this proposal was sensible.

The affair took an unexpected and critical turn a few days later when Tserendorj and the Sain Noyon Khan visited Ch'en Lu and told him of an unprovoked attack five days earlier on the Yegüzer monastery by Chinese troops. Not only had people been killed and monastic property pillaged, they asserted, but the Yegüzer Khutukhtu himself together with several other lamas had been arrested. The delegation protested that the Chinese had unlawfully crossed the border without giving advance notice and had destroyed the monastery.

Ch'en had not been informed of this incident by

his government, although he did know that Chinese troops were under instructions to pursue and destroy Bavuujav, presumably wherever he could be found. He replied that Republican troops were naturally more concerned with apprehending a dangerous bandit than with honoring border distinctions; Mongolia moreover was part of China, and Mongolia's borders consequently were the borders of China--how much more difficult was their task, he stressed, when the borders of Inner and Outer Mongolia were still undefined. One wonders if Ch'en did not blush slightly at pressing an argument so clearly in contravention of the Tripartite Treaty, which forbade Chinese troops in Mongolian territory.

Ch'en then skillfully turned the attack against the Mongols by accusing the Yegüzer Khutukhtu of harboring Bavuujav and the Urga government of failing to control him. The Mongols replied that Bavuujav had broken with Urga and that they could not take responsibility for his activities. They proposed instead that Ch'en Lu and the Mongolian government select representatives to visit the monastery, where the Chinese troops could be ordered to surrender the Khutukhtu and return south, and damage to the monastery could be assessed.

Ch'en was unyielding. He told his visitors that Bavuujav's surrender was the minimum condition for the withdrawal of Chinese troops. Tserendorj and the Sain Noyon Khan finally agreed that the Khalkhas would take responsibility for expelling him across the border. It is clear from Ch'en Lu's record of this meeting that the Khalkhas were measurably less interested in the fate of Bavuujav than in the presence of Chinese troops on Mongolian territory and the attack on one of their monasteries.

Following this visit Ch'en received a secret letter from the commander of the unit which was then occupying the Yegüzer monastery stating that on November 22 his troops had seized the monastery after a battle lasting six hours. A thousand of Bavuujav's men had been killed and five hundred captured (these figures are surely exaggerations). Although Bavuujav was able to escape with a large number of his men, the letter continued, troops had been sent in pursuit and the Khutukhtu placed in custody "because he was the cause of the disturbance."

Ch'en also learned from an agent of his in Urga that Bavuujav had escaped northeast to the T'ao-nan-Barga area in western Heilungkiang. The report asserted that the Outer Mongolian government had sent a thousand men to the Yegüzer monastery and another thousand to Zamyn Üüd and some other areas lying in the direction of Barga on the pretext of cutting Bavuujav off, but in reality to block the advance of Chinese troops further into Outer Mongolian territory. Ch'en immediately passed this information on to Peking, warning that if China withdrew its troops, the Mongols would interpret this as weakness. He proposed that the Mongols should be demanded to surrender Bavuujav, assume responsibility for the tranquility of the border, and reimburse the Peking government for expenses incurred in repressing the bandits.

Although these demands clearly reflected Ch'en's conviction that Bavuujav was operating under orders from Urga, it is more likely that by this time Urga had indeed broken with Bavuujav, just as it had abandoned pan-Mongolia. This "two thousand-strong" Mongolian army, moreover, was probably ordered to push Bavuujav out of Khalkha, as Ch'en was informed later by Tserendorj and the Tsetsen Khan. Manlai baatar Damdinsüren and the Commander of the Tsetsen Khan aimag Dorjtseren had even been sent by Urga to persuade Bavuujav to accept the treaty and disband his troops, but they failed.

On the next day Miller visited the Chinese High Commission and protested that the presence of Chinese troops north of the border was a violation of the Tripartie Treaty, and asked that the Yegüzer Khutukhtu be released and that the government of Yuan Shih-k'ai take responsibility for any losses suffered by the monastery. Bavuujav was an officer of Outer Mongolia, Ch'en retorted, and it was Urga which must accept responsibility for these events. Once Bavuujav was turned over to Chinese authorities, there would be no difficulty in recalling these troops. Ch'en quickly wired Kalgan reporting that a large Mongolian force was being sent south to rescue the Yegüzer Khutukhtu and suggested strongly that additional troops be sent north to reinforce the Chinese unit at the monastery.

Feelings were running high in Urga. The city was

throbbing with rumors of Chinese soldiers marching north, and even the Russian Consulate and concession area were placed under martial law. The Mongols were in such a belligerent mood that Chinese merchants began preparing frantically to protect themselves, while Ch'en Lu was considering measures for defending the High Commission. When Ch'en learned that Chinese troops had been directed to continue their pursuit of Bavuujav, he realized that a clash was inevitable if they were to meet the Mongolian units supposedly moving south. He advised Kalgan to order these troops to remain where they were.

In the event, this advice was not necessary. The Russian Minister in Peking had warned Yuan Shih-k'ai that failure to agree to the three demands of the Mongols (withdrawal of Chinese troops, release of the Yegüzer Khutukhtu, and reparations for damages to the monastery) would produce a crisis in Russo-Chinese relations. Yuan, who at that time was beginning to press forward with his plans to restore the monarchy, was in no mood for unnecessary distractions and on November 30 ordered that the Chinese commanders stop their advance. A sudden mellowing on the part of the Mongols also became apparent. On December 4 at the invitation of the court, Ch'en was received in audience by the Jebtsundamba Khutukhtu and his consort; and on the following day the Mongols agreed either to hand over or to expel Bavuujav and to take responsibility for the security of the commercial routes between Inner and Outer Mongolia.

Although the withdrawal of Chinese troops from Yegüzer monastery in December and the flight of Bavuujav to Manchuria, where he was given sanctuary by the Russians, brought the Bavuujav affair to a close as a political issue in Sino-Mongolian relations, there was still the matter of the Khutukhtu's release. The Chinese commander, claiming to have discovered evidence at the monastery that the Khutukhtu had "plotted secretly with foreigners" and had been in communication with rebel factions in Heilungkiang and Kirin, decided to hand him over to Peking for trial. Although the Mongolian government asked Ch'en Lu several times to seek the release of the Khutukhtu, Ch'en received a telegram in early January 1916 stating that the Khutukhtu had expressed his desire to "submit" to China and requested an interview with the President; the Yegüzer Khutukhtu would be released as soon as this meeting had taken place. The Mongols were evidently satisfied with this explanation and the affair was permanently closed.

A second matter which occupied much of Ch'en's attention during the early part of his term in Mongolia was the question of the "investiture" (ts'e-feng) of the Jebtsundamba Khutukhtu as the "Bogd Jebtsundamba Khutukhtu Khan," the style-name recognized by the Tripartite Treaty.[77] Politically, the act of investiture was irrelevant. That the atmosphere of Chinese-Mongolian relations had cleared to the point where it could take place at all, however, was not. Investiture was the first unmistakable sign of the composed, even harmonious character of relations between Peking and Urga by the end of 1916 and of the growing detente between the two countries. A new relationship which, significantly, excluded Russia was in the process of being formed. Chinese and Mongols were talking directly with one another.

The investiture question, notwithstanding its happy conclusion, had a troublesome beginning. In June 1915, following the signing of the Tripartite Treaty, the President of China announced that envoys were to be sent to invest the Urga Khutukhtu. In a move obviously calculated to show that China was actively exercising its suzerain rights, he also confirmed the legitimacy of all titles and ranks granted to the lay and church nobility of Mongolia during the Ch'ing and Bogd Khaan years.

Both the Office of the Prime Minister of Outer Mongolia and the Russian Foreign Ministry protested that the Kyakhta treaty had empowered only the Khutukhtu to grant such titles, since it was clearly a matter which concerned internal administration and was a privilege which could not be arrogated by the President of China. The Chinese Foreign Minister in his reply to Krupenskii tried to dismiss its importance by saying that investiture had a "purely ceremonial and provisional character" and equated the confirmation of Mongolian titles and ranks with the custom of granting decorations to foreign citizens. The Russian Foreign Ministry was plainly not satisfied, referring to these as "rather equivocal excuses," and complained that the Peking government was endeavoring "arbitrarily to expand the rights accorded to it" by the Kyakhta treaty.

The Russians were right. The imperial prerogative of investiture was a well-known and essential element in Chinese relations with the frontier peoples. This move by Yuan Shih-k'ai to force the Khutukhtu into accepting a Chinese patent and seal of office was a transparent attempt to restore the traditional symbols of Chinese rule over Mongolia.

Ch'en Lu first raised the issue when he visited Damdinsüren on October 26 bringing with him a draft plan for the investiture ceremony worked out in Peking. Ch'en had not anticipated any objections, but he discovered from this short conversation that the Mongols believed that the June wire from Yuan Shih-k'ai informing the Khutukhtu of his confirmation of rank had satisfied the requirements of investiture as stipulated in the Tripartite Treaty. Sensing that there might be a problem, he decided to push the matter through without any delay while the memory of the treaty and its obligations was still fresh in everyone's mind. He quickly copied out the draft plan and dispatched it to the Mongolian government, while at the same time telegraphing the two investiture officers to depart immediately.

Ch'en's apprehensions were not misconceived. On November 1 he received a reply from the Urga government stating that article four of the treaty had not mentioned a gold seal or a patent and that the Mongols consequently were under no compulsion to accept them. Ch'en was insistent. He sent two more notes to the Urga government but received the same answer. An audience with the Khutukhtu scheduled for November 5 was canceled at the last minute on the excuse that the Khutukhtu was ill. By mid-November, however, the Bavuujav was absorbing Ch'en's attention and the investiture question was temporarily shelved.

In the first part of December, after the Bavuujav crisis had passed and Chinese-Mongolian relations had taken a distinctly improved turn, there occurred a most extraordinary thing which clearly demonstrated the new Sino-Mongolian rapprochement and perhaps even a certain dimunition of will among Mongolian leaders to preserve their independence. On December 6 Yuan Shih-k'ai had sent the Khutukhtu and his consort some gifts, and a few days later in the course of conversation with Tserendorj, Ch'en proposed that the Mongols reciprocate with their own mission to Peking. Ch'en thought that this gesture would help to show the warm regard which the Chinese and Mongols held for each other.

This suggestion was passed on to the Bogd Khaan, who agreed, and Ch'en learned that the Tsetsen Khan was to be sent to Peking with "tributary articles" (kung-p'in). A delegation of around thirty persons, headed by the Tsetsen Khan, left Urga on December 13 bringing the Bogd's present of two camels and four white horses, and the Ekh Dagina's present of two camels and four black horses. Ch'en suggested to his government that a detachment of soldiers be sent to Zamyn Üüd to escort the delegation to Peking and that the Bureau of Mongolian and Tibetan Affairs greet this delegation with particular warmth. The parallels with Ch'ing procedure for receiving tribute missions can hardly have been accidental.

While Mongolian sources do not tell us how the Mongols themselves interpreted the gifts to the President, Ch'en Lu immediately recognized in them the old "Nine Whites" tribute of the Ch'ing: "Although the tribute rendered on this occasion was not handled (strictly) in accordance with the code of the Bureau of Dependencies, it sufficiently testifies nevertheless to the fact that Chinese and Mongolian feelings were daily growing closer."[78]

It is impossible that the Mongols were unconscious of the similarity between their gift of camels and horses, and the camels and horses of the "Nine Whites," especially in view of their proven sensitivity to all of the other historic symbols of Chinese-frontier relations. We can only conclude that the Mongols, in their unceasing and thus far disappointing search for a patron, had moved full-circle and were now offering to the Chinese the tantalizing prospect of restoring the relationship as it had existed during the Ch'ing.

The Chinese government followed Ch'en suggestion and received the delegation with honor. Fifty soldiers met the mission on the border at Ereen khot

(Erh-lien) and escorted it to Kalgan, where it was given a ceremonial reception. In Peking the Tsetsen Khan met with various governmental officials and on February 10 was received by Yuan Shih-k'ai--as the self-proclaimed Hung-hsien Emperor, Yuan had a marvellous opportunity to try on his new clothes--to whom the gifts of the Bogd Khaan and his consort were offered. Yuan presented the delegation with twenty thousand dollars for "road expenses," another echo of Ch'ing tributary practices, and in mid-April the delegation returned to Urga.

Mongolian resistance to investiture was beginning to weaken. When Ch'en again broached the subject to Tserendorj on March 3, he received a very different reply. The Foreign Minister did cite several objections to the investiture plan: the investiture officers and their staff, who would surely number fifty or sixty persons, were too many for the Mongols to provide for adequately; moreover, "foreigners," that is, Russians, would "be suspicious of China's motives;" and finally, the Khutukhtu had lost not only his eyesight but also movement in his limbs and could not maneuver about easily. The plan submitted by Ch'en, however, called for the descending of steps and repeated bowing. If the High Commissioner himself were to preside over the ceremony and if, in view of the Khutukhtu's disabilities, there were no "vexatious demands" made on the monarch, investiture could go ahead. Tserendorj did insist on the right to inspect the inscription on the patent in advance. Ch'en accepted these conditions on the spot.

Chinese benevolence toward the Mongols now seemed limitless. In March the Khutukhtu was awarded the highest decoration of merit China could offer, the Ta-hsün-wei; a variety of other decorations was conferred on other Mongolian officials. On March 23 Ch'en delivered the draft text of the patent inscription. The text was innocuous, suffused with fulsome and hyperbolic references to the founding of the Chinese Republic, Sino-Mongolian friendship, and veneration of the Khutukhtu. Predictably, the Bogd Khaan was delighted with it. On July 8 the ceremony of investiture took place with appropriate flourish.

Another problem which Ch'en had faced on his

arrival, the history of which followed very closely the pattern of the earlier two, was the question of the taxation of Chinese merchants. Now that Russian loans had dried up, taxation on Chinese commerce was the single most important source of revenue for the Mongolian government, and the Urga government was under such financial pressure that the Mongols decided to squeeze the Chinese even harder by levying a poll and house tax.

The Chinese were naturally resentful, and Ch'en, who regarded the protection of these merchants as his primary charge, brought the subject up with the Sain Noyon Khan on November 6, followed by a note of protest to the Urga government three days later. The Urga government responded by curtly reminding the High Commissioner that all commercial matters came under the exclusive jurisdiction of the Mongolian government. The Bavuujav affair, now dominating the attention of Ch'en Lu, led to a brief hiatus in these exchanges. But on December 10, after the crisis had passed, Ch'en received a conciliatory letter from the Mongols promising that the advice of the High Commissioner would be solicited in the future on any matter affecting the interests of Chinese merchants and not covered by the Kyakhta treaty. The poll and house taxes were quietly withdrawn.[79]

Ch'en Lu had served the interests of his government in Mongolia so ably that Peking was in no hurry to transfer him. But his southern constitution was ill-adapted to the rigors of the northern climate, and since early May 1916 he had been suffering from a stomach complaint and was forced to take medicine to induce sleep. His condition deteriorated so markedly that he wired the Cabinet Secretariat (Kuo-wu yuan) in June and then twice in July requesting that he be allowed to resign. It was to take almost a full year before a satisfactory replacement could be found. In the meantime, Ch'en's illness continued to worsen, and the Secretary-General of the Urga Commission had to assume the duties of high commissioner. On May 7, 1917 Ch'en Lu received permission to return to Peking. He left the following day.

---

Historians have generally credited Ch'en Lu, singling out his ability and tact, with responsibility for the new detente between China and Mongolia after the Kyakhta conference. Ch'en unquestionably deserves much credit for the upturn of Chinese fortunes in Mongolia, although it must be remembered that, unlike either his predecessor (San-to) or successor (Ch'en I), he was able to serve at a time when there was relative peace on the northern frontier and when problems in Mongolia were more tractable. Nevertheless, his intelligent and generally tolerant treatment of the Mongols undoubtedly created a congenial ambience for the improvement of Chinese and Mongolian relations. The best support for this impression comes from the Mongols themselves, who appear to have genuinely liked Ch'en and were distressed when he left.

The main reason for the Sino-Mongolian rapproachement, however, was the profound disillusionment of the Mongols with Russia. By the early part of December 1915 the first concrete signs of this revival of Chinese influence appeared with the decisive handling of the Bavuujav affair by Ch'en Lu and the Peking government. This contrasted with the relatively ineffectual response of the Russians: if in 1912-13 the mere threat of a Chinese military advance into Mongolia had brought several Russian units streaming into the country, the Chinese border crossing of 1915 brought only protests. The Mongols must have taken note. In this sense, therefore, it was the Bavuujav affair which marked a turning point in Chinese and Mongolian relations.

Between the years 1911-17 the Mongols had moved full circle, from vassalage to independence to autonomy, and by 1917 were subscribing once more to most of the essential elements of the Ch'ing tributary system. The corollary of this is that the Mongols were starting to reject the principles upon which the Bogd Khaan state had been founded and were returning to more tested and familiar patterns of political life. This swing gained momentum during the next two years.

## CHAPTER IV

## CHINESE TROOPS IN MONGOLIA, 1918-1919

The shot that killed Francis Ferdinand in June 1914 echoed throughout northern Asia and signaled the contraction of Russian interests in the Far East. As the European war continued and increasingly turned against Russia, there was a proportional decline in the capacity of Tsarist representatives in Asia to act with the same boldness they had before. The security of Russian interests in the East was nevertheless guaranteed to a certain degree by Russia's stature as a great power and by its treaties with China and Japan. Russian diplomacy in Asia during the war, consequently, was able to coast on the momentum generated in earlier years--albeit at a slackening tempo. The effects of Russia's diminishing presence in Asia can be seen particularly vividly in Mongolia.

The Chinese were nettled by "autonomy" for Mongolia but had little choice other than to submit to this arrangement, leaving it to their resident officials to salvage what they could. Although the issue of Mongolia receded into the background of Chinese politics as more important domestic problems demanded attention, the 1917 February (March) Revolution and especially the October (November) Bolshevik Revolution in Russia changed that. Civil war in Asiatic Russia catapulted the Chinese frontier question into the foreground and gave it new urgency.

The seizure of power by the Bolsheviks brought disorder, civil war, and foreign intervention, and a host of governments of different political complexions, each claiming to be the authentic voice of the Russian people, sprang up across Siberia and Russian Central Asia. As Chinese officials anxiously surveyed this situation, they became increasingly conscious of the powerlessness of these regimes and of Russian diplomatic officials in

China, who continued to act on behalf of the "legitimate" Russian government. This quickly led to a new logic, that the moment had arrived to reassert Chinese influence on the frontier and to end some of the more obnoxious concessions to Russia which China had been compelled to make over the years. But as every attempt to dislodge the Bolsheviks quickened the political and military exhaustion of the White Guards, an even more radical reformulation of Chinese frontier policy occurred between 1918-19 aimed at completely restoring Chinese sovereignty over the frontier zone of Mongolia and Manchuria. Happily for the Chinese, this coincided with the search of the Mongols for a new patron.

## Negotiations for Chinese Reinforcements

The revolution in European Russia in 1917 had a rippling effect in Siberia, where a number of executive councils, or soviets, seized power for themselves, a process which was essentially completed by the summer of 1918. The attitude of the Chinese government toward the Bolshevik government and these soviets was equivocal. Like the Western powers, the Chinese were appalled by the determination of the Bolsheviks to challenge and destroy the old order in Europe. Their withdrawal from the war and repudiation of Tsarist war debts to the Allies (Russia was the largest debtor), their rejection of "secret diplomacy" and publication of classified documents from the archives of the Tsarist Foreign Ministry, their mysterious communal philosophies and advocacy of revolution, were hardly calculated to win the sympathy of the Allies.

The policy of the latter was to deal with the Bolsheviks unofficially and on an ad hoc basis, withholding recognition until the situation in Russia had stabilized. Although the Chinese were intrigued by a Soviet offer in early 1918 to abrogate all of the "unequal treaties" (including the Russo-Japanese agreements signed between 1907 and 1916) concluded between Russia and China, pressure from the Allies and fears that unilateral action might prejudice Chinese bargaining strength at the European conference expected to follow the war, however, eventually forced the Peking government to take a conservative line. In February 1918 the Peking government decided that China must act uniformly with the Allies and take a "watch and wait" attitude without showing partiality to either the Bolsheviks or those Russian groups still loyal to Tsarism. Although its behavior toward the Whites and Reds was not nearly so even-handed as this policy recommended, Chinese strategy was cautious and generally conformed to that of the Allies.

While the Bogd Khaan government responded sympathetically to news of the February Revolution, the reaction of the Mongols to the formation of soviets in Siberia generally and Transbaikalia in particular was not so charitable.With the organization of soviets in Verkhneudinsk, Chita, and Troitskosavsk in February 1918 the Bolsheviks were now standing at Mongolia's front gate. When the new Diplomatic Agent in Urga Orlov approached Foreign Minister Tserendorj with a request that the Mongols follow the example of their suzerain China and deny recognition to the new government in Petrograd, the Mongolian Minister agreed on the spot.

The presence of Bolsheviks so close to the Mongolian border was no less obnoxious or disturbing to Chinese diplomats in Mongolia, and especially to Chang Ch'ing-t'ung, the Deputy High Commissioner in Kyakhta. In the early months of 1918 this office, perhaps more than any other Chinese outpost on the frontier, was ensnarled in the tangles and confusion of the revolution in Siberia. The town was convulsed by fear, uncertainty, and political and social turmoil. Chang, reminding his government repeatedly of Kyakhta's importance as a major crossroads and warning that he had too few troops to deal with the disorder, urged Peking to adopt a more aggressive line toward the frontier in view of the unsettled conditions there. In mid-February Chang reported that Verkhneudinsk had been taken by the Bolsheviks and predicted that there would certainly be trouble for Outer Mongolia if Kyakhta were similarly seized. Again, Chang urged Peking to take "measures."

The Chinese sources are almost totally silent

about the debate, as there surely must have been, within the government regarding the proper reply to these appeals. A precedent of sorts for direct military action had been established less than two months earlier when Chinese troops moved into the Russian concession at Harbin in late December, dispersed the soviet recently formed there, disarmed the Russian railway troops, and reorganized the administration of the Chinese Eastern Railway to ensure Chinese domination. But the Chinese had overplayed their hand and had aroused protests from other powers, which interpreted this move more broadly as a challenge to the entire system of privilege and immunity they enjoyed in China. It was perhaps because of this reaction that the Peking government, in order to mute criticism from the Allies, was to show a certain amount of sensitivity to form when dealing with Mongolia.

In spite of the obvious need for caution, concern for the safety of Chinese citizens (and, to a lesser extent, of the Mongols) living on the frontier, and the hope that a fortified presence might lead to the reestablishment of real Chinese authority in Mongolia, persuaded the government to make a positive response to Chang's appeals. But China's freedom of action was circumscribed by the Kyakhta treaty, which explicitly limited the number of troops it could have in Mongolia. The Foreign Minister then hit upon a strategem which, it was hoped, would both satisfy the Allies and reassure the Mongols.

On February 14 Ch'en I, the new Urga High Commissioner and former Deputy High Commissioner of Uliastai, was instructed to inquire of the Mongolian government what measures it contemplated to resist a Bolshevik invasion and to suggest that the Mongols formally request China to increase its troops in Mongolia, until the "disturbance" had quieted. Without waiting for a reply, Peking decided to apply even stronger pressure. Four days later the High Commissioner was directed to warn the Mongols that unless they were prepared to accept responsibility for the safety of the Deputy High Commission and the Russo-Asiatic Bank in Kyakhta, they must request Chinese troops. With a remarkable disregard for the spirit and letter of the Kyakhta treaty, Ch'en I was instructed to add that such a request would not violate the 1915 agreement.[80]

As the Foreign Ministry was certainly aware, the Kyakhta treaty strictly limited the number of troops which China or Russia could have in Mongolia, nor was there a provision for an emergency force (the Chinese delegation at the tripartitle talks had unsuccessfully sought recognition for such a right). Peking probably hoped that a "spontaneous" Mongolian appeal for Chinese reinforcements would create a sufficiently ambiguous legal situation to blunt foreign criticism.

In a formal and detailed reply on February 23, the Urga government gave a characteristically evasive answer. For itself, the government noted, the idea was welcome; but it was feared that the Mongolian people would not understand the need for calling upon outside help and would become alarmed at the presence of more Chinese troops; the proposal was respectfully declined. The Bogd Khaan Government did promise to assign fifty additional troops to Kyakhta, where they would join the hundred Mongolian and Chinese soldiers already there, and Ch'en I was asked to send another fifty men from his own escort. Should this be inadequate, the government promised to send a thousand more Mongols north. The letter concluded by reassuring Ch'en that if the situation were to change later, the subject of Chinese reinforcements could be raised again.

Ch'en detected the subterfuge and remarked in his transmission to Peking that it was really the Mongolian government, and not the Mongolian people, which objected to the offer. He recommended that the Chahar Governor T'ien Chung-yü be urged to send troops to Zamyn Üüd and Pang-chiang on the Sino-Mongolian border as a reserve force for Urga.[81]

These appeals from the diplomatic representatives in Mongolia repeatedly warning of an imminent Bolshevik invasion, as well as the growing conviction among many in the Peking government that the moment was now ideal to reassert control over the northern frontier, stimulated a vigorous interministerial debate regarding a proper course of action. At this stage, however, the dispute was still somewhat academic. The situation in Siberia continued to remain fluid and no real threat to Mongolia had yet materialized, with the exception of communications from anxious Chinese agents reporting the presence of Bolsheviks.

But the debate obscured the real reason why the Peking government throughout the Republican period appeared to lack the resolve to take the Mongolian question more firmly in hand. The decision to send troops or not into Outer Mongolia ultimately did not turn on treaty restrictions, fear of adverse foreign reaction, or the gravity of the Red or White danger. It was warlordism.

With the death of Yuan Shih-k'ai in 1916 China was divided into a number of independent regions ruled by military governors (tu-chün), or warlords. Tax revenue from these regions seldom found its way into the coffers of the central government but remained within these areas, generally to maintain the armies of the warlords. This fact is central to understanding the chronic poverty of the Peking government. The warlords were incessantly preoccupied with enlarging their territory at the expense of their neighbors or with resisting similar encroachments on their own fiefs. Because an army was the principal instrument of their power, the warlords in the north were exceedingly chary of committing their forces to such a remote region as Mongolia. The impecunious Peking government, moreover could not have been counted on to subsidize the rather considerable costs of such an expedition. This more than anything helps to explain the failure of the Chinese to act more decisively in Outer Mongolia.

The tumultuous domestic politics of China between 1917 and 1918 also complicated the political situation in north China and worked to reduce interest in Mongolia. In June 1917 Sun Yat-sen, along with many members of the Peking parliament prorogued by Li Yuan-hung, had formed a military government of six provinces in Canton which disputed Peking's authority to govern China. This led to a series of military expeditions launched in September 1917 by the leading northern warlord Tuan Ch'i-jui against the southerners lasting for two years. A split, moreover, had rent the Peiyang clique, the umbrella organization for all warlords in north China, into two factions after the death of its founder, Yuan Shih-k'ai. The question of Mongolia figured only indistinctly among the more pressing issues facing the central government.

The High Commissioner in Urga was undaunted by the complexities of the political situation at home and continued to flood his government with near-hysterical telegrams. Ch'en, transfixed by the prospect of a Bolshevik invasion, gave total credence to every rumor without making the slightest effort to determine its veracity. In April he addressed himself to the problem of Chinese reinforcements in Mongolia with even greater intensity, but this time he concentrated his energies on obtaining agreement from the Mongols and the Russian Diplomatic Agent. The vulnerable, uncertain diplomatic status of Orlov (the Soviet government's refusal to recognize Tsarist diplomats was a useful lever with which Ch'en was able to shift him into a more obliging frame of mind).

In mid-April Orlov informed Tserendorj that the Soviet government had appointed a new consul-general to Urga, who was on his way to Kyakhta accompanied by armed troops; he was then to proceed to Urga. Orlov feared that his presence would prejudice the safety not only of his own staff but of the entire Russian community in Urga. If his worst fears were realized, would the Mongols, he asked, place the Russian settlement under their protection? Tserendorj reiterated the policy of the Urga govern- not to permit the Soviet Consul to cross the Mongolian border and assured Orlov that, in any event, he and all Russian citizens in Mongolia would be granted sanctuary.

Orlov was still not satisfied and in a visible state of panic visited Ch'en I, to whom he expressed concern that the Mongols might yet recognize the Bolsheviks without fully appreciating the consequences of such an act. Orlov begged Ch'en I to impress upon the Mongols the importance of protecting the expatriate Russians and advised him that "if the situation becomes critical, it will be necessary to ask the High Commissioner to send more troops to protect the Consulate." Ch'en agreed to accept this responsibility.[82]

Orlov undeniably had reason for concern. His status and authority had been seriously undermined in the eyes of the local Russian population by the February and October Revolutions. More alarming, however, was the challenge to his leadership from the more radical members of the Russian communities in Mongolia, now swollen with refugees from Siberia escaping either Red or White persecution.

Friction developed almost immediately between Orlov and the Executive Committee (a group of radicals which claimed to represent the interests of the Russian colony in Urga), and the latter sent several requests to the Provisional Government in Petrograd for the replacement of the Consul-General. Mutinies of the Cossack consular guards in Mongolia eroded the authority of Orlov still further. In February 1918 the consular guard at Kyakhta had absconded; in May the Cossacks in Uliastai turned on the Vice-Consul, forcing him to seek refuge with the Chinese Deputy High Commissioner (these Cossacks were eventually disarmed by Chinese and Mongolian troops and escorted out of the country); and by May the consular guard at Khovd had also deserted. The Cossack unit at Urga, if it remained intact at all, must have been completely unreliable by mid-April.

On April 17 the Peking government unconditionally authorized Ch'en I to seek Mongolian approval for Chinese reinforcements. A telegram from the Foreign Ministry on that day informed him of a letter received from Prince Kudashev, the Tsarist Minister in Peking, expressing concern over news of the impending arrival of a Soviet-designated consul to Urga and the danger this might present to the Russian community. The Foreign Ministry suggested that this fear could be used to "extend Chinese power in Outer Mongolia." Ch'en was directed to inform the Mongols that, in the opinion of the Peking government, they lacked sufficient strength to protect the lives and property of Russians in Mongolia and that they should formally apply for Chinese troops in order to "repress fear."[83]

Although the Chinese sources do not explain the reason for this renewed initiative after the rather inconclusive debate within the Chinese government earlier, the answer is probably to be found in the generally strengthened foreign and domestic circumstances of the Peking government, the cumulative effect of which was to stiffen Chinese resolve regarding Mongolia. Chinese diplomatic confidence had received a shot in the arm when Peking declared war against Germany, thereby giving China a coveted place among the Allies. This, added to the growing concern of the Allies over Bolshevik gains in Siberia, surely encouraged the Chinese government to believe that Western reaction to Chinese troops in Mongolia (if a suitable pretext could be found) would be nominal. Another important factor was the so-called Nishihara Loans to the government of Tuan Ch'i-jui between January 1917 and September 1918. This money, ostensibly to be used for projects that would contribute to the commonwealth of China, was in fact spent by Tuan to bolster his political and military position in the country.

Ch'en was only too happy to comply, but he immediately encountered Mongolian resistance. On April 27 he was visited by Tserendorj, who told him that the Khutukhtu's cabinet, after meeting twice over the question, had decided unanimously that an increase of Chinese troops was a good idea insofar as the Mongols were concerned. However, Tserendorj continued, the Tsarist Consul Orlov opposed it on the grounds that such a step contravened the Kyakhta treaty and Ch'en was advised to seek Orlov's approval first. This "agreement" of the Bogd Khaan's government was undoubtedly another evasion. Counting on the certain objection of Orlov to any Chinese reinforcements, the Mongols probably hoped to finesse their way out of this difficulty.

Ch'en then met with the Consul-General and pointed out the contradiction of appealing for troops one moment and then withdrawing it the next. On the contrary, Orlov replied, there was no contradiction: his request had applied only to the escort guard of the High Commissioner, not to additional troops from China. Ch'en countered with a spurious interpretation of the Kyakhta treaty, pointing out that the limitation on troops applied only to peacetime, not to periods of crisis. There was no crisis, Orlov replied, and it was very unlikely that the Bolsheviks would send anything more than a small escort guard to accompany the new Consul. Ch'en I was thoroughly exasperated by Orlov's new confidence and responded that the Russians could simply evacuate Mongolia if the situation became difficult; the Chinese could not. Orlov would not yield.[84]

Ch'en I, reporting this stalemate to his government, speculated that the Mongols continued to oppose the introduction of more Chinese troops despite the approval which they had voiced to the plan. Ch'en believed that they were influenced by rumors circulating in Urga of a large Chinese force at Zamyn Üüd, five to six thousand-strong, which was preparing to march on Urga, and were wary of openly opposing China. For this reason they had shifted the responsibility on to the shoulders of the Consul-General, counting on his resistance to such a scheme. Ch'en recommended that Orlov be by-passed in favor of direct negotiations with the Mongols.

By the beginning of May the threat of a Soviet consul in Urga had faded and attention was now turning to the western part of Mongolia, where there were disturbing rumors, apparently originating from the Russian diplomats there, that large numbers of Bolsheviks were heading for the area. According to the Tsarist Vice-Consul in Uliastai, three hundred Bolsheviks were then on their way to Khovd and another thousand were already in Uryankhai preparing to march on Uliastai (these Russians probably were part of the "Mongolian Expedition" sent by the Soviet government in the spring of 1918 to purchase livestock). Ch'en I asked that two or three companies of Chinese troops at Zamyn Üüd be transferred immediately to Uliastai. At the urging of Ch'en, the Urga government also mobilized three hundred fifty Mongolian troops from the western aimags.

Letters were exchanged between the ministries of the Peking government at a dazzling speed. Each called the other's attention to the gravity of the situation and asked that the matter be "investigated," but one proposed any useful suggestions and every one of these communications was couched in a vague and cautious language.

Finally, the Ministry of the Army arranged a meeting of the relevant ministries and departments for May 20. Although its proceedings have never been published, it evidently did decide on a firm course of action: on the following day Ch'en I was informed that Chinese troops were being sent from Zamyn Üüd to Uliastai via Urga, and the High Commissioner was instructed to forewarn the Mongols of this step in order both to allay their suspicions and to coax them into a more receptive attitude toward the subject of Chinese reinforcements. There was no mention of securing Mongolian permission in advance. Ch'en, in a display of caution quite out of character for him, immediately wired Peking that he was in the midst of negotiating with the Mongols over this very problem and recommended that the troops at Zamyn Üüd remain there until he gave the signal.[85] The High Commissioner obviously anticipated a successful outcome of these discussions.

Ch'en I earlier had made it very clear to the Mongolian government that it must accept complete responsibility for all losses suffered by Chinese residents in Mongolia resulting from its refusal to permit additional troops in the country. The Mongols, naturally troubled by this threat, became even more anxious when reports began coming in from Kyakhta,Uliastai, and Khovd warning of Bolshevik movement across the border. Tserendorj sought Ch'en's views and the latter urged that the Mongols must allow China to help them resist the Soviets. Tserendorj simply nodded and left. He visited Ch'en again on the following day and related that Orlov had approached him "imploring" protection. When the Foreign Minister replied that Mongolia could not assume responsibility for the Russian Consulate by itself, Orlov had inquired whether the Mongols truly wanted China to send in troops. Tserendorj asked if there were any alternative; Orlov departed in silence.

After relating this story to Ch'en, Tserendorj offered his opinion that Orlov's silence was a tacit recognition of the need for Chinese troops, but measures still had to be devised to assuage Mongolian suspicions. A formula was then worked out between the two men by which China would temporarily assign one battalion of Chinese troops to Mongolia until the end of the European war and the restoration of peace.[86]

Until more archival material is published, it is

impossible to know the attitude of Mongolian political leaders toward the Bolsheviks or why they finally agreed to Chinese troops. The evidence is thin, but what there is suggests that senior Urga officials were by no means united on the question of the seriousness of the Bolshevik threat or the need for Chinese reinforcements. Ch'en I, for instance, had heard that the Khutukhtu's cabinet had been evenly divided on the question of recognizing Soviet Russia; the Khutukhtu opposed it when the issue was put before him. According to a Russian account, in the early part of 1918 the Sain Noyon Khan headed a delegation to the Central Executive Committee of the Soviets of Siberia (Tsentrosibir') in Irkutsk, where the Khan was alleged to have complained that the Chinese were moving troops to the Mongolian border with the aim of ending Mongolian autonomy, and that some high personages in the government, alarmed by the spectre of revolution, were helping them.[87]

There may be some basis for the argument of Communist historians that the Mongolian aristocracy feared the Bolsheviks because of their potentially revolutionary influence on the arats. It is not yet possible to gauge the seriousness with which the lay and church princes regarded the chances of social revolution in Mongolia. Chinese sources, however, show clearly that many Mongols were indeed mistrustful of the Bolsheviks, less because of their political philosophy than because of fears that their presence in Mongolia would be generally disruptive--anxieties which Tsarist and Chinese officials were fueling regularly. By May the situation in western Mongolia did indeed appear critical with rumors of a thousand or more Bolsheviks moving south. Orlov clearly lacked the power to help; there was no one else to whom the Mongols could turn except China.

Ch'en I was genuinely alarmed by these reports from western Mongolia of a Soviet invasion, but he was also quick to take advantage of the situation. His May 29 telegram to Peking, reporting the agreement reached with Tserendorj for a limited number of Chinese troops, was memorable for its cunning. Noting that the Kyakhta treaty forbade China to increase its troops in Mongolia, he pointed out that a precedent had now been established nullifying this article and that it could be used again if necessary. Ch'en did advise the government to prove its honorable intentions by adhering strictly to this agreement with the Mongols and withdrawing the troops when the situation in Mongolia had settled. He also suggested that the two cavalry battalions at Zamyn Üüd be amalgamated into one (Ch'en and Tserendorj had agreed that the reinforcements were to be limited to one battalion) and that the number of its troops not exceed two hundred (this apparently was a condition laid down by the Mongols).[88]

Although the procrastination and evasions of the Chahar Governor delayed the arrival of the much discussed Chinese force for another three and a half months, two battalions from Suiyuan, probably numbering between two hundred and two hundred fifty men under the command of Kao Tsai-t'ien, finally arrived in Urga between September 14 and 24.

By the time these troops appeared, however, the political situation in northern Asia had changed dramatically. The uprising of the Czech Legion, the Allied intervention, and a reinvigorated White Guard assault had forced the Soviets to relinquish their cities and towns one after the other: Red units abandoned Irkutsk on July 11, 1919; on August 20 Soviet detachments evacuated Verkhneudinsk and retreated toward Chita; and on August 26 Chita itself fell to the Whites. A decision was taken in late August to form partisan bands for guerrilla warfare in Siberia.

In Mongolia the feared invasion of a thousand Bolsheviks proved to be no more than a party of seventy men who came to Uliastai in mid-June to purchase livestock. In mid-August the Uliastai Deputy High Commissioner was able to declare that they were behaving themselves and had honored an order directing them to camp outside the city.

The Mongols were alert to the changed situation in Siberia and realized how groundless were their fears of a Bolshevik invasion. When Ch'en I informed Tserendorj on September 1 that Chinese troops in the vicinity of Zamyn Üüd were ready to move (actually some of them had already left on August 23), the Minister replied two days later with an answer that must have surprised the High Commissioner. Pointing out that although three months had elapsed since the agreement to additional Chinese troops, not one Chinese soldier had arrived. The letter went on to enumerate the measures taken by the Mongols to secure the border against Bolshevik intrusions and concluded:

> Fortunately, not only has no one from the "disorderly party" (samuun nam) crossed out border, but members of the (White Guard) Provisional Government have taken power (in Siberia). Therefore, the situation in the border areas of Khovd and Uliastai is no longer critical. In addition, because the "disorderly party" in such areas of Russia as Irkutsk, Verkhneudinsk, and Kyakhta has in recent days been suppressed and members of the "old party" have taken power, the situation on the Kyakhta border is no longer critical.[89]

The Bogd Khaan Government suggested that these troops remain in China, since they would only be an "unnecessary burden" in Mongolia. Chʻen I was not easily dissuaded. He replied that China had announced its support for the Czech soldiers and that it would be best to send some troops to the border in the event of "something occurring unexpectedly;" later, he promised, they could be either withdrawn or reinforced depending on the European war.

Tsarist diplomats were equally unhappy. Orlov protested to the Mongolian government but was told that while the Mongols had agreed to these reinforcements with reluctance, this was a temporary measure and they were confident that the situation would improve in the near future. Between September 6 and October 5 Kudashev sent four protests to the Chinese Foreign Ministry stressing that the defeat of the Bolsheviks ahd obviated the need for additional Chinese troops in Mongolia and that they must be recalled immediately. Kudashev tried without success to interest the Allied representatives in Peking in this matter.

The Chinese government was not prepared to recall these troops. Peking authorities did not believe that the threat to the security of the Mongolian border was yet over. The situation in Siberia was still in flux and it was impossible to know whether the Bolsheviks might not reestablish their position as quickly as they had lost it. Moreover, an even greater peril loomed on the eastern border of Mongolia in the person of Grigorii Semenov and his pan-Mongolian movement. But there was another, perhaps more persuasive reason for rejecting these protests. Many individuals in the Chinese government hoped that this violation of the Kyakhta treaty was the first step toward abrogating the entire tripartite settlement, and that the treaty could be whittled away until the pre-1911 relationship between China and Mongolia had been totally restored.

## Reclaiming the Frontier: Uryankhai and the Altai Region

By the end of 1918 and the beginning of 1919 a new confidence animated the policy of the Peking government toward the northern frontier. From 1912 until the Russian revolution the Republican government was generally circumspect in its declarations and activities which affected the frontier and carefully avoided more ambitious measures that were certain to arouse Mongolian or, more importantly, Russian opposition.

But the Bolshevik seizure of power in Siberia, the upheavals in Manchuria which were linked with the Russian civil war, and the uninterrupted flow of appeals from Chinese representatives in Mongolia warning of disaster unless immediate action were taken, forced the government slowly to turn more attention to the frontier. During the same period there was a growing consciousness that the Russians, fragmented and consumed by mutual hatred, were powerless to resist China in the management of its frontier affairs. Although the Allies had assumed responsibility for Russian interests in China until the formation of a "legitimate" government, the Chinese soon realized that, under the guise of fighting Bolshevism, they could dismantle the Sino-Russian condominium over the nothern frontier with minimal Western interference.

One area on the frontier where the Chinese were keen to consolidate effective control was Uryankhai. China was far too distracted during the early years of the Republic to force the Uryankhai question with Russia, especially since this region had been absorbed into the Tsarist empire in April 1914 as a protectorate. Its interest in the area was revived in early 1916, however, with a series of appeals from Buyan-Badarkhu, chief of the largest Uryankhai banner Kemchik, asking China to accept the submission of this banner. Uryankhai was by this time in ferment because of the anger of Tuvins over Russian colonization, which was particularly active between 1912 and 1914, and the forceful Tsarist measures to bring this area under control. In June the Chinese Minister in Petersburg Liu Ching-jen was instructed to negotiate with the Russians over Uryankahi and to inform them: "The fact that Tannu-Uryankhai is subject to Outer Mongolian jurisdiction can be proven from history and treaties and is absolutely beyond doubt."[90] Foreign Minister Sazonov refused to acknowledge China's claim.

After the outbreak of the February Revolution Ch'en I, then Deputy High Commissioner of Uliastai, recommended that Chinese troops be sent into Uryankhai to enforce Chinese claims. Faithful to the generally cautious tone which was struck during this early period, however, the Peking government decided that such a step would violate the Kyakhta treaty and conceivably lead to an armed clash with Russian troops. Liu Ching-jen was again directed to aproach the Provisional Government on this question.

The outbreak of the October Revolution ended any prospect of a negotiated settlement of the Uryankhai problem, but the diplomatic isolation and military vulnerability of the Soviet government encouraged the Chinese to believe that a unilateral solution was now possible. The Peking government was being scourged by Chinese merchants and its own agents in Mongolia with demands for decisive action. A more powerful argument, however, was the instability of the new Russian regime and the unlikelihood that it had the means to resist a Chinese attempt to reclaim the region. On February 7, 1918 the Chinese Foreign Ministry proposed to the Cabinet Secretariat that an official be sent to Uryankhai to survey the situation and suggested that unless there were serious obstacles, a deputy high commissioner be appointed to the region. "Because of the existing confusion in Russia, we believe it is doubtful that (the Russians) will have the ability to interfere in this matter."[91]

Ch'en I composed a plan with the Urga government for a joint force of something over three hundred men to occupy Uryankhai. The expedition advanced so smoothly that in January 1919 Yen Shih-ch'ao, commander of the Chinese unit, was appointed by the Peking government deputy high commissioner for Uryankhai. although this force encountered unexpected resistance from the White Guards, forcing it to retire temporarily into Mongolia, a revolt of Uryankhais together with an attack on the White Guards by Siberian partisans allowed the Sino-Mongolian force to return. By early September 1919, when the partisans departed, the Chinese and Mongols were in control of western Uryankhai.

Although neither Chinese nor Russian sources are very forthcoming on Yen Shih-ch'ao's activities in Uryankhai after this, the broad outline of events is fairly clear. Yen could not possibly hope to dictate events in Uryankhai with such a paltry number of troops, especially after the recall of the Mongolian unit by the end of July 1919. Red units entered Uryankhai at the end of 1920 and in early March 1921 Yen's force, which was never reinforced despite his energetic appeals, was routed by a surprise attack of some armed Tuvins. On August 13-16 a congress of representatives of the Uryankhai banners, chaired by the political chameleon, Buyan-Badarkhu, declared Tuva an independent "people's republic" and Tuva's international relations were placed under the protection of Soviet Russia. Uryankhai had moved full circle.[92]

Another frontier zone which the Chinese regarded as vulnerable to both Russian and Mongolian encroachment was the Altai region in the northeastern part of Sinkiang. Sparsely populated and weakly defended, this area was inhabited by one Khoshuud and two Torguud banners which had returned from the Volga in the early eighteenth century, as well as by seven Altai-Uryankhai banners, which nomadized on both sides of the Altai mountains. Until 1907 both the Khovd and Altai districts had been administrated from Khovd, but in that year Shara sume (Ch'eng-hua ssu; present;day Altai) was designated by the Ch'ing government as the administrative center of the Altai region.

According to the provisional agreement for the cessation of hostilities between China and Mongolia signed by the Tsarist Consul in Shara sume and the Altai Superintendent in December 1913, the Altai mountains were defined as the provisional border between China and Mongolia. The Mongols, however, who at this time were still actively campaigning for pan-Mongolia, refused to accept this arrangement as final and at the Kyakhta conference had argued that the Altai region belonged to Outer Mongolia since it had been governed by the Khovd deputy military governor. The Russians forced the Mongols to yield.

Chinese frontier commissioners were conscious that the Altai region was potentially an explosive problem, especially in view of the approaching deadline (June 7, 1917) for the demarcation of the Sino-Mongolian border as provided for by article eleven of the Kyakhta treaty, and were fearful that the Mongols might be spurred to contest Chinese sovereignty. Just as these commissioners had worked so faithfully to enlarge Chinese sovereign rights over Outer Mongolia and Uryankhai, so they worked with equal industry, and greater success, to moor Altai securely to the Republic. In January 1917 the Deputy High Commissioner in Khovd and in August 1918 the High Commissioner in Urga advised the government to incorporate Altai into Sinkiang as a district (tao). Ch'en I again petitioned Peking in January 1919 emphasizing the strategic importance of the Altai region and predicting that Chinese dominion over the area would surely be endangered once Russian power was restored in Siberia. Pressure brought its desired results, and on July 1, 1919 the President of China announced the incorporation of Altai as a district of China.[93]

Semenov and Pan-Mongolia

Mongolian agreement to the introduction of Chinese reinforcements into the country and the Uryankhai expedition just then in progress had a euphoric effect on those quarters of the Peking government charged with frontier responsibilities, and more ambitious plans began to unfold for restoring full Chinese sovereignty. As usual, it was the Chinese officials in the field who were the catalysts of action.

In September 1918 Hung Chen, before leaving Peking to take up his new appointment as deputy high commissioner of Khovd, was asked by the Foreign Ministry to submit recommendations for future Chinese policy in Mongolia. He urged the government to adopt a more forceful posture toward the frontier and pointed out what was surely in the front of everyone's mind, that the presence of Chinese reinforcements then in Mongolia was merely the first step toward abrogating the entire Kyakhta settlement.

In December 1918 the Cabinet Secretariat asked the Foreign Ministry to comment on a suggestion from the Kyakhta Deputy High Commissioner that the question of Mongolia be referred to the Paris Peace Conference for international arbitration. The reply of the Foreign Ministry, important because it was the first statement of this new policy which had been in operation already for several months, opposed the idea of raising the problem of Mongolia before the conference:

> As far as the restoration of (Chinese sovereign) rights is concerned, the Russian disturbance is presently in full swing and (the Russians) do not have the time to be involved in the East. If we can take advantage of this opportunity and apply ourselves to (improving) our links with the Mongolian government, we can (thereby) demonstrate the sincerity of our government in 'beckoning and leading by the hand' and 'cherishing the distant. (When) the Mongolian government realizes that it cannot fully rely on the strength

> of the Russians, perhaps they will move into our sphere. If any matter arises affecting Chinese interests, we can at any time conclude an agreement with the Outer Mongolian government and there will be no way for the Russians to oppose it.[94]

In brief, the Ministry was arguing for a policy of moderation aimed at restoring Chinese sovereignty over Mongolia, not through coercion or intimidation, but by exhortation. This was good Confucian stuff. It also reflected the personality of Ch'en Lu, who was at that time the acting foreign minister. This strategy of leaving Mongolia with the appearance of autonomy while reclaiming the more vital rights and powers of sovereignty was more clearly expressed in a January 1919 telegram from the Cabinet Secretariat to Ch'en I: China "should seek to control the reality, but there is no need to abolish the empty name of autonomy."[95]

In pursuit of this objective, Ch'en was directed in early January 1919 to negotiate a new treaty with the Mongols which would transfer Russian commercial rights to China and end any restriction on the number of Chinese troops permitted in Mongolia. Ch'en did warn his government that the Mongols were by temperament suspicious and that this matter must be approached cautiously. Ch'en met with Tserendorj, who seemed to approve fully of the idea and even claimed that for some time half of the Mongolian nobility had such thoughts of their own but did not dare voice them. Tserendorj told the High Commissioner that negotiations would have to be dealt with by the Sain Noyon Khan and that they should be kept strictly secret. Discussions, however, did not advance further. The death of the Sain Noyon Khan (possibly murdered at the orders of the Khutukhtu's court) and the sudden emergence of the pan-Mongolian threat forced Ch'en I to shelve the project.[96]

The Chinese may have regarded the Bolsheviks as a menace to the security of the frontier, but it was the White Guards who ultimately proved to be the gravest threat. Forced into flight from Siberia, they congregated in the railway zone of northern Manchuria, where they deferred infrequently if at all to Chinese law and authorities. While the Peking government would have preferred to keep a tighter check on their activities, the Chinese lacked the military power to deal with these Cossack bands and were under constant pressure from the Allies to grant the Whites unconditional sanctuary in northern Manchuria. Ironically, it was the professed champions of order who were the most contemptuous of Chinese sovereignty. It was the firebrands of revolution who most scrupulously observed international convention in their relations with China. Had the Peking government grasped this fact, the history of Mongolia might have taken a radically different course.

The anti-Bolshevik forces in Asia were fragmented into a number of governments and armies led by men whose personal ambitions infinitely eclipsed their loyalty to the old regime. One of the best known and most ruthless of these was the twenty-nine year-old Grigorii Semenov. After an unsuccessful effort in late January 1918 to dislodge Soviet forces in Transbaikalia, he had returned to Heilungkiang, where he reorganized and trained his Special Manchurian Detachment with the assistance of Japanese advisers. This force, numbering about twelve hundred men, included one Buryat and two Kharchin (Inner Mongolian) cavalry regiments. In April he launched another offensive against the Bolsheviks and declared himself head of the Provisional Government of the Transbaikal Region, but a successful Soviet counterattack pushed Semenov back toward the Manchurian border. The uprising of the Czech Legion in July brought timely relief to Semenov's position, and the Chinese government, under pressure from the Allies, allowed Semenov's disorganized and routed troops to cross the border.

Following his ignominious flight into Manchuria Semenov began once again to rebuild his military organization. This time, however, the balance of forces in East Asia augured for greater success, for by the fall of 1918 Soviet forces in Siberia were in disarray after the uprising of the Czech Legion and the Allied intervention. By January 1919 Semenov had assembled a following of Buryat and Inner Mongolian nationalists for the creation of a pan-Mongolian state embracing Khalkha, Buryatia, Barga, and Inner Mongolia.

It is unclear when or exactly why this plan was devised, but it is possible that Semenov's past ties with Mongolia (it was reported that he was half-Buryat) may have attracted him to the idea. The plan itself was fantastic, ill-conceived, and without the remotest chance of succeeding. Such a state would have aroused inevitable opposition from both the Chinese government and the Allies, which were pledged to defend China's territorial integrity. Nor would the Tokyo government have been indifferent to the transferrence of eastern Mongolia, regarded as part of Japan's sphere of influence, to the rule of such an obstreperous and unpredictable Russian as Semenov. Semenov's separatist plans were not received sympathetically by other Russian loyalist political leaders either.

Whatever its political flaws, pan-Mongolia did strike a responsive chord among a number of Buryats and Inner Mongolians, particularly at a time when President Wilson's statements regarding national self-determination were arousing such interest in China. Since the turn of the century many Buryat intellectuals had been particularly active in promoting a Buryat self-consciousness through their research into various aspects of Buryat and Mongolian culture and history. Others found a political outlet for their nationalism by joining the Russian revolutionary movement. These men were the product of two cultures, one Mongolian and the other European, which tended to give their nationalism a special sharpness. But it was the steady encroachment on Buryat land by Russian colonists which gave it special urgency.

Until the 1917 revolution Buryat intellectuals advocated more cultural and administrative autonomy. After the revolution, however, like some other national minorities in Central Asia and Siberia, a strong independence movement quickly blossomed. At an all-Buryat congress in Chita in October 1917 a Buryat National Committee (<u>Burnatskom</u>) was organized as the principal administrative organ of the Irkutsk and Transbaikal Buryats and imediately enjoined the natives to expel Russian settlers. In around June 1918 Semenov reformed it into the

People's Duma of the Buryats of Eastern Siberia (Burnarduma). The second major group to participate in Semenov's pan-Mongolia was the Inner Mongolians, the most important of whom were Fushenge, who according to Chinese reports commanded over fifteen hundred men in early 1919 (this apparently was the core of Semenov's army), and an obscure Inner Mongolian khutukhtu, Niis Gegeen Mendbazar.

The first step Semenov took to launch pan-Mongolia was to summon representatives from different parts of ethnic Mongolia to work out the organiztional structure of the state. A preliminary meeting was held in Dauriya in February and a formal congress met in Chita from the end of that month to early March, attended by sixteen representatives from Inner Mongolia, Barga, and Buryatia (only Outer Mongolia refused to send a delegate), and a few other observers, including Semenov and some Japanese officers. It was the Buryats who dominated the congress.

The most important decision to issue from this meeting was a call for the formation of a pan-Mongolian state organized on a federal basis in which the four major "aimags" (Inner Mongolia, Outer Mongolia, Barga, and Buryatia) enjoyed broad autonomous powers under a central government. This accent on regional autonomy was unavoidable given the different historical and cultural paths which these areas had followed since the seventeenth century. A constituent assembly was to decide later whether a constitutional monarchy or a republic would be adopted. Niis Gegeen was elected prime minister, while other ministerial positions were distributed amongst representatives from the four "aimags." Hailar was selected as the capital of the new state, although provisionally the seat of government was to be Dauriya, probably because Semenov's troops controlled the town.

A decision was also taken to create an army composed of troops recruited from all over Mongolia. In order to finance both this army and the new government, Semenov stepped forward with a promise of a million ruble gift and a six million ruble loan (presumably from Japan), guaranteed on the mineral deposits of Mongolia; the lending country was also to be given the exclusive right to build railroads in the new state. Before the congress adjourned it resolved to send delegates to the Paris Peace Conference, where they were to seek international recognition for this new government. A telegram was transmitted to President Wilson asking for his support, and wires were sent to other countries inviting their governments to recognize pan-Mongolia.[97]

The Peking government was not inattentive to Semenov's activities, and beginning in January 1919 it was receiving regular reports from various officials in Mongolia and Manchuria warning that Semenov was "inflaming" the Mongols. In March concern over pan-Mongolia quickened. Ch'en I's report that Semenov and the Japanese were exploiting the differences between the nobles and lamas by inciting the former to revolt against the Khutukhtu, as well as the disheartening news that Yen Shih-ch'ao's Chinese-Mongolian expeditionary force into Uryankhai had been forced to retreat, stimulated fresh debate within the government.

Ironically, the Chinese Foreign Ministry by this time had come to reject diplomacy in favor of more aggressive military action on the frontier. It proposed to the Ministry of the Army that a force be sent to Barga and a few days later urged the Office of War-Participation Affairs, headed by Tuan Ch'i-jui, to send troops into Siberia, Outer Mongolia, and Barga in order to counter the expansion of Bolshevik power. Tuan endorsed the idea, perhaps because he hoped that a more visible and aggressive posture toward the frontier, sure to appeal to the patriotic instincts of all Chinese, might mollify domestic and foreign criticism of his War-Participation Army. Significantly, the question of Chinese troops in Mongolia no longer appeared to require consultation with the Outer Mongolians.

If more troops were to be sent to Mongolia, the Foreign Ministry had to prepare for almost certain opposition from Western quarters. Allied representatives in Peking had barely noticed the dispatch of Chinese soldiers to Mongolia in the late summer of 1918 since it appeared to be a move directed against the Bolsheviks. Even Tsarist diplomats, who knew better, could not persuade the Allies to intervene.

But now the situation was different. Siberia was occupied by Whites, supported to various degrees by the Western powers, and the European diplomats in China, who were pledged to support the old Russian regime and its interests, took a much less benign view of an action so obviously designed to abrogate the entire treaty system with Tsarist Russia. Disturbed by rumors that yet more troops were being sent to Mongolia, the American, British, and French Ministers met with Ch'en Lu during the end of March and the beginning of April, but Ch'en, keeping them at arm's length, refused to divulge the intentions of the government and feigned ignorance over the matter while emphasizing that any military action taken in Mongolia was aimed not only against Semenov but against the Bolsheviks as well. The Ministers left, evidently not having detected the evasion. Kudashev was not so easily taken in, but the Foreign Ministry replied to his protest with a curtly worded message that China had the proper duty to defend its own borders.

Despite their disappointment over the Urga government's refusal to send representatives to Dauriya or Chita, the Pan-Mongolists went ahead and formed a government while continuing to put considerable pressure on the Khalkhas to join. Although the Khutukhtu's court had already decided that Outer Mongolia would not participate in pan-Mongolia, a formal decision was taken by the Ministry of Foreign Affairs on April 13 announcing that Outer Mongolia would not split off from China nor would it support the plan of Semenov and the Japanese. A note was sent to Ch'en I two days later with a request that Semenov's troops in the Chita-Manchouli area be disarmed and sent home. Otherwise, the note warned, the eastern banners of Outer Mongolia would surely be endangered.[98] On April 16 orders were issued by the Urga government for the mobilization of two thousand men for service on the eastern frontier.

Although Mongolian sources do not explain why the Khalkhas refused to join pan-Mongolia, the reasons are sufficiently clear. The Khutukhtu's government resented having to take a back seat in a movement in which the Khalkhas would play a comparatively minor role. Khalkha was the ancestral homeland of the Mongolian people, the land where

Chinggis himself had been born. It was inconceivable to them that anyone but Khalkhas, and certainly not Buryats, should be the spirit behind such an undertaking. It was the Khalkhas who seven years earlier had defied the armies of China in 1913 in their struggle for the unification of all Mongolian tribes. What incentive was there, beyond the vague persuasion of nationalism, for the Bogd Khaan, his court and government, to deliver themselves over to a group of unknowns led by an upstart lama?

The deep Khalkha mistrust of the Buryats and, to a lesser extent, of the Inner Mongolians was a second and equally important reason. Urga's brief experience with its own pan-Mongolian project--which excluded, it is important to stress, the Buryats--between 1912 and 1915 had ended ingloriously. The Inner Mongolians bitterly resented the insouciant treatment they had received from the Khalkhas, and the Bogd Khaan's government was so disenchanted with what it regarded as a tepid Inner Mongolian reaction to the scheme that it was never revived. Now, the Buryats had produced a similar plan of their own which pushed the Outer Mongolians into the background.

The Outer Mongolians were no more enthusiastic about enlisting in a movement led by Buryats than they had been in defining Buryatia as part of ethnic Mongolia. It was not so much that they feared the russification of the Buryats. The Khalkhas resented Buryat arrogance. Here perhaps lies the nub of the problem. Each of the three--Khalkhas, Buryats, and Inner Mongolians--regarded itself as the natural leader of the Mongolian people: the first two because they were culturally superior, the third because it was culturally purer.

Yet a pan-Mongolia in which the Khalkhas played no part could hardly claim to represent all the Mongolian people. Bad luck continued to dog the movement when in March the Japanese government decided to withdraw it support. The Japanese, who by the turn of the century had thrown off the coarser inequities of their relationship with the West, had begun taking a greater interest in the fate of their fellow Asians. After Japan's stunning victory over Russia in 1905 had tested the bond of its synthesis of East and West, this island nation thrust itself forward as the self-annointed savior of the Asian people. The Japanese, and especially the moribund samurai class, adopted a militant ideology of Asia for Asiatics, and championed a doctrine of Pan-Asianism under Japanese leadership.

It was inevitable that the pan-Mongolian movement, which harmonized so faultlessly with the pan-Asian outlook of the Japanese, should have attracted their attention. Contemporary sources record the presence of Japanese officers and civilians in Urga claiming to be visiting the country on matters relating to trade. They were received suspiciously by the Chinese and Tsarist diplomats in Mongolia, especially when it was learned that some of these travellers were encouraging certain Mongolian leaders to adopt a more pro-Japanese course.

We do not know precisely who these Japanese were, under whose instructions they were operating (if they had instructions), or what these instructions were. The evidence suggests that they were nothing more than a handful of adventurers, not unlike many others who could be found throughout northern Asia at that time working without the knowledge or blessing of the Tokyo government. Indeed, the striking paucity of information about them or their activities in Mongolia would indicate a minimum of serious Japanese interest in the country. Following the disembarkation of Allied troops at Vladivostok in August 1918 there were around seventy thousand Japanese troops in northern Manchuria and Siberia (to which one must add an indeterminate number of Japanese civilians). Yet there were probably not more than twenty or thirty Japanese in all of Outer Mongolia, nor did Japan have an official representation in Urga.

An official decision came on March 16, 1919 when the Japanese cabinet decided that all participation of its citizens, both civilian and military, in the pan-Mongolian movement must end. The cabinet acknowledged that Japanese living in Manchuria and Siberia were playing a role and that this was well known to Chinese officials. It was felt that aid to pan-Mongolia would only aggravate anti-Japanese feeling in China, Europe, and the United States, and would complicate relations with the indigenous Russian forces in northern Manchuria and Siberia. The Foreign

Ministry, therefore, refused to help finance the formation of the pan-Mongolian army.[99] Once again, Mongolian nationalism had been sacrificed to great power politics.

When the Japanese government refused to underwrite pan-Mongolia with the expected money, arms, and advisers, the movement was doomed. The fact that the pan-Mongolian delegation to Paris was stopped in Tokyo was another discouraging blow. At the eleventh hour the pan-Mongolists realized that their objective would elude them altogether unless the Khalkhas were induced, or coerced, into joining. A meeting held in Chita at the end of May decided to send the Inner Mongolian Fushenge, the Buryat Tsedenov, and a personal representative of Semenov Colonel Levitskii to Urga, where they were to invite the Bogd Khaan to preside over a "Great Mongolian State" with the title of emperor. In the event of the Khutukhtu's refusal, it was reported, they were to engineer his overthrow.[100]

They arrived in June to a very frosty welcome from the Urga government and were totally snubbed by the Khutukhtu. These men apparently did contact a small number of nobles with whom a coup d'état was planned, but for unexplained reasons the plot never materialized. When persuasion failed, they tried intimidation. The Outer Mongolians were warned that it might be necessary for the "Chita government" to send in troops to "force an attitude of recognition."[101] The Mongols took this threat very seriously indeed.

Although the War-Participation Office had at the end of March agreed to send additional troops to Mongolia, there was still no sign of them. Ch'en I had proposed on April 1 that at least two mixed brigades (roughly four thousand men at full strength) should be stationed along the border between Inner and Outer Mongolia, and in the next two months he sent seven emotionally worded telegrams with the same appeal. The Cabinet Secretariat in letters to the Foreign Ministry expressed concern over these disturbing telegrams and asked the Ministry to take "measures." The government was temporizing again.

Although the cabinet in mid-June did decide to send two divisions immediately to support Urga, no more than fifty men from the Northwest Frontier Army actually reached Urga (on July 8), and it was not until mid-September, a few months after the Semenov crisis had passed, that the Chinese troops which Ch'en I believed were so urgently needed arrived.

The Mongols faced a dilemma. It is clear from the Chinese records that they were profoundly disquieted by the thought of more troops from China and yet feared that they had insufficient strength to repel a pan-Mongolist attack by themselves. The Khutukhtu's cabinet met twice over this problem and concluded that while joining Semenov would be fatal for the Khalkhas, they were not strong enough to resist him. Therefore, the cabinet decided to stall in the expectation that Mongolian defenses could be fortified in the meantime. The representatives of Semenov were told that their proposal was much too important to be decided by the Urga government alone. They must wait until the annual assembly of league chiefs, military commanders, and banner princes scheduled for later in the summer.[102]

Ch'en I did what he could to disarm Mongolian apprehensions about these new Chinese units. He counseled Tserendorj that the Mongols and Chinese must "join their hearts and unite in defense," and assured Tserendorj that Chinese policy was fair and honest, and that the central government had no intention of interfering in Mongolia's internal autonomy. The Chinese government was annoyed, he explained, only at the limitations placed on its freedom of action by the treaties with Russia. The High Commissioner also vowed that all Chinese soldiers in Mongolia would be kept under strict discipline.

It was these very treaty limitations, of course, which safeguarded Mongolia's limited independence. But the Mongols were probably lulled by Ch'en's pledges; more importantly, they were alarmed by the prospect of a Semenov invasion of Outer Mongolia. Neither the Mongols nor the Chinese yet realized that the Japanese government had renounced all association with Semenov's scheme, nor were they aware of rapidly widening fissures within the pan-Mongolian movement itself. Even the threat of an invasion was probably a desperate bluff.

On June 28 Ch'en I was informed by Tserendorj that the Mongolian government, with the approval of the Khutukhtu, had decided to request China to send troops against Semenov. The Mongolian Foreign Minister suggested that Chinese troops be moved up to the border by the time of the general assembly of the Khalkha princes. These soldiers should then be dispatched across the border on the following day, an act which would emphasize to the pan-Mongolists the resolution of Khalkha princes to defend themselves.

The assembly, attended by senior aimag officials and banner princes of Khalkha and western Mongolia, finally met on August 4. It was decided to reject the Buryat overtures and to resist the pan-Mongolists, with arms if necessary. On August 13 the Mongolian government sent a note to Ch'en I formally requesting Chinese military aid to end the Semenov threat: "We have already sent Mongolian troops to different places on the Tsetsen Khan aimag border and request (China) to take immediate measures to prevent these bandits from harassing our Mongolian borders...." Ch'en asked his government to send troops from Fengt'ien and Heilungkiang to the eastern border of Mongolia and to transfer the Third Brigade of the Northwest Frontier Army to Urga.[103]

While the Mongolian note was rather vague on this point, the Mongols probably did not intend a general strengthening of the Chinese garrison in Urga, but rather the dispatch of Chinese units across Mongolia to the eastern frontier in order to deal directly and immediately with Semenov. Significantly, the note had not asked for more troops in Mongolia itself, although this subtlety had either escaped Ch'en or he preferred to ignore it.

The feared invasion never materialized, but not because of Chinese intervention (there is no evidence that the authorities in Manchuria made even a token effort to deal with the pan-Mongolists). Semenov's pan-Mongolia, virtually still-born, ended ignominiously in early September, when a clash occurred at Dauriya between the Buryats and Inner Mongolians. Fushenge's army was routed and Fushenge was killed. Pan-Mongolia died with him.[104]

## CHAPTER V

## ABOLITION OF MONGOLIAN AUTONOMY, 1919-1920

On January 1, 1920, almost eight years to the day since the Bogd Khaan was installed as emperor of Mongolia, theocrats and princes ceremoniously renounced their "autonomy" and accepted full membership in the Chinese state. The exaggerated fear of the Bolsheviks, encouraged as well as shared by the Chinese, followed by a more ominous threat from the White Guards and pan-Mongolists, marked the end of Russia's importance as a patron of the Mongolian aristocracy. The incapacity of the Urga government to deal with both Red and White Russians underlined the urgency of recruiting another protector--the choice was obvious, the precise form of the relationship was not.

### Discontent in the Bogd Khaan State

Nine years of quasi-independent government under the Bogd Khaan had demonstrated to all but the most unyielding partisans of the court that theocracy had not worked. By the fall of 1919, the eighth year of the Bogd Khaan's rule, the great experiment in state-building was in a shambles. The Urga court and government had shown themselves to be ineffectual and philistine masters.

Most Mongols had expected that the the different taxes rendered during the Ch'ing and the cause of various uprisings against the Manchus would end once independence was announced. Just the opposite happened. Money and labor were so essential to the new government that demands on the banners actually increased. Had the Urga government used its country's human and physical resources intelligently and fairly, the population might have made their sacrifices more cheerfully. But almost from the beginning of its existence it failed to appreciate the limits of those resources or the indulgence that could be expected from the people. The Russian Diplomatic Agent coolly noted in a dispatch to Petersburg in 1913: "The aimless and aggressive policy of the Urga authorities, which has cost dearly, has exhausted the country. More and more often one hears complaints about the impoverishment of entire hoshuns (i.e., banners)."[105] Similar dissatisfaction was echoed by another Russian living in western Mongolia at this time, A. Burdukov, who wrote that 1914 was the turning point when disenchantment with the results of the revolution had become widespread.[106]

Although the Russian government sought to impose a modicum of fiscal responsibility on the Urga government by insisting on the presence of a financial adviser, his office was closed down by the Mongols in 1918. At the same time Urga's financial worries must have been increasing. The Russian ruble, which over the years had become the most popular currency, used by Russians and Chinese alike, was well on its way to collapse. Chinese merchants, who were seriously affected by the inflation of the ruble and were suffering considerable losses as a consequence, even feared that unless the government intervened, they would no longer be able to operate in the country. Incomplete customs reports from the Bogd Khaan Ministry of Finance indicate that trading activity in the Urga markets had diminished catastrophically, that prices had increased from five to thirty times, and that the number of native Mongols trading in the city had halved by 1919.[107] As trade declined so did customs revenue--the most important source of income for the government--and even the real value of this income was depreciated by inflation.

Unrelieved taxation, payment of debts to Chinese merchants, and the venality of banner princes continued to aggravate social tensions in the countryside. Throughout the Bogd Khaan years the same symptoms of social and economic deterioration which prevailed during the latter part of the Ch'ing were visible in every part of the country. With increasing frequency banner princes and league chairmen were petitioning the government for temporary remission of taxes, while arats and khamjlaga fled their homes as they had been doing since the end of the nineteenth century for the imagined prosperity of Urga, where they were submerged in a sea of refugees who came with the same purpose in mind. The Mongolian government was no more sympathetic to arat grievances than Manchu officials had been and were similarly inclined to equate disobedience to the local banner princes with sedition. In short, nine years of self-government had brought little relief to the arats--indeed, the evidence points only to an exacerbation of their condition.

Although it is difficult to know how the arats assessed the record of the Bogd Khaan government, the attitude of the princes and other secular nobles by contrast is much clearer. The lay aristocracy was plainly dissatisfied, and this dissatisfaction was all the more bitter because of its high expectations in the early years. Independence had gratified the yearning for self-rule, and the nobility was well represented in the government. And while there were not a few setbacks in the process of state-building, the nobles and officials couls still be reasonably content with their achievements.

But their participation in government was a sham. The real source of power lay in the Khutukhtu's court, from which laymen were for the most part excluded, and lama appointees of the church controlled the key ministries of Finance and Internal Affairs. The prestige of the court had suffered since public opinion held it responsible, rightly or wrongly, for the deaths of influential princes during these years. But perhaps most important of all, the greed of the church was impinging directly on the living standards of the nobility. Although the Ministry of Finance had undertaken to resume payment of government salaries to the princes, interrupted during the final years of the Ch'ing, the financial condition of the state was never equal to the task, and as the reserves of the Mongolian treasury were steadily depleted, salaries were paid more infrequently. The deteriorating circumstances of the arats, moreover, could not but adversely affect the local nobility.

One reason for the worsening situation of the banners which can be traced directly to the church was the growing number of state arats, especially wealthy ones, who became shav' nar in order to evade their banner obligations. With the tax burden falling increasingly on a diminishing proportion of the banner population, state and banner finances suffered. To be sure, there were reformers in the government who sought to correct this situation. The Bargut general Damdinsüren had so incurred the wrath of the lamas by a reform bill which he had drafted that he was forced to seek the protection of Korostovetz. Deputy Minister of Foreign Affairs Tsedensodnom in March 1916 had submitted to the upper hourse of the Mongolian parliament various proposals for increasing state revenue, one of which was to tax the shav' nar. Although the response of this house to the motion has not been recorded, the proposal was never implemented.[108]

The princes were particularly angered in August 1919 when the Khutukhtu was asked to allow his shav' nar, as a patriotic sacrifice, to be conscripted into units being organized against Semenov. The refusal of the Khutukhtu vexed the nobles, who were alleged to have complained that the church princes "regard banner troops lower than their shav' goats." Many routine religious expenses were shouldered by the general population rather than by the shav' nar, and part of the state revenue was regularly funneled into the Ikh Shav' for projects of doubtful economic benefit. The cumulative effect of these claims upon the local economy was to impoverish many banners. A letter from the League Chairman of the Sain Noyon Khan aimag to the Erdene Shanzudba in 1918 testifies to this: "Offerings to the Bogd Gegeen (i.e., the Bogd Khaan), the Ekh Dagina, and you, and the expenses of the Yonzon Khambo and religious ceremonies are piling up. Even if the men and women (of our aimag) were dispossessed of all their personal belongings, it would still be impossible (to meet the tax demands)."[109]

As the princes became increasingly isolated from the decision-making process and as ecclesiastical politics collided with the historic privileges of the princes, the delicate balance between church and state, carefully maintained during the Ch'ing, was upset. The harmony of conviction and unity of purpose so much in evidence in 1911 had yielded to bitter wrangling between the two estates. The resentful princes began to question the fundamental principles upon which independence had been declared and now came to believe that Mongolia was better off governed by China than administered by its own grasping theocrats. When these notions became a consensus, as they had by August 1919, the curtain rose on the last act of the Bogd Khaan era.

## Separatist Movement in Western Mongolia

In western Mongolia dissatisfaction with the Urga government had occurred earlier and was even more widespread than in the east. Even in 1912 some Oirat nobles, notably the Dalai Khan, Chairmen of one of the two Dörvöd leagues, had misgivings about casting in their lot with that of Khalkha. There were linguistic differences, although comparatively minor, between the Eastern and Western Mongols; the Oirat nobles did not trace their descent from Chinggis Khan nor did they call themselves "Mongol;" and during the Ming and first part of the Ch'ing dynasties the two groups had frequently been at war with one another. According to many contemporary observers, there were also noticeable differences in temperament between the two.

There were also differences in the historical development of Lamaism. Ecclesiasticism had grown relatively more slowly among the Oirats, and it was only in the nineteenth century that the building of monasteries really gathered momentum. The church consequently never had the opportunity to develop the institutional organization and authority to compete with the lay princes as it was able to do in Khalkha. The Oirat princes, moreover, played a larger role in the administration of local monasteries than did the princes of Khalkha, where monasteries were often independent of and occasionally in conflict with the secular banner administrations.

These facts suggest that the Oirat nobles had a very different perception of the role which the church should be allowed to play in secular affairs, and it is likely that the Oirat nobles chafed even more than did the Khalkhas under the Urga theocracy. If Urga authorities had adopted a more charitable and even-handed approach, the government might have been better supported in the west. Instead, the Khalkhas chose to ignore the need for delicacy in their relations with the Oirats and exhibited the same insensitivity and chauvinism that had characterized their relations with the Inner Mongolians--with the same results.

Within a year or two after the fall of the Khovd garrison Oirat princes were already having doubts about the wisdom of their earlier decision to join the Eastern Mongols.[110] The decentralized and autonomous tax structure of the Bogd Khaan government was responsible for some of the earliest grievances of the Oirats. Although the 1911 revolution passed almost unnoticed in most of Khalkha, by contrast the Ch'ing garrison at Khovd held out for several months until it finally had to be taken by force. The local population expected to be compensated by the Urga government for its expenses and losses, inasmuch as the expulsion of the Chinese from Khovd was a matter of national rather than simply regional importance. But Urga understood its obligations differently. There was no compensation.

In the following year, when the west was reinforced by Russian and Mongolian troops because of a threatened Chinese invasion from Sinkiang, the Oirats were again expected to shoulder all the costs. The practice in the early years of appointing only Khalkhas as governors of the Khovd region and excluding Oirats from membership in the government caused further mischief to Oirat relations with Urga (it was only in 1916 that Oirats were appointed as governors of Khovd, although there was always a Khalkha assistant).

It was precisely at this time that a colorful adventurer, Ja Lama Dambiijantsan, a Kalmuck Russian, was making a bid to carve out a kingdom for himself in the west. One of the new princes of the church designated by the Bogd Khaan after 1911, he soon claimed an ecclesiastical authority equal to that of the Urga Khutukhtu.

We are informed by most writers that Ja Lama's success in attracting the support of the local Khovd princes was due to an exotic and terrible power which he exercised over the population. Superstitious fear, however painstakingly cultivated by Ja Lama, explains only part of his hold on the people. Much of the explanation lies in his ability to exploit Oirat separatism (it was surely the very likelihood that Ja Lama would be successful in detaching the Khovd region from Khalkha, and the inability of the Bogd Khaan Government to deal with this threat, that forced the Russians in 1914 to arrest and deport him back to Russia). When the Urga government proceeded to confiscate Ja Lama's property and valuables, including silver religious objects belonging to the local monasteries, and to transport them to Urga, the population became indignant and complained that these things rightfully belonged to the Oirats.[111]

By the middle of the Bogd Khaan period, Khovd separatism had become a serious issue. An assembly on the Khovd river at Tsagaan bulan in the summer of 1915, attended by prominent officials of the region, demanded more equitable treatment from Urga, and many of those present openly called for a return to China or annexation by Russia. So concerned was the government that the Khalkha Governor was recalled and the Dörvöd Dalai Khan was appointed in his place. Manlai baatar Damdinsüren, himself a non-Khalkha, was sent with some troops to the region in August ostensibly to investigate a legal case but in reality, or so it appeared to observers, to demonstrate Urga's determination to keep the region under its control.[112]

With the arrival of the Chinese Deputy High Commissioner in late 1915 agitation for restoring the pre-1911 relationship with China, led by the prominent Oirat noble Natsagdorj, quickened. This movement acquired an additional impetus when the Peking government began awarding titles and emoluments to Khovd princes who secretly "submitted" to the Sinkiang Governor. By June 1919 the Khovd Deputy High Commissioner could report gleefully that all Dörvöd princes, with the exception of the Zorigt Khan, were eager to reunite with China. The Khovd Governor Dalai Khan had even inquired of the Commissioner when Chinese troops could be expected to arrive in the region so that he could declare his allegiance to Peking without fear of reprisal from Urga.[113] The princes of Khalkha were equally attracted by these Chinese inducements. Thus, by 1919 support for the Bogd Khaan Government from both the western and eastern Mongolian princes had eroded dangerously.

## Ch'en I and Negotiations for the Abolition of Autonomy

Negotiations over the abolition of autonomy proceeded logically from the earlier discussions between Ch'en I and Tserendorj in December 1918 and January 1919, when the Mongols had agreed to negotiate a new treaty with China to supercede the 1912 agreement with Russia. The Russo-Mongolian Agreement, the Sino-Russian Declaration, and the Tripartite Treaty, however, were the keystones of Mongolian autonomy, without which the entire system collapsed. The three were inextricably linked, since each endeavored to define Mongolia's relationship with China and Russia--it was a short step from discarding one treaty to rejecting the entire concept of autonomy.

Ch'en I appreciated the importanct of having obtained Mongolian consent to a new treaty and realized that the bridge to more serious discussions about the very nature of Mongolia's autonomous relationship with China was now in place. Between January and August 1919 the High Commissioner carefully tried to insinuate himself into the favor of the lay princes and to emphasize the feelings of affection which the central government held for the Mongols. The princes, though, were prepared only to negotiate a new treaty with China, not to abolish autonomy itself.

When the question of theocratic rule came up at the August 4 assembly of princes called to take a decision regarding Semenov's invitation to join pan-Mongolia, however, there was clearly a consensus of a very different order. The lay princes decided that the country could be liberated from church rule only by sacrificing the autonomous government itself. The sources do not explain whether this was a formal resolution of the assembly (unlikely) or a conspiratorial decision taken by some of its participants. Nor are we told why the question should have been brought up at this particular moment when one would have expected the two estates to close ranks against the common enemy. But by 1919 murmurs of resentment against the court and government were growing louder. The pan-Mongolist threat probably stimulated many nobles to ask themselves what they were defending.

The August assembly gave them an opportunity to answer that question.

On August 13 Tserendorj visited Ch'en I with a message from the "representatives of the four aimags" (Minister of Justice Tsetsen Khan Navaannarin acted for the Tsetsen Khan aimag, Deputy Minister of Internal Affairs Darkhan Wang for the Tüsheet Khan aimag, Deputy Minister of the Army Jam'yandorj for the Sain Noyon Khan aimag, and the Jalkhanz Khutukhtu for the Zasagt Khan aimag), stating that the princes were very concerned about the Semenov threat and implored the Chinese government to come quickly to Mongolia's aid. The Khalkha nobility, moreover, was unanimous in its desire to abolish autonomy and to restore the old Ch'ing system.

Tserendorj submitted an outline of administrative changes which the nobles wished to see implemented. In addition to the present Chinese commissioners, the princes wanted the creation of an assistant commissioner (presumably a Mongol) responsible solely for the banners; he and the high commissioner would be the senior administrative officers in Mongolia. Thus, Tserendorj explained, the power of the lamas would be "invisibly eliminated."

The proposals also called for the present five ministries of the Mongolian government to be placed directly under the jurisdiction of the high commissioner instead of the Bogd Khaan, and for local autonomous assemblies to be set up to handle important matters in the banners. It was asked that the lamas continue to receive favored treatment from the Peking government but, as the outline stressed, the princes of Outer Mongolia must be regarded as the genuine leaders of the Mongolian people. Ch'en suggested that the nobles compose a document stating that this petition had been made voluntarily; Tserendorj agreed.[114]

In an "eyes only" telegram to Ch'en Lu, Ch'en I recommended that the government accept this proposal but that it maintain absolute secrecy lest the Russians or the lamas be alerted and try to thwart negotiations. It was in this, however, that his strategy was so seriously flawed. According to Ch'en's scheme, a set of informal articles were first to be drafted with the participation of the lay princes, after which they would be presented to the court for ratification. The lamas, in other words, were expected to consent to a new constitutional arrangement for Mongolia in which their own powers were substantially curtailed while at the same time being denied a role in the discussions. The High Commissioner assured Ch'en Lu that neither the lamas nor the Khutukhtu would raise any objections to the articles.

Although the court was ultimately included in the discussions (the sources do not explain how or precisely when), Ch'en's promise that the court would acquiesce quietly was either culpably obtuse or he hope to beguile Peking with promises of a smooth passage for the plan. Intentionally or not, Ch'en I in his communications to Peking distorted the affair by giving it a false unanimity while glossing over the potential snares. Ch'en realized that his government's consent was required quickly and he probably feared that the Foreign Ministry was unlikely to give its speedy blessing to a project so fraught with uncertainties. The High Commissioner was derelict in not anticipating the keen hostility which the articles provoked in court circles and in not foreseeing the desperate measures that the high lamas were prepared to take to preserve autonomy. But in regarding the nobility as the historical and legitimate representatives of the Mongolian people and in believing that it was exclusively with them that he should treat, Ch'en seriously underestimated the power and resourcefulness of the court.

The Peking government believed that a petition signed in the name of the Mongolian aristocracy was the first priority; later conditions for the abolition of autonomy could be negotiated. The Mongols naturally were unwilling to abolish their autonomy without a clear idea of what would replace it; Ch'en had to concede. In the negotiations that followed, from the second half of August to the end of September, the princes were represented by Tserendorj and the court by Badamdorj, and on October 1 the High Commissioner was able to send Huang Ch'eng-hsu, a member of his staff, to Peking with a draft copy of sixty-three articles detailing the new system for Mongolia. The fact that the talks required a month and a half before an agreement acceptable to Ch'en I, the princes, and the court was reached reflects no doubt the difficulty of the negotiations.

The criticism of Communist historians, that these articles did no more than advance the interests of the ruling class, is to my mind far too harsh. This was by all means a conservative document which sought to revive the essential features of the administrative system as they had existed during the Ch'ing and to restore the privileged position enjoyed by the aristocracy before 1911. Both ruling and non-ruling nobles were guaranteed an annual salary to be paid by the Chinese treasury; there were provisions for the yearly rotation (nien-pan) to Peking and an audience with the president; and the Mongolian nobility and their khamjlaga, and the officials and shav' nar of the Ikh Shav' were exempted from military service.

It is important to stress, however, that every one of these privileges and immunities, far from being new, had been in practice since the early part of the Ch'ing dynasty and for the most part continued in force during the Bogd Khaan period. Rather than seeking broader rights, the princes wanted to guarantee constitutionally the observance of existing ones. In criticizing these articles one is merely commenting on the entire social and political structure of Outer Mongolia since the seventeenth century. The articles did include one provision for which there was no parallel during the Bogd Khaan period: church princes were ordered to confine their attention to religious matters and not to meddle in the secular government. But even this had been a prominent element of the Mongolian policy of the Manchus.

In one important respect the sixty-three articles were an important departure from Ch'ing practices because they sought firmer guarantees for Mongolian autonomy. There were a large number of articles which preserved the territorial, social, economic, and religious system of the Mongols, not to mention various stipulations permitting the Mongols a more active role in the administration of their country. Article two, for example, explicitly denied the Chinese government the right to alter the aimag and banner system or to permit colonization or the transfer of land to Chinese immigrants; article fourteen provided for league assemblies of nobles with consultative rights on important affairs affecting the banners.

Some of the worst abuses under the Ch'ing were eliminated. Salaries and living expenses of Peking-appointed authorities and Chinese troops were to be paid by the central government, not by the Mongols. There were limitations, albeit vague, on the number and length of service of Chinese troops in Mongolia. Livestock for the Chinese army was to be purchased at market prices. There were restrictions on the use of the postal relay and the maltreatment of relay workers was prohibited. Those Chinese wishing to farm, trade, erect buildings, or cut timber were required to obtain the permission of the local banner princes.

Ironically, it was China that received the fewest tangible returns for these concessions. The articles did acknowledge the right of the Peking government to appoint its senior officials to Mongolia, to invest Mongolian nobles, to station troops, to manage all railway, postal, and telegraph affairs--important foundations, to be sure, for the economic development of Mongolia and the strengthening of China's political control in the future, but of little immediate consequence. Possibly, most important from the Chinese point of view was the reaffirmation of Peking's sovereignty over Mongolia.[115]

## The Lamas Fight to Save Autonomy

The court had consented to the articles primarily because they preserved the "substance and form" of the Khutukhtu's position and included a promise of "generous treatment" of the lamas. But after the articles were already on their way to Peking, the court changed its mind, perhaps because it realized that the end of autonomy meant the end of theocracy. This forced the nobles into action. A petition for the abolition of autonomy was hastily drawn up and secretly transmitted to Ch'en I on October 14, but with the request that it not be sent to Peking because of the hope that the court might yet come around. In this event, another petition could be composed. The petition was signed by three ministers (but not by Minister of Internal Affairs Badamdorj or Minister of Finance Da Lama Luvsanbaldan), six deputy ministers, and "all the nobles and khutukhtu lamas residing in Urga." Other signatories included the four league chairmen, the Zasagt and Tsetsen Khans, and the Jalkhanz Khutukhtu.

When Ch'en informed his government of this development he tried to give the petition a semblance of national consensus by stressing the representative character of its sponsors. He neglected to mention, however, that there were no Oirats among the signatories, and his remark that the Jalkhanz Khutukhtu had signed on behalf of all lamas came dangerously close to prevarication.[116]

The court was determined to preserve autonomy. Badamdorj informed Ch'en I that an assembly of aimag and banner nobles was scheduled for October 28 to discuss certain articles which the court wanted to have revised (there is no evidence that this assembly ever met). Ch'en agreed, although he suspected that Badamdorj was stalling, hoping that a delegation which had just left for Peking would successfully block further attempts to abolish autonomy. (On October 19 five lamas, headed by Mergen Khambo, a man reputedly close to the Ekh Dagina, left Urga by car ostensibly to buy goods in Peking but in reality to convey a letter from the Khutukhtu to the President of China complaining of Ch'en's efforts to abolish autonomy. The letter asked the President to intervene.)

Ch'en's carefully orchestrated march to the abolition of autonomy was quickly falling out of step, and his earlier promises of untroubled negotiations were now seen to have been premature. Ch'en also was worried by information he received from Premier Chin Yun-p'eng that the Northwest Frontier Commissioner Hsu Shu-cheng would be arriving shortly in Urga to inspect the troops. As though anticipating Ch'en's fears, the Premier explicitly told him that Hsu would have no "direct responsibilities" regarding Mongolian civil affairs.[117]

Ch'en may have believed that unless his differences with the court were settled before Hsu's arrival, the latter would intervene and either undo or reap the benefits of Ch'en's patient toil. The High Commissioner went straight to Badamdorj and severely reprimanded him for reversing his earlier agreement to the articles and for daring to send a group of lamas to disturb the President. According to Ch'en's description of this meeting, Badamdorj cowered at these stern words and promised to meet with the Khutukhtu and recall Mergen Khambo

But a letter which Ch'en received that evening from the Khutukhtu included only hopeful expressions of bringing these talks to a successful conclusion. There was no mention of recalling the lamas. The letter also remarked that a decision on the articles must await an assembly of "outer" nobles, that is banner princes not residing in Urga, scheduled for October 28 (the court perhaps believed that it could exert more influence on the provincial nobility). The court was indeed stalling. The Urga nobles, like Ch'en I, were agitated by this delegation of lamas and, possibly fearing that the Peking government would assent to the Khutukhtu's request, decided to ask Ch'en to send their earlier petition to Peking immediately but without making it public yet.

A week after the departure of Mergen Khambo, the Jalkhanz Khutukhtu was also sent by the Bogd Khaan with a letter for the President of China claiming that the abolition of autonomy was not desired by the princes, by the officials, or by the people of Mongolia, and that it was solely the contrivance of the High Commissioner. The Khaan asked that autonomy be preserved and Ch'en recalled.

The choice of the Jalkhanz Khutukhtu as a courier was a curious one. Although a prominent ecclesiastic, he was well known for his progressive views and his eagerness for the modernization of his country. He objected to the rule of the state by the church and was the only church luminary to join the movement for the abolition of autonomy. It was because of his opposition that the court may have decided to get him out of the country, and with a fine sense of the ironic, it instructed the Jalkhanz Khutukhtu to deliver the Bogd's message to Peking. As a special precaution, however, he was provided with some travelling companions who, as the Jalkhanz Khutukhtu learned, were ordered to poison him should he defy the court's instructions.[118]

On the morning of November 3 the Jalkhanz Khutukhtu, accompanied by Ch'en Lu, met with Premier Chin Yun-p'eng, who limited himself to expressing his joy at seeing the Mongols' affection for China rekindled, especially at a time when the chaos in Russia was growing so dangerously; Chin met Mergen Khambo later in the day and repeated these sentiments. On November 8 the Jalkhanz Khutukhtu was received by President Hsu Shih-ch'ang. Neither Chin nor Hsu appear to have addressed themselves to the real objective of these delegations.

The Peking government was not prepared to indulge in a recondite argument whether a consensus existed in Mongolia for the abolition of autonomy. After Huang Ch'eng-hsu brought the articles to Peking, the various ministries were immediately invited to express their views on all sixty-three points. The general feeling was that the government should deal moderately with Mongolia, which explains the surprisingly few alterations recommended for the document. On October 28 the articles were approved by the National Assembly. A conciliatory letter to the Jebtsundamba Khutukhtu was drafted by the Foreign Ministry and signed by the President pledging respect for Mongolian feelings and reverence for the Khutukhtu and the Yellow Faith.

## Hsu Shu-cheng and the Abolition of Autonomy

By the end of October the Chinese government was thus poised to cancel autonomy despite the opposition of the Khutukhtu's court. The articles had been approved by the Chinese National Assembly and all that remained was for the Mongols to agree to Peking's amendments and allow the Peking government to publish the secret petition of the nobles. The sudden appearance of Hsu Shu-cheng in Urga, however, signaled a new and final phase in this affair.

Hsu's arrival in Urga, hardly fortuitous, was linked with events at home and the waning fortunes of the Anfu clique, of which Hsu himself was a very prominent member. China was at that moment experiencing a momentous social and intellectual upheaval called the May Fourth Movement. The questionable ties of the Anfu government with Japan, a country which only four years earlier had present China with the notorious "Twenty-one Demands," seized Shantung on the pretext of joining the Allies in their war against Germany, and pressured the Chinese government into signing unpopular military and naval treaites, had aroused the patriotic indignation of the intellectuals and the business and professional communities. But the Chinese were truly excited to a paroxysmal nationalist fervor when news arrived in April that the Versailles Conference, on which the Chinese had pinned their hopes of securing a just settlement of the Shantung question, had recognized Japan's claims to this peninsula. Anger at the government's feeble resistance to the Allies in Paris erupted in the famous May Fourth Incident.

In addition to the broader criticisms of the Peking government, there were also criticisms of Tuan Ch'i-jui's War-Participation Army. Unlike most warlords of this period whose power was guaranteed by control over territory and an army, Tuan had been forced to maintain his position of leadership in the Peiyang clique through a delicate manipulation of slippery and ephemeral alliances with other warlords in the north. Realizing that his political future depended on controlling his own military force, Tuan founded in March 1918 the War-Participation Office, the publicly stated objective of which was to form and train units for duty in Europe (the office was also responsible for frontier defense), and organized an army with Japanese financing (the famous Nishihara Loans), guns, and instructors.

When fighting on the western front in Europe ended in November 1918, Tuan's force no longer had a convincing reason to remain in existence. There were angry calls for its amalgamation into the national military, and Tuan's army became a major issue at the Shanghai Peace Conference, which opened in February 1919 with the aim of ending the war between north and south China. In order to counter this criticism, Tuan simply rechristened his office the Bureau of Frontier Defense and his army the Frontier Defense Army. The invocation of "frontier defense" gave his organization a suitably patriotic image, although Tuan himself never showed more than a marginal interest in frontier matters.

Hsu Shu-cheng, Tuan's chief lieutenant, was appointed northwest frontier commissioner on June 13, and commander-in-chief of northwest frontier defense on June 24. Hsu was now not only the senior military officer of Outer Mongolia but the senior civilian officer as well, with responsibility over such matters as communications, land reclamation and animal husbandry, timber, mining, commerce, and education.

According to the accepted wisdom, the Anfuists sent Hsu Shu-cheng into Mongolia at this time in order to divert public attention from some of their less popular activities and to burnish their reputation by recovering a piece of the frontier lost to Russia. This proposition is especially compelling to many writers when the Anfu policy toward Mongolia is set against the inaction, if not indifference, of Republican governments in previous years. According to many writers, Hsu, who knew that negotiations for the abolition of autonomy were about to be concluded, hoped to intervene in order to seize the glory for himself and his clique.

To the extent that this theory stresses the timing of his intervention as a calculated act, I believe it is correct. But it misses his larger aims in Mongolia. It is reasonable to assume that the appointment of such a powerful man to such a relatively obscure post was based on more than simply patriotic service. Seven months earlier, in April 1919, Hsu had submitted to the government a visionary plan (approved by the National Assembly on June 10) for the social and economic reconstruction of the Mongolian frontier with a thinly disguised suggestion that he should execute it.

He proposed an ambitious program of railroad construction, land reclamation and cultivation, mining, and banking. Hsu urged an energetic program of education be carried out among the Mongols and even suggested--highly uncharacteristic of a Chinese--that Chinese officials, merchants, and laborers in Mongolia learn Mongolian in order to promote closer feelings between the two peoples. More pernicious from the Mongols' point of view was his suggestion that colonization and intermarriage be encouraged in order to "transform the customs of the Mongols" and break down one of the barriers between them and the Han Chinese. Hsu wanted nothing less than the total sinification of Mongolia.[119]

Although Hsu repeatedly stressed that it was

only patriotism which prompted him to recommend these measures, they in reality must be regarded as the blueprint for the formation of a warlord empire in Inner and especially Outer Mongolia to rival that of Chang Tso-lin's in Manchuria. Hsu's contemporaries certainly drew this conclusion and gave him the sobriquet "King of the Northwest" as distinct from Chang Tso-lin, the "King of the Northeast."

Indeed, Chang's readiness to ally with Ts'ao K'un and Wu P'ei-fu in the spring of 1920 against the Anfu may indicate that he was alive to Hsu's ambitions. Hsu had earlier served as an officer in Chang's Fengtien Army and probably was impressed enough with Chang's military power, which derived from the wealth and geographical isolation of Manchuria, that he was persuaded to create the same powerful base for himself and Tuan Ch'i-jui in Mongolia. Hence the stress on economic development. It is wise to recall also that Tuan's army had been financed by Japanese loans, which had now dried up. New sources of revenue were needed.

The threat of a Semenov invasion was Hsu's pretext, but it was Ch'en's negotiations with the Mongols for the abolition of autonomy which was his real motive for intervening in Mongolia at precisely the moment he did. Despite the clash between the Inner Mongolians and Buryats in early September, of which Ch'en I apparently knew nothing, rumors continued to fly that Semenov was planning to invade Mongolia with a large Buryat army. On September 13 the Chinese Foreign Minister asked the Bureau of Frontier Defense to respond to Ch'en's anguished appeals for help.

In fact, the Seventh Regiment of Ch'u Ch'i-hsiang's Third Infantry Brigade at Hsuan-hua was already on its way to Urga, arriving on September 15, but Ch'en complained that it was insufficient and asked for the Eighth Regiment to be dispatched immediately. On September 23 this Office replied that Hsu had been ordered to send more troops, but that there was a problem of money, which Hsu was carefully studying. It may be significant that the communication of September 23 made no mention of Hsu Shu-cheng personally leading any troops to Mongolia.

According to Hsu himself, he came to Mongolia in

late October to set in motion his vast plan for the reconstruction of that country and to reinforce the garrison at Urga. He later protested to Peking that Ch'en I's negotiations with the Mongols had nothing at all to do with his trip and claimed that he did not obtain a copy of the sixty-three articles until October 22, the day before leaving the capital, although he did admit knowing that a certain Mr. Huang had brought a draft plan for the abolition of autonomy to Peking. It was only after examining these articles "day and night" on his journey to Urga and recognizing their flagrant inadequacies that he decided to intervene.[120]

Hsu's denial is unconvicing. Whether or not he intended to develop Mongolia into a prosperous and secure warlord base for himself--as all the evidence suggests that he did--Hsu certainly had very ambitious plans for the region which he was keen to see implemented quickly. It is inconceivable that the chief civilian and military officer of Outer Mongolia would have been indifferent to negotiations in Urga which had such enormous implications for his Mongolian scheme. If the sixty-three articles were put into effect, Hsu would have been forced not only to revise his plans but to scrap them altogether. He had to act carefully, however, lest he arouse the suspicions of other warlords. Therefore, he presented his intervention as spontaneous and patriotic.

It is far more probable that Hsu was monitoring Ch'en I's progress and had discreetly obtained a copy of the articles brought by Huang to Peking around October 5. Even a casual examination of the terms would have alerted the Frontier Commissioner to the dangers they held for his project. Three weeks later he came to Urga with troops, not only to reinforce the escort guard but to press upon the Mongols a very different set of conditions.

Hsu left Peking on October 23. Over a hundred motor vehicles were quickly purchased in Kalgan, and they transported the remainder of the Third Brigade. Perhaps as many as two thousand Chinese troops were now in Outer Mongolia.[121] In a telegram to Peking two days arriving in Urga, he specified seven objections to Ch'en's articles. Hsu complained that the articles ignored the need for developing the Mongols materially and intellectually and they lacked any provisions for the exploitation of Mongolia's natural resources. Although lip service was paid to China's administrative sovereignty, he wrote, there were ten articles which sought to enlarge the power of the princes at the expense of the central government. The articles were silent, furthermore, on such matters as custom duties, finance, agriculture, commerce, and mining.

Hsu recommended that Ch'en delete the numerous inconsequential clauses which merely encumbered the document and draw up a briefer set of articles focusing on administration and finance. These should include statements guaranteeing generous treatment of religion, payment of state salaries to the princes, and recognition of current ranks and titles. There should also be statements that the government was responsible for the preservation of peace in the rural areas and that diplomacy was the sole prerogative of the government. Any more provisions than these would in Hsu's opinion simply handicap the articles and provoke disagreements. He asked that the Foreign Ministry instruct Ch'en to discuss the drafting of new articles with himself. Afterwards, Ch'en could again take charge of negotiations and Hsu would return home once his military duties were completed.[122]

Not only did the two men disagree over strategy, they differed over tactics as well. Hsu believed, first of all, that Ch'en was fundamentally mistaken in collaborating with the nobles against the church. He thought that in the long-run Peking must adopt an even-handed approach to the princes and lamas, favoring neither one nor the other. But in the short-run, the agreement of the church to the abolition of autonomy was essential. Hsu asserted that it was the church which propped up the secular rule of the princes, and if the church were to withdraw its recognition, the mandate of the princes would end immediately. He epitomized his tactics with the aphorism: "to catch a thief you must catch his master."

Hsu also advocated a balanced application of both "generosity" and "coercion," or the "hard" and the "soft," to achieve China's aims in Mongolia. He did caution that the Mongols were by nature suspicious (a favorite Chinese stereotype) and that in the immediate future only generosity would succeed in creating the initial bonds of friendship--later, he added, coercion could be employed to make them submit.[123]

Although Chin Yun-p'eng had refused to approve these objections, arguing that the articles of Ch'en I had already been accepted by the cabinet, he was overruled by the President, who instructed Hsu to formulate with the Urga High Commissioner a plan for their implementation. Because neither Hsu nor Ch'en had been put in charge of negotiations for the abolition of autonomy, the Frontier Commissioner apparently felt that he had to reinforce his authority among the Mongols by actively courting the more influential lay and church figures in Urga with banquets and gifts (he had a secret audience with the Khutukhtu on November 6).

On November 11 he met with Ch'en I to discuss the articles of abolition. Li Yuan and En-hua (the deputy high commissioners of Kyakhta and Uliastai respectively), Ch'u Ch'i-hsiang, and Counsellor Yang Chih-ch'eng were also invited to attend, as he explained, "in order to avoid disagreement (caused by) the prejudices of one or two persons"--a clear reference to Ch'en I. The High Commissioner had been watching Hsu's activities with growing apprehension and warned Ch'en Lu that his interference would rally the lamas and encourage them to greater opposition. He implored Ch'en to apprise the President of the situation.

At the meeting Hsu presented Ch'en I with four "suggestions:"(1) Chinese policy must focus on promoting education; (2) political power must belong to the central government and not to the princes; (3) church and lay princes must be treated impartially; and (4) the northwest frontier commissioner was the chief officer of Outer Mongolia. Ch'en I capitulated and agreed to revise the articles in the sense recommended by Hsu.[124]

Hsu's primary instrument for persuading the Mongols to abolish their autonomy was the aging Badamdorj, one of the most interesting personalities of this period. Although much disliked by the princes for his dogged efforts to enlarge the prerogatives of the church at their expense, contemporary observers consistently described him as crafty, acquisitive, very capable, and pro-Chinese. Such qualities, not to mention his membership in the cabinet and access to the Khutukhtu, made him the obvious target for Hsu's attentions. Hsu cultivated Badamdorj with unctuous flattery and deference, even suggesting that he was the logical heir of the Khutukhtu should the Bogd die (the Khutukhtu was seriously ill at this time).

Acting at Hsu's request, Badamdorj met several times with the Bogd Khaan between November 10 and 13 to persuade him to agree to the abolition of autonomy. The Khutukhtu submitted the matter to his cabinet on November 10 but no decision was reached. With an unusual sensitivity to parliamentary democracy the court declared that questions affecting foreign affairs required consultation with the parliament. On November 13 the matter was submitted to the assembly, and although the result was inconclusive, there was nevertheless an indication of the mood of the two houses: the upper house agreed to abolish autonomy while the lower house was undecided.[125] Hsu was at the end of his tether. His "soft" policy had not worked, now he would test the "hard." It was at this point that he initiated a train of remarkable events which finally beat the Mongols into submission.

On that evening Hsu visited Badamdorj and explained why the Bogd Khaan's objections were unacceptable. First, foreign relations were solely the charge of the central government; and secondly, since the Khutukhtu had ruled until now without ever consulting parliament, its consent was unnecessary. He warned that the conflict between the church and lay princes was at a flashpoint and its explosion would mean the end of Outer Mongolia. Hsu demanded that the Khutukhtu either give his decision the next day or he would be deported immediately to Peking. In the event of the Khutukhtu's refusal, Hsu also threatened to arrest four of his closest advisers, including Badamdorj, on the charge that they were unable to advise him properly. In a wire to Peking Hsu confided that this threat was made to instill fear: "The hard and the soft aid one another and the majesty of the Chinese state remains unimpaired."[126]

On the next morning Badamdorj unexpectedly arrived at Hsu's residence and told him of the Khutukhtu's agreement to discarding Ch'en I's articles and discussing new ones, and of his willingness to compose a petition to the President of China requesting the abolition of autonomy. The Khutukhtu only asked that Ch'en I, because of his proven hostility to the court, the princes and the lamas, be excluded from these new discussions. Hsu agreed, promising to accompany Badamdorj to meet the Khutukhtu that evening.

Hsu then drew up a set of eight articles which contained most of his criticisms of Ch'en I's sixty-three points adumbrated in the November 1 telegram. This document, having almost nothing in common with the sixty-three articles, was a set of economic and social objectives for the development of Mongolia calling for an increase in the population, the development of commerce, industry, and agriculture, the exploitation of Mongolia's natural resources, and the promotion of education. Because it was considerably tougher than the articles of Ch'en I, Hsu, perhaps anticipating hostile reaction from the Mongols, decided that an additional show of force would be helpful. On the evening of November 14 he placed troops around the Khutukhtu's palace (the Tsagaan süm on the banks of the Tuul' river) and Badamdorj's yurt in the Ikh Khüree monastery.

Accompanied by Ch'u Ch'i-hsiang, General Staff Officer Li Ju-chang, and En-hua, Hsu arrived at Badamdorj's home by car and presented him with the eight points. Hsu pointed out that a Mongolian representative could be sent later to Peking to discuss more detailed measures for Mongolia. For the moment, however, the Jebtsundamba Khutukhtu must lead his people in presenting a petition for the abolition of autonomy. He "generously" gave the court twenty-four hours in which to reply; otherwise, both the Khutukhtu and Badamdorj would be sent to Peking. Badamdorj, in Hsu's words, became "extremely apprehensive." The Bogd Khaan had no choice but to yield.

A second assembly of the Mongolian parliament was convened by Badamdorj on the morning of November 15 to ratify the Bogd Khaan's decision. The upper house agreed to accept the articles, and representatives were then sent to the lower house to relate the events of the previous evening and to impress upon it the necessity of confirming the decision of the upper house. For a long time no one dared to say anything, but the stillness of the chamber was finally broken by murmurs, gradually rising to shouts, calling for armed resistance to Hsu's ultimatum. A vote was taken which declared that Mongolia must not abolish autonomy and that Hsu and his troops must be expelled if they tried to force it. The upper house, after learning of this decision, sent back the following message: "The few cannot vanquish the many, nor the weak overcome the oppressor. Therefore, we cannot be guided by (your) ill-considered views." The decision of the upper house prevailed.

Victorious, Hsu could afford to be generous. He agreed to shelve, temporarily, the eight articles which had so upset the Mongols and to receive the petition for the abolition of autonomy without fanfare. On November 17 in the presence of only five Chinese officials Hsu accepted the petition, signed by the ministers and deputy ministers of the Bogd Khaan's government--but not by the Bogd Khaan himself.

Before leaving Urga there were still two matters which required Hsu's attention. The first was to assuage the anxiety of Mongolian leaders over the sudden abolition of their autonomy and to reassure them about their future. He visited many of the lay and church princes, pledging that the central government would treat both estates impartially. Hsu also left special instructions with Chinese officials that the Mongolian people were to be treated with greater respect and consideration than they had been formerly. Hsu's second task was to organize a temporary administration to operate in his absence. He placed the Northwest Frontier Commission under the direction of Ch'u Ch'i-hsiang and advised the Mongols that all business must be conducted with this office, not with the High Commissioner under Ch'en I. Hsu left Urga on November 21.

On the very next day a special ceremony was held

in Peking to celebrate the abolition of autonomy and a presidential mandate was issued accepting the petition of the Mongols. Hsu arrived in Peking a few days later to a hero's welcome arranged by the Anfu Club. On December 1 Hsu was appointed superintendent of Outer Mongolian reconstruction affairs and on December 2 investiture plenipotentiary. At his request, the post of high commissioner was abolished and Ch'en I was recalled.

Hsu returned to Urga on December 27 carrying with him a gold seal of office, engraved with seven lions, which he had received from the President for the Khutukhtu. The ceremony for the investiture of the Bogd Khaan (he was allowed to retain his title) was observed on January 1 with appropriate pomp. Soldiers were lined on either side of the road from the Ikh khüree monastery to the Khutukhtu's palace, and the diploma of office and portrait of the President of China were borne in a specially prepared palanquin draped in yellow silk. The standard of the Chinese Republic followed accompanied by a marching band of cymbals and drums. Mongolian officials, lamas, and citizens were obliged to prostrate themselves repeatedly before these symbols of Chinese sovereignty. The capitulation of the Mongols seemed complete. It was not. That very night arats and lamas gathered outside the Khutukhtu's palace and angrily tore down the five-colored flags of the Chinese Republic hanging from the gate.[127]

Hsu immediately turned his attention to the task of implementing an ambitious program of development for Mongolia. The first step was to dismantle the old Mongolian government and to replace it with an administration specially designed to execute these reforms. A new government of eight departments was organized: general affairs, finance, commerce and transportation, postal, land reclamation and animal husbandry, timber and mining, ceremonies and education, and military defense. Soon after the ceremony of investiture the doors of the Mongolian ministries were locked and Chinese sentries posted in front of them, and the seals of the ministries were handed over to Hsu. The Mongolian army was demobilized and its arsenal seized.

The banner administration in the countryside was also transformed by the reorganization drive.

"Responding to the popular will of the Mongols," the Chinese government in February announced the Law for the Reorganization of the Leagues and Banners of Mongolia, the general thrust of which was to create a new form of banner government superficially at least more consonant with modern Chinese republicanism. Titles of banner officials (such as _tuslagch_ and _zakhiragch_) were replaced by the general term "officer of banner affairs." Each banner government was to be composed of two offices, general affairs and administrative affairs. And assemblies of officials and elected representatives were to be convened in every banner.[128] It must be emphasized, however, that this law left the authority of the banner princes undiminished.

If the Mongols were uncertain about the broader implications of Hsu's reforms, such doubts vanished in March when his eight articles were publicly issued as the charter of the promised reformation of Mongolia. Foreign specialists were invited to the country to conduct preliminary investigations of the country. Hsu revived the scheme, dormant for the past ten years, of a railroad from Kalgan to Kyakhta (he was appointed superintendent of the project). And a Frontier Bank, subject to the Northwest Frontier Commission in Urga, opened for a brief spell.[129]

Hsu's effect on Chinese commerce is more controversial. The Frontier Commissioner did cancel the aimag and banner official debts to the Ch'ing bank of the Board of Revenue and Population amounting to 500,000 taels (the interest on this debt had previously been annulled). Nevertheless, there apparently were no restraints on Chinese collecting the official banner and private debts, and according to Mongolian historians the Chinese merchants took advantage of their strengthened position to demand payment of old loans plus the interest which had accrued on them during the Bogd Khaan period. Chinese merchants presented the Khovd district with a bill of over one million head of livestock as compensation for property destroyed during the capture of Khovd in 1912, a claim which appears excessive.[130]

Hsu left Urga in January or early February for Peking, and Li Yuan was put in charge of the Frontier

Commission in his absence. He returned to Urga for a third and final time at the end of May or beginning of June. The growing power of the Anfu clique and its apparent intention to expand into central China had united the Chihli generals Ts'ao K'un and Wu P'ei-fu with Chang Tso-lin not long before in an "Eight Province Alliance." Tuan's continued association with Hsu Shu-cheng and the ambitions of the latter in Mongolia were also serious issues which troubled the relations of Chihli warlords with the Anfu. When war appeared imminent, Hsu was ordered by Tuan in May to move his Frontier Defense Army to Peking. Hsu was probably in Urga to arrange for the transfer of these troops south, although events in China moved so quickly that few of them actually left Mongolia. Hsu returned to Peking, arriving on June 17, and was never to bother Mongolia again. Tuan Ch'i-jui was easily beaten in the war with the Chihli group and Hsu Shu-cheng had to seek refuge with the Japanese.

On August 15, at the request of the Mongols, the new Chihli government appointed Ch'en I northwest frontier commissioner, but probably because of the post's association with the despised Hsu Shu-cheng, it was renamed pacification commissioner of Urga, Uliastai, Khovd, and Tannu-Uryankhai. Deputies were appointed to each of these four areas (both Chinese and Mongols were eligible, and perhaps as an act of conciliation the new government appointed Mongolian deputies to Khovd and Uliastai).[131]

---

The abolition of Mongolian autonomy has been the subject of no little debate among Western and Asian scholars. Chinese historians have singled out Hsu Shu-cheng for special criticism. It was his abusive handling of the negotiations for the abolition of autonomy, they believe, which so disaffected the Mongols that they eventually turned to Russia for help. Russian and Mongolian historians, on the other hand, have blurred the distinctions between Ch'en I and Hsu, regarding both as instruments of unrelenting Chinese imperialism, and have attacked the church and lay princes for their treachery to the Mongolian people and pusillanimity toward the Chinese. The truth, I think, is more complex.

The conflict between Ch'en I and Hsu Shu-cheng was more than simply a difference of style. The issue was historical and universal. In its simplest construction it turned on the question, familiar to many governments in other parts of the world, of whether an interventionist or non-interventionist strategy was to be pursued in raising (or changing, depending on one's viewpoint) the cultural patterns of a relatively backward minority.

This was not simply an economic or political problem--it was an ethical dilemma. Ch'ing policy toward the frontier for most of its existence had been indulgent and laissez-faire. But Western and Russian encroachments and the growing reform movement of the nineteenth century brought the frontier policy of the government under increasingly critical scrutiny and a new logic, that only the economic and social integration of the frontier with the interior would guarantee China's borders, soon governed the thinking of late Ch'ing reformers. Besides strengthening China, it was argued, the cultural and material lives of the Mongols would be signficiantly improved. The Mongols interpreted this less as progress than as transformation--hence the revolution of 1911.

Whereas the sixty-three articles of Ch'en I were unmistakably shaped in the mold of Ch'ing tradition, Hsu's program, whatever his personal designs on Mongolia, was comparatively far-sighted and progressive and was firmly rooted in the new thinking. Hsu hoped to emancipate the Mongols from their "benighted" condition and bring the prosperity of the twentieth century to the northern frontier. In isolating Hsu Shu-cheng for criticism, therefore, we are ignoring the deeper reason for China's "loss" of Mongolia. Although the Frontier Commissioner's two-fisted methods of dealing with the Khutukhtu's court and government undeniably angered the Mongols, it was his plan for the modernization of Mongolia and its integration with China which terrified them. Hsu never understood the depth of Mongolian nationalism or the fact that the coincidence of Chinese and Mongolian interests was more evident to the Chinese than it was to the Mongols.

But Hsu's prejudices were shared by an entire culture. Throughout the Republican period Chinese governments showed a striking insensitivity to the national aspirations of the Mongols. Their cynicism was particularly well illustrated by the practice of working exclusively through the hereditary chiefs of the Mongolian people who, it was believed, were moved solely by self-interest and could be bought off with the bangles and beads of rank. While this perception may not have been entirely inaccurate, it was incomplete. Most of these Mongolian leaders were at the same time desperately worried about the survival of their people and anxious that they be allowed to continue living in the traditional ways. Republican China could never fathom the complexity of the Mongolian character or the justice of its ambitions.

The immediate consequences of Hsu Shu-cheng's intervention, however, are fairly clear. His eight-point program reawakened Mongolian fears of China, and in the wake of this nationalistic feeling two small group of men who were opposed to Chinese domination came into being;they were later to merge into the Mongolian People's Party. They won the sympathy of both secular and church leaders, whose differences were temporarily laid aside, and obtained their support for an approach to Soviet Russia for help. It is unlikely that either group would have appeared, let along develop as each did, had the comparatively more generous conditions of Ch'en I been accepted as the basis for the abolition of autonomy.

Mongolian historians have been very severe in their judgement of those men who endorsed the abolition of autonomy. I cannot agree with their tendency to reduce the choice facing Mongolian leaders in 1919 to that between freedom or slavery, and to condemn _en masse_ as traitors those princes who voted to abolish autonomy. The issues were more difficult, and the solutions were less evident, than they are today. The patron-client psychology of the Mongols, the belief that only the destruction of the Bogd Khaan state itself could liberate Mongolia from the shackles of ecclesiastical Lamaism, and the overpowering might of the Chinese military, convinced many Mongolian leaders, such as Tserendorj, that there was no alternative.

The end of the Bogd Khaan Government brought to a close one of the most important eras in modern Mongolian history. This was a crucial transitional period which bridged the divide between the premodern and modern eras of Mongolia. The most outstanding theme of these eight years was the heightened interest in the outside world and the eagerness to adopt European practices. By imitating the West the Mongols hoped to stand shoulder-to-shoulder with other nations of the world. This aspiration was shared, to varying degrees, by men of the most diverse backgrounds. Most, if not all of them, believed at first that modernization could occur while still retaining traditional Mongolian institutions. In this many were disappointed.

Although progress was undoubtedly made during this period--a national army was formed, primary schools were set up in some banners, a modern government was organized,diplomatic relations were sought, and economic development was encouraged--many of these reforms came about only through Russian pressure and were emasculated wherever possible by the forces of reaction, especially the Khutukhtu's court. The Bogd Khaan's entourage never enthusiastically committed itself to reform, and it was here that it progressively undermined its claims to leadership. But an elite of non-noble, educated men living in Urga and employed by the national government had for perhaps the first time witnessed the possibilities of the twentieth centurn. For them there could be no return to the old ways.

## CHAPTER VI

## THE MONGOLIAN PEOPLE'S PARTY, 1920

Throughout Mongolian society there was confusion and uncertainty. The political and economic upheavals of 1918 and 1919 in Mongolia were unsettling, and only the most remote, apathetic herdsman was untouched by the vexations of these years. The economy was in an irretrievable decline; contradictory and exaggerated reports of imminent Bolshevik or White Russian invasions multiplied; and the split between the court and banner princes made unified resistance impossible--just as the moment when unity was so desperately needed.

But when Mongolian princes were poised to accept Chinese sovereignty under the rather generous conditions offered by Ch'en I, Hsu Shu-cheng intervened with his regiments and imposed a very different arrangement on Mongolia. Differences between the church and lay princes now paled in the face of this new threat to the very existence of the Mongolian people themselves. It was to be neither group, however, which initiated and led resistance against the Chinese. It was the new class of civil servants and intellectuals which played this role.

### Formation of the Consular Hill and East Urga Groups

Of all the recognizable elements of Urga society it was the members of the Bogd Khaan's government whose position was the most emphatically imperiled by the abolition of autonomy. Although arats of ability had always been able to find employment in the Ch'ing or shav' bureaucracy, the creation of a native Mongolian state with an elite of administrative and military officials offered new and enlarged scope to ambitious young commoners. Through service to the state such men as Tserendorj, Magsarjav, Damdinsüren, and others were able--impossible a decade earlier--to participate in government at the highest levels. As a result, government officials and army officers (unlike the banner population of nobles and arats) came to regard their livelihood as indissolubly linked with the fate of the government. The end of the Bogd Khaan state not only put them out of work, it removed them from their positions of power and privilege.

But their resistance to Hsu Shu-cheng was generated not simply by the material impact which the abolition of autonomy had upon their lives. Many of these young officials and officers were deeply influenced by the reformist spirit of the Bogd Khaan years, and were intellectually and emotionally committed to the concept of an autochtonous, modern, bureaucratic state. In this they were squarely in the mainstream of twentieth-century nationalism. The determination of these officials to cling to autonomy was reflected most clearly in the vote of parliament on the question of its abolition. But Ch'en I also recognized the link between the opposition of the lower house and the employment of a majority of its members in the Bogd Khaan government.[132]

Some of these men who were especially angered by Hsu's peremptory dissolution of the Bogd Khaan state and fearful of the consequences for Mongolia's future began to coalesce into two groups, much in the traditon of secret arat *duguilans*. It is clear that, with the possible exception of Choibalsan, they were untutored in the political philosophy of Marxism-Leninism, nor does the published evidence support the conclusion of Communist historians that in the first few months of 1920 they hoped to couple their opposition to the Chinese with the democratization of the country. This was to come somewhat later.

These groups, one known as the Consular Hill Group (*Konsulyn denj büleg*) and the other as the East Urga Group (*Züün khüree büleg*), came into existence in response to Hsu's military occupation of the city and his unceremonious dismantling of the Bogd Khaan Government. They were not organized in any formal sense, but seem to have had a comparatively fluid membership, coalescing around, rather than under, one or more of their more influential members. Throughout the lifespan of the two groups and during the early period of the Mongolian People's Party recruitment was adventitious, ideology was vague.

The lack of published material has obscured the origins and activities of both groups, a problem which has been aggravated by the insistence of Communist and many Western historians to exaggerate the contributions of Sükhbaatar and Choibalsan to the the revolution at the expense of other men, especially Bodoo and Danzan. The task of assessing the historical roles of these four is a particularly sensitive and difficult one. Almost from the moment of their executions in 1922 and 1924, and particularly during the Choibalsan years, Bodoo and Danzan have been stigmatized by Communist historians as traitors and counter-revolutionaries and their services to the revolution have been for the most part ignored or de-emphasized. On the other hand, Sükhbaatar's premature death in 1923 and subsequent "beatification," and Choibalsan's "cult of personality" have dominated historical thinking so completely that it is these two who are primarily credited with guiding the revolution to its ultimate victory. In the course of refurbishing the discolored reputations of Bodoo and Danzan, I hope to show through the remainder of this book that the reality was very different.

It must be said, however, that a more balanced appraisal of Sükhbaatar and Choibalsan, in which both men are properly credited with major contributions to the revolution but without the effusive descriptions characteristic of earlier years, has been gradually emerging in Communist historiography since the second half of the 1960s.

In contrast to the East Urga Group, whose beginnings are rather conjectural, we have a relatively clearer picture of the origin of the Consular Hill Group. The prime mover behind its formation was a well educated thirty-five year-old lama, Dogsomyn Bodoo (1885-1922), who was well known for his progressive views. He had belonged to the Ikh Shav' and was literate in Mongolian, Chinese, Tibetan, and Manchu. It was because of his education that he was employed as a clerk in the Shav' Yamen, although for reasons which are unknown he fell out of favor with the Erdene Shanzudba and other officials of that office. He then went to work as a teacher of Mongolian in the Russian Consulate's School of Translators, where he became acquainted with Ts. Zhamtsarano and aided the Buryat in his various liberal enterprises. They had endeavored to form a cooperative, the objective of which was to promote "democratic work" among the people, but the Urga government refused to approve such a plan, believing that it was merely a fiction for a political party. Bodoo also assisted Zhamtsarano in publishing his journal New Mirror, which was a popular forum for progressive even radical ideas, and in publishing other works, some of which, such as The Reception of the Ordos Gunj Gegeen and Tolstoy's Buddha, had an explosive effect on the Urga establishment.

By 1920 Bodoo was already a prominent journalist, conversant in foreign and domestic affairs, a regular contributor to Mongolian-language gazettes, and well connected in Urga society. At the same time his feet were firmly planted in the traditional culture, and he could be seen studiously reading the Buddhist scriptures and historical chronicles of Mongolia.[133] Of all the Mongolian revolutionaries he was probably the most gifted, though his intellectual attainments made him a rather difficult character: one Russian described him as "expansive and somewhat affected by Russian culture," a criticism substantially repeated by Danzan, who accused him of being "proud and haughty."[134]

Bodoo's pre-revolutionary career, as well as his work during the revolution, suggests that he was genuinely committed to left-wing politics, although too little has been published to ascertain the extent of his commitment to social revolution. He was executed in 1922 along with Chagdarjav, Puntsagdorj, and others, ostensibly for planning a coup against the People's Government with the aid of high lay and church princes, Dambiijantsan, the American Consul in Kalgan S. Sokobin, and Chang Tso-lin. A potpourri indeed of rogues, warlords, and Western agents. Another, more contemporary accusation has it that he sought to subordinate the Central Committee of the party to the government, that he opposed certain social and economic reforms, and that he tried to undermine Soviet-Mongolian relations.

It must be stressed, however, that with the exception of a brief quote from Bodoo's alleged "confession," there is no published documentary proof to support these accusations. But because they have had such a powerful effect on Communist and consequently Western historians, it will be useful to review what is definitely known about the events leading up to Bodoo's execution.

While the truth of this affair may never be known, there is enough evidence to justify the suspicion of the English historian C.R. Bawden that Bodoo's execution was the result of a factional struggle which he lost.[135] It appears, moreover, that his fall, far from resulting from a "counter-revolutionary" conspiracy, was the consequence of his desire to push the revolution farther and faster than his colleagues wished. Sometime in November 1921, while Danzan and Sükhbaatar were in Moscow, Bodoo, then Prime Minister, issued an order for men to cut off their queues, for women to limit their hair adornments, and for the elimination of the high shoulder (*mör*) of the traditional Mongolian costume, the *deel*. Mongolian historians claim that Bodoo hoped to bring the party into disrepute among the people by these measures.

This is totally unconvincing. The queue, imposed on Chinese and Mongols alike by the Manchus at the beginning of the Ch'ing dynasty, was regarded as an offensive reminder of Mongolia's colonial past and in post-1911 China as reactionary and anti-republican. A democrat would have been similarly ruffled at the sight of hair adornments, which were a popular way for women to display their wealth--the rich wore silver ornaments, the less privileged worn embellishments of baser metals. The reason for wanting to cut off the high shoulders is less clear, unless they were regarded as too old-fashioned.

There was such an uproar over this order that Bodoo soon came under criticism from members of both the party and government. In a pique, and perhaps with an eye to forcing a showdown with his critics, he announced in early 1922 his wish to resign from all his party and government offices. Although most of the Mongolian leadership wanted to refuse this resignation, Sükhbaatar (and undoubtedly Danzan, because of the personal hostility between the two men) was happy to see him step down.[136] Bodoo was executed a few months later.

During the Bogd Khaan period Bodoo had worked in various capacities in the Russian Consulate, where he became acquainted with several Russians, among them a certain M. Kucherenko, a mechanic and typesetter in the Russo-Mongolian printing office. Kucherenko had formerly served in the Tsarist army and like so many other Russian political refugees sought shelter in Urga from repression at home. He was also a member of the underground Revolutionary Committee of Russians in Urga headed by a small group of Bolshevik sympathizers in the Consulate. Kucherenko occasionally used to visit Bodoo's yurt, located in the courtyard of the printing office, where they discussed current events in Russia, China, and Mongolia. We are told by an eyewitness that he took great pains to explain the Russian revolution and the importance of the establishment of a people's government in Petrograd.[137]

Present at these conversations and serving as translator was Khorloogiin Choibalsan (1895-1953), ten years younger than Bodoo but a man who was eventually to eclipse--and outlive--all of his revolutionary comrades. The illegitimate son of a poor woman named Khorloo, he was born in one of the most impoverished areas of all Mongolia, the Sansraidorj banner in the Tsetsen Khan aimag, which was notorious for its social unrest. Like Stalin, with whom he has often been compared, Choibalsan was placed in a monastery at the age of thirteen, but finding the discipline uncongenial, escaped with a companion to Urga in 1911-12; there he found work in various menial jobs. A fateful meeting in 1912 with N.T. Danchinov, a progressive Buryat who headed the School of Translators, however, changed the course of his life. Choibalsan enrolled in the school, where he studied until 1914; then he, along with several other Mongolian youths, was sent to Irkutsk for further education. He studied the Russian language, culture, and history until the outbreak of revolution in 1917, when he and the other students were ordered by the Urga government to return home. While in Irkutsk he lived with a Russian of "democratic leanings," Chelpanov, and the Buryat Elbegdorzhi Rinchino, a Left Social-Revolutionary who was to play a prominent role in Mongolian political life until 1925.[138]

There is very little information on his life from 1917 to 1919. According to one source he enrolled in the Urga Communications School, which trained students in telegraphy, but was dismissed. Another claims that he was employed in the Urga telegraph office. By late 1919, when we can pick up the threads of his life again, he was sharing a yurt with Bodoo. The pair may have been drawn together by a common political philosophy. Circumstantial evidence certainly suggests that Choibalsan held radical political views or at least may have been sympathetic to them.

Another frequent visitor to Bodoo's home who also participated in these conversations was the lama D. Chagdarjav, an old friend of Bodoo. He is perhaps the most enigmatic character of the entire revolution and biographical information is exceptionally meagre and contradictory. Although he was one of the seven men sent to Russia and briefly held major positions in the party and government, he is mentioned only casually in the contemporary documents and memoir literature, and his revolutionary record was totally undistinguished.

This, according to Choibalsan himself, was the nucleus of the Consular Hill Group. On occasion Kucherenko was accompanied by a friend, Ya.V. Gembarzhevskii, an important figure in the underground Russian revolutionary movement in Urga. Originally a postal official, he had been imprisoned in Irkutsk for eight years because of his involvement in the 1905 revolution, whereupon he came to Urga after his release and was employed as an accountant in the office of the Russian Export Company. From 1917 he became active in the trade union movement in Urga and in the radical Public Duma. These conversations, which surely centered on the Russian revolution and the political situation in Mongolia, must have made a deep impression on this small group of patriots and intellectuals.

The meetings of Kucherenko and Gembarzhevskii evidently struck a responsive chord. Bodoo contacted

O. Jam'yan, an official in the Ministry of Finance, the lama D. Losol, and Jigmiddorj. Soon these men were meeting regularly in the home of Bodoo or Jam'yan, where they discussed the increasing oppression by Chinese authorities and the "short-sighted policies" of the princes and lamas. Several other men also began joining these discussions.

It is difficult to draw any firm conclusions from the little information available about this group. There was a higher proportion of lamas (three) than in the East Urga Group (none?), but this was fortuitous and there is no reason to conclude that the Consular Hill Group had a religious or conservative bias; there were governmental officials (four?) and possibly a few arats. The only statement which can be made with any confidence is that the social composition of this group was possibly more representative than that of the East Urga Group, including as it did a cross-section of Mongolian society (with the exception of hereditary nobles).

The suggestion of Owen Lattimore, that the Consular Hill Group was more revolutionary--if by that we mean each of its members, to a greater or lesser extent, subscribed to a democratic-social philosophy--while the East Urga Group was more nationalistic, is possibly correct.[139] Bodoo and Choibalsan were by the standards of Mongolia at that time left-wing intellectuals whose patriotic and political convictions must have been given sharper ideological focus by their meetings with Kucherenko and Gembarzhevskii. Whether and how much the political ideas of the other members of this group were shaped by these discussions is unknown. Certainly, the "intellectual" character of the Consular Hill Group differ sharply from the activism of the East Urga Group, and perhaps to describe it as a study club rather than a revolutionary band would be more accurate.

While the Consular Hill Group was blessed with a chronicler who carefully recorded its beginnings, the origin of the East Urga Group by contrast is very dim and only brief references to its birth can be found in the various sources. Although Communist orthodoxy has it that Sükhbaatar founded the group, an obscure but invaluable article based on Mongolian memoir literature by A. Kallinikov helps to shed light on this mystery.[140]

According to Kallinikov--it is worth noting that the link between these events and the beginnings of the East Urga Group appear to have been missed by Kallinikov, as well as by other scholars working on this period--some of the more militant members of the lower house (Danzan, Dogsom, Dendev, Jam'yan Kung, Nyamjav Kung, Lkhundai, Tsend, Togtokh, and others) met secretly on the first night following the dissolution of the parliament (November 15?) and drew up a petition to the Russian Consul Orlov appealing for assistance against the Chinese. A delegation was selected to ask the Khutukhtu to place his seal on the document. This deputation was received by the Bogd Khaan, but his answer, delivered by attendants later, was disappointing: "Your intention to defend religion and state, which are threatened by terrible sufferings, deserves great appreciation. But the time has not yet come, and right now it is necessary to forebear. Do not forget, however, these intentions of yours."

It was this November 15(?) meeting which can be regarded as the birth as the East Urga Group, although it is hardly conceivable that those present intended at this stage to form a secret band. Only gradually did the association change from a loose collection of parliamentary patriots to a conspiratorial group. Although the Bogd Khaan had refused their request, he obviously was sympathetic to the idea, objecting only to its timing. This support must have been tremendously encouraging and undoubtedly fortified the will of these men to cooperate further.

There were other meetings during November and the following month. At one of them, probably in late December (just before the public ceremony for the abolition of autonomy), it was decided to try again, but this time with a direct appeal to the Russian Consul-General in the name of the now disbanded lower house. A new delegation of Danzan, Dendev, M. Dugarjav, Galsan, and Dogsom took the same November document which they had previously submitted to the Khutukhtu and presented it to Orlov. The Tsarist diplomat declared that the lower house represented only Urga officialdom and could not claim to speak on behalf of the country. He advised them that he would happily transmit the petition to his government should they obtain the seal of the Bogd Khaan. Danzan, Dogsom, Dendev, Dugarjav, and Sükhbaatar (who had joined the group by now[141]) met secretly with the Khutukhtu, to whom they reported Orlov's answer and explained the urgency of obtaining the Bogd's consent. At dawn on the following morning they were given the Khutukhtu's answer: "I have already said that the moment has not yet arrived. Wait quietly for my instructions." According to Kallinikov, certain members, discouraged by the Bogd Khaan's refusal, quit this company. Those who remained constituted the nucleus of the East Urga Group.

Despite the claim of many historians that Sükhbaatar founded and led the group, it appears that during the several months of its existence Danzan and Dogsom were the central figures while Sükhbaatar occupied a lesser though not insignificant position. Danzan and Dogsom were eight to nine years older than Sükhbaatar, better educated, and held higher positions in the government. Indeed, the bulk of the existing evidence points to the fact that it was Bodoo and Danzan, because of their age, ability, and political experience, who led the two underground groups and eventually the party following the merger of the two secret societies in June 1920. It was only when the military objectives of the revolution superceded the political ones, that is, when the party began organizing a partisan army near Kyakhta in early 1921, that the soldier Sükhbaatar came into his own and a new triumvirate of Bodoo, Danzan, and Sükhbaatar emerged.

There is a surprising dearth of biographical information about Danzan (1885-1924) considering his importance in modern Mongolian history. It is known that he was born in the Süjigt Beise banner (Sain Noyon Khan aimag), was the illegitimate son of a poor arat woman Sol', and before the dissolution of the Bogd Khaan Government had been employed as an official in the Ministry of Finance.[142] He was accused at the Third Party Congress in 1924 of planning a coup against the party and posthumously of a variety of other anti-party activities, although a study of the records of the congress suggests that Danzan's real "crime" was crossing swords with E. Rinchino.

Dansranbelegiin Dogsom (1884-1939), only one year older than Danzan, was in 1919 an official in the Ministry of the Army. He had been born in the Tsetsen Khan aimag and began his study of the written Mongolian language at the age of twelve. His progress attracted the attention of the local authorities and he served in the banner and aimag administrations and as a sumun chief. After the 1911 revolution he came to Urga and was first employed in the Ministry of Finance and then in the Ministry of the Army. Dogsom was regarded as the best educated of the East Urga Group and was probably well known in government circles.[143]

Today, of course, the most famous member of the East Urga Group is D. Sükhbaatar (1893-1923), who was only twenty-seven years old at the time of its formation. His life is particularly interesting for it epitomizes so much of Mongolian social history during the late nineteenth and early twentieth centuries. His family originally came from the Tsetsen Khan aimag, where his great-grandfather had died in prison for participating in an uprising against the banner prince. Sükhbaatar's father fled the poverty of the banner for Urga, where Sükhbaatar was born three years later. They continued to live in indigence, however, on the western slope of Makhur tolgoi mountain alongside many other refugee families. But unlike most youths from poor arat backgrounds who were destined to repeat the lives of their fathers, Sükhbaatar was able to escape this treadmill when he was accepted by O. Jam'yan as a student. He studied for two or three years and obtained a basic education in the written language and mathematics.

Following the 1911 revolution he joined the new Mongolian army and was commissioned as a commander of a machine-gun unit after an exemplary training record at Khujirbulan. He soon saw action in Inner Mongolia and later in 1917 along the eastern border. Although associated with a couple of minor mutinies over food and discipline he nevertheless distinguished himself in military service and was generally recognized as a courageous and capable soldier. In 1918 he was temporarily assigned as a typesetter in the Urga printing office, where he worked until it was closed down following the abolition of autonomy.[144]

Another, less distinguished, member of the Urga group was M. Dugarjav (son of the famous Magsarjav Khurts), who had served as a clerk in the ministries of Foreign Affairs and the Army. There were in addition other "members" of the group such as Galsan, Togtokh, Dash, Tsend, Dendev, Balsan, Jam'yan Kung, and Namjav Kung (the last two were government officials who, in recognition of their services to the state, were made non-hereditary nobles). With the exception of Dendev, whom we know to have been in charge of the Urga arsenal, there is no biographical information on these men nor is their stature or work in the group clearly understood.

Based on this rather sketchy biographical data it is possible to draw a rough profile of the members of the East Urga Group. Similar to the Consular Hill, they were young (thirty-six or under), came from arat families, and had acquired at least a working knowledge of the Mongolian written language. There were, however, two noteworthy differences. First, the East Urga Group had a higher representation of middle-level officials from the defunct Bogd Khaan Government, especially from the Ministry of the Army (this connection with the government was so clear at the time that Bodoo once derisively referred to it as a "party of officials"). Unlike the members of the Consular Hill Group, these men had a more material interest in the fate of the Bogd Khaan Government, which may partially account for their greater activism.

Secondly, although there is circumstantial evidence to suggest that some social and political reforms were envisaged by the Consular Hill Group, there is nothing to show that the members of the East Urga Group sought anything more than the expulsion of Chinese from Mongolia. The democratic platform adopted at the founding meeting of the Mongolian People's Party in June 1920 was probably due above all to the influence of the more liberal Consular Hill Group.

Although the two groups were aware of one another's existence, it was to be several months before they began cooperating, even on a limited scale, and it was not until June 25, 1920 that they formally amalgamated into the Mongolian People's Party (the present name, Mongolian People's Revolutionary Party, was adopted in 1924). All the sources agree that the two groups maintained a watchful distance from one another for several months, that each suspected the other of spying for the Chinese, and that each was mistrustful of the other's political aims (this may be an allusion to the comparative radicalism of Bodoo's circle, which contrasted with the more limited, nationalistic objectives of Danzan's group).

During the months of January and February the East Urga Group worked feverishly, but futilely, to organize resistance to the Chinese. In January a decision was taken to obtain weapons, probably in preparation for an armed revolt. Dendev, the superintendent of the Urga arsenal, was instructed to take charge of this, but the plan had to be scrapped when Chinese troops on the next day were posted at the door of the arsenal. A more desperate scheme, apparently concocted also in January, was to assassinate Hsu Shu-cheng himself. It was learned that Hsu was scheduled to visit Kyakhta, and Dogsom and Dugarjav were to lay an ambush for him. In the event, however, an explosion in the gunpowder warehouse of the old Ch'ing barracks forced Hsu to delay his trip and possibly saved his life.

A month or so later they tried to contact the Soviets in Siberia. It is possible that they had learned of the August 1919 "Soviet Declaration to the Mongolian People and the Government of Mongolia," which had denounced all Tsarist treaties with Japan and China regarding Mongolia and declared the right of the Mongols to independence. Danzan and Sükhbaatar went to Kyakhta in the first lunar month (February 20 to March 20) to learn more of this new government and whether it would aid the Mongols, but strict surveillance by Chinese troops on the frontier prevented the two from crossing the border.[145]

## Founding of the Mongolian People's Party

In another part of Urga a war of a different sort, the result of which was to have profound consequences for the fledgling Mongolian revolutionaries, was coming to a temporary close. The Russian community in Urga was divided by the same issues and engulfed by the same hatreds as their countrymen to the north. Indeed, the struggles of this small settlement were an exact, if marginally less homicidal, microcosm of the larger conflict in Russia itself.

The Russian part of Urga was a typical frontier town, and descriptions of it evoke memories of the nineteenth-century American West. It was much like backwater settlements in Siberia, crowded with low woodframe or log buildings and interlaced with broad dusty streets. Only the presence of camel caravans, begrimed Mongolian yurts, and colorful Buddhist temples reminded the Russian that he was transplanted in a more exotic culture. Life was hard in Urga, and one could find the very best, and the very worst, of Russian society. There was a saloon and brothel (the good citizens had tried unsuccessfully to expel the proprietor). Murders, particularly at the gold mines of Mongolor, were not rare, and suicides were appallingly frequent.

A few years before Mongolian independence there had been an influx of Siberians hoping to make their fortune in commerce, and the Russian community grew from a hundred-plus in the late nineteenth century to between five hundred and eight hundred by 1912-14. After the 1917 revolution, the arrival of Russian refugees in Urga swelled the colony to a couple of thousand. Within this colony were also revolutionaries, most of whom had fled to Urga after 1905 to escape Tsarist repression, who held a degree of influence in the community disproportionate to their numbers. It was these men who directed the Russian revolutionary movement in Urga and who aided the Mongols in establishing contact with the Comintern.

Although the restoration of White rule in Siberia in the fall of 1918 had forced the revolutionaries temporarily underground, when the Soviet position in Siberia was restored with the advance of the Red Army in late 1919 the radicals became active again. In November 1919 a secret Revolutionary Committee was formed and included men who were later to have special links with the Mongolian revolutionary movement: Kucherenko, Gembarzhevskii, the Buryat Erdeni Batukhanov (Minister of Education of the MPR from 1924 to 1929), and I. Maslakov. In December the Trade Union of Workers and Employees of Urga was revived, and in early 1920 elections were held for a Public Duma, in which Bolshevik sympathizers won a clear majority. Such revolutionaries as V.N. Chaivanov, S. Popov, Sheineman, I. Maslakov, and I. Sorokovikov were elected to the executive organ of the Duma, the Uprava.

At its opening session on March 1, the day before White Guards were forced out of Verkhneudinsk, the Duma assumed control over the entire Russian community. The radicals launched a repression against the Whites, ordering a general registration of Russians in the city to ferret out White officers, many of whom were executed or deported to Troitskosavsk.[146] The failure of Danzan and Sükhbaatar to contact the Soviets in February-March must have been a blow to the hopes of the East Urga Group. But the election of the Public Duma and its ascendancy over the Russian settlement were to present unexpected opportunities for both groups.

Although we are given the impression by Communist historians that the Russian revolutionary administration in Urga was keenly interested in the work and ideological development of the two groups, this does not appear to be consistent with the known facts. Kucherenko and Gembarzhevskii, and somewhat later I.S. Maslakov (telegraphist and member of the Uprava), were left alone to work with the Mongols, and Mongolian contact with other Russian revolutionaries was rare. It seems, furthermore, that these three Russians had no independent contact with members of the East Urga Group, and that all communication with it was managed by the Consular Hill people.

Kucherenko, Gembarzhevskii, and Maslakov were undoubtedly keeping the Uprava current on the activities of the two groups, and by March these Mongols were beginning to be taken a little more seriously. In the early part of that year the Bolshevik Naum Burtman, while passing through Urga on his way to Irkutsk from Peking, was reported to have become "closely acquainted" with "such Mongolian revolutionaries as Choibalsan," that is, with the Consular Hill Group.[147] It is perhaps no coincidence that only four or five months later, in July-August 1920, the Section of the Eastern Peoples in the Siberian Bureau of the Central Committee of the Russian Communist Party was formed in Irkutsk under Burtman and included a Mongolian-Tibetan Department headed by S.S. Borisov.

Influenced perhaps by Burtman's assessment of these Khalkhas, a decision was taken by the Uprava to provide Irkutsk with a more detailed analysis of the Mongolian revolutionary movement. Sorokovikov, a member of the Revolutionary Committee and Uprava, was being sent to Irkutsk with a report concerning the status of the Russian colony, and the Consular Hill Group was invited to transmit a message to Soviet authorities regarding their own situation.

It is not clear either when or how the two underground circles made contact with one another, but Bodoo's invitation to Danzan and other members of the East Urga Group to meet with Sorokovikov in March certainly indicates that some form of communication existed between them by this time. We are told that Bodoo, after meeting with some of the East Urga members and satisfying himself that the two groups shared similar goals, recommended that more be learned about them with the view to future cooperation. Although the Consular Hill Group did decide to merge with Danzan's association, the union did not occur for another three months (several months later Danzan was to blame Bodoo's pride and arrogance for preventing an earlier merger).[148]

A gathering of perhaps five Mongols representing the two circles met secretly with Sorokovikov in the middle or, more likely, latter part of March at the home of Kucherenko.[149] The meeting was a fascinating one. The Mongols, erroneously thinking that Sorokovikov had come from Soviet Russia especially to see them, tried to gloss over the imperfections of their organization and to present an image of confidence and strength. The Mongols began by pointing out that nothing had been done by the princes and lamas to strengthen Mongolia since independence. Indeed, they said, their country had only recently been betrayed to the Chinese, and it was for this reason that a party (<u>nam</u>) had been formed to fight the occupiers, whose troops, however, were too strong. They concluded by saying that Comrade Gembarzhevskii and others had described the Soviet revolution to them and now they, the representatives of the Mongolian people, had been appointed to receive Sorokovikov's instructions. This, incidently, was the first clear statement in the sources of the objectives of the Mongols: the liberation of their country from the Chinese.

Sorokovikov explained that he had met the Mongols only to learn of their situation and to report this information back to the authorities in Russia, not to give instructions. "But if your country is oppressed, and if there are comrades who are struggling for freedom, I am to help in opening a path of communication to your country." Sorokovikov then posed a set of questions regarded the age, size, achievements, and social composition of their "party," the answers to which he hoped would clarify their situation.

One can image how the Mongols must have squirmed at this reply. As Dogsom recalled in his memoirs, they feared that a candid answer to the representative of such a powerful country and an explanation of how truly feeble they were in men and arms would have jeopardized the success of this approach to the Soviets.[150]

The answers of the Mongols may generously be described as exaggerations. It is puzzling, however, that none of the three Russian "advisers" to the Mongols, either then or later, corrected Sorokovikov's report. This helps to support the theory that the familiarity and contact of these Russians with even the Consular Hill group was considerably less than the secondary sources have led us to believe.

The Mongols, ignoring momentarily their lack of political or organizational unity, replied that their "party" had been in existence for two years (it had yet to be formed), that it numbered several thousand "members" (a maximum of twenty for each group would have been more accurate), and that it possessed several hundred repeating rifles (they had a few dozen at most). The Mongols claimed that they were busily recruiting new members and that their "party" was growing daily. They reassured Sorokovikov that no aristocrats had been enlisted (true), nor had contact been made with any organization other than the "Red Party of the Soviet country." The arats, they stressed, were being oppressed by the Chinese, while the princes and khutukhtus were fawning upon the Peking officials in their quest for rank and privilege.

Sorokovikov listened intently as they spoke and recorded their answers. He urged them to hasten their revolution and promised to acquaint the Soviet authorities in Irkutsk with the results of this meeting, and to return as soon as possible with an answer. The Mongolian delegates then reported back to their respective groups.

The Mongols did not meet Sorokovikov again until June 20, and very little is known of their activities during the intervening three months. But by the time Sorokovikov did return, the Mongols had accomplished very little: their numbers were as small as ever, and they were just as ill-prepared to lead the country in a national uprising. The presence of Chinese troops and spies in the city, of course, did inhibit serious work, and perhaps the only sensible course open to the Mongols was to tread water until they had a clear idea of what could be expected from Soviet Russia. The success of their entire enterprise hinged on that reply.

Sorokovikov left for Russia shortly after this meeting and reported to Ya. Yanson, Chairman of the Irkutsk Military Revolutionary Committee and concurrently representative of the Soviet Commissariat of Foreign Affairs for Eastern Siberia. We do not know either the contents of the report or his recommendations, but the Soviets evidently decided that they would like to have a closer look at the Mongols. After returning to Urga Sorokovikov met with ten of them on June 20 and said that the Soviet government welcomed their struggle for the national liberation of the Mongolian people and that it would render "assistance of all kinds" to the Mongolian "workers." The Mongols were advised to send delegates immediately to Soviet Russia for consultations. Sorokovikov informed them that the Russian Consul in Troitskosavsk, Makstenek, had been apprised of the situation and would expedite their passage.[151]

The Mongols went to work with renewed enthusiasm

and a sense of mission. Whatever impediments to cooperation existed in the past between the two groups now had to be put aside and delegates, able to represent a united, disciplined party, had to be selected to go to Soviet Russia. It was to this end that an historic meeting of both groups took place at Danzan's yurt on June 25. During the intervening five days between Sorokovikov's visit and this meeting the Mongols had clearly done some soul-searching, seeking new answers to old problems. The result was the June 25 meeting at which they formally organized the Mongolian People's Party (MPP).

The first item on the meeting's agenda was the adoption of the "Party Oath," a document strongly influenced by Leninist ideas of party organization, indicating perhaps that it was drafted with the assistance of their Russian "advisers."[152] The introduction of the oath began:

> Although Mongolia separated from Manchu-Chinese rule and established an independent autonomous government, the power-holders did nothing for the benefit of the people but thought only of themselves and the old ways. This continued to the ninth year (1919), when a few ministers and officials, (wishing) to destroy the state, insulted and deceived the people and, taking advantage of the unsettled conditions in our neighbor Russia, arbitrarily conspired with the Chinese (to abrogate) the rights of the (Bogd Khaan) Government. They deceitfully issued a certificate stating that Outer Mongolians had voluntarily abolished autonomy and then sent it to the central government (of China). Because this is a departure from the path which has forever been in accord with the hearts of the people, it is important that the members of the party firmly unite in mind and strength to devise suitable and decisive measures --invulnerable to the internal and external enemy--for our people to restore the rights which have been seized by others, to strenghen and protect the

> affairs of our race, and to improve our own internal government.

There followed nine articles which collectively were a statement of the aims and pledges of the party. Some were perhaps naive by Western standards --for example, a member who violated the pledge of absolute secrecy was allowed to commit suicide, provided he acknowledged his error; otherwise, he was to be executed--yet they were an expression of an unyielding commitment to a new faith. Each member, for instance, was to work for the party without regard for his own life or property. Another article provided for the continued growth of the party by enjoining each member to recruit ten more, who would then form a new cell.

Of all the articles, the first is the most interesting for its unequivocal declaration of the objectives of the party:

> The goals of the Outer Mongolian People's Party are: to liquidate the foreign enemy which is hostile to our religion and race; to restore lost rights; to improve sincerely the internal government; to give total attention to the interests of the poor and lowly masses; to preserve forever our internal rights; and to live, neither oppressing nor being oppressed.

Although this was not a document suffused with the Marxist-Leninist cant which we have come to expect of so many twentieth-century revolutionary movements, when it is examined against the history of hereditary rule in Mongolia it is an authentic revolutionary statement. These Mongols may not have been Jacobins, but they had an intuition of a different political and social order, expressed by the tantalizingly vague phrase "to improve and reform sincerely the internal government." The social orientation of the party was clarified somewhat by article six: "Members of the People's Party, with one mind and strength, from beginning to end, will strive to consider the interests of the poor and lowly people and will endeavor by any means they can to eliminate anything which is unjust or injurious to the people."

There was still the ticklish problem of selecting party representatives to Soviet Russia. For understandable reasons no one was anxious to undertake such a hazardous trip. Chinese troops still patrolled the frontier, as did troops of the new Far Eastern Republic (FER), whose relationship with Moscow and Peking was unknown to the Mongols, and to many European observers as well. Since there were no volunteers, it was decided to draw lots. The names of Danzan and Choibalsan were drawn, and money was collected for their travelling expenses.

## Mission to Russia

Danzan and Choibalsan did not leave Urga until June 28 or 29. Only a couple of days earlier the Mongols met with Soviet representatives sent from Irkutsk, S.S. Borisov and the Buryat Ts. Tseden-ish, who had arrived to inspect first-hand the situation of the MPP. The Soviets in Irkutsk must have been intrigued by this faint apparition of revolution in Mongolia and now had dispatched their own agents to investigate it more fully.

A tent was set up on the banks of the Tuul' river, away from the prying eyes of Chinese soldiers, and a modest supper of Mongolian tea, dairy products, and *airag* was prepared. The Mongols detailed the events leading to the abrogation of autonomy and described the history of the MPP. Borisov explained the importance of the Bolshevik revolution and the Soviet policy of rendering assistance to backward countries. He approved of their struggle for the liberation of the Mongolian people and of their decision to send delegates to Russia, but urged them to accelerate their work. He made one other important suggestion. Warning that the party must be alert to the potential danger represented by the lay and church princes, Borisov advised them to solicit the support of the Bogd Khaan by emphasizing their intention to protect the church. With the patronage of the Khutukhtu, he assured them, the reactionaries in Urga would be unable to oppose the party.[153]

The members of the party were in total accord on the need to send delegates to Russia and to obtain assistance from the Soviets, but a bitter quarrel broke out over whether Danzan and Choibalsan were to take a letter impressed with the seal of the MPP or that of the Bogd Khaan. Although later Communist historians have been purposely fuzzy on the issues and personalities of this debate, Choibalsan, Losol, and Demid state plainly that it was Danzan and Losol who argued for a letter with the Bogd's seal, and that it was Bodoo who opposed them, reasoning that a party seal should be sufficient. This argument was to continue into August and almost resulted in the rupture of the party.

The sources do not explain the logic behind the two positions, but it was probably grounded in tactics rather than in ideology. Danzan had been conditioned since November 1919 to think in terms of an appeal signed by the Bogd Khaan, the acknowledged leader of the Mongolian people. The Russian Consul Orlov had refused to act without it, and Danzan may have thought that the Soviets were more likely to give credence to an appeal signed by the head of the Mongolian state. Bodoo, possibly believing that the Russians would be more receptive to an appeal from a revolutionary party than from a theocrat, argued that a letter with the Bogd's seal should be "evidence of the last resort."

The Mongols settled for a compromise. While Danzan and Choibalsan were for the present supplied only with documents authorizing them to speak on behalf of the party, it was decided that if the Bogd's seal became necessary after all, they could inform Urga. The pair was directed to proceed to Troitskosavsk, where, as Sorokovikov promised, they would receive further instructions. Various tasks to be carried out during the absence of Danzan and Choibalsan were then assigned to the party members remaining in Urga. Some were to maintain contact with Kucherenko and Gembarzhevskii; others were to keep the activities of the princes, lamas, and Chinese in Urga under surveillance; and the remaining members were to recruit Khatanbaatar Magsarjav, the Jalkhanz Khutukhtu, the Dilowa Khutukhtu, and Da Lama Puntsagdorj to the party, and to persuade the Bogd Khaan to impress his seal on a letter to Soviet Russia in the event this became necessary.[154]

In the early part of July Danzan and Choibalsan

reached Kyakhta and contacted O.I. Makstenek, representative of the Soviet Ministry of Foreign Affairs for Mongolia, who told them that he knew of their mission and that they would have to travel on to Verkhneudinsk. A few days later passage was booked on a steamship which regularly plied the Selenge river between Kyakhta and Verkhneudinsk. Although Makstenek promised to send a special telegram to advise the authorities in Verkhneudinsk, then the capital of the Far Eastern Republic, of their arrival, the two Mongols were disquieted by what seemed to them to be excessively casual arrangements and insisted on knowing who their contacts were in Verkhneudinsk. Makstenek only scribbled out an address where they were to stay in the city.

The choice of Verkhneudinsk was a curious one. The Far Eastern Republic was in a very delicate position, militarily and politically, vis-a-vis China and Japan, and aid to these revolutionaries could have had undesirable consequences for its foreign policy, particularly at a time when the Verkhneudinsk government was trying to project an image of moderation and responsibility. Furthermore, Soviet authorities had just organized an office in Irkutsk to deal with Mongolia, probably in anticipation of the Mongols' arrival, and it seems more logical, therefore, that Danzan and Choibalsan should have been directed to that city. Why Makstenek sent them to Verkhneudinsk is not known. He may have misunderstood his instructions, or these instructions may have been incorrect.

When Danzan and Choibalsan arrived in Verkhneudinsk there was no one to meet them at the wharf, nor were they expected or met at the address given them by Makstenek. It was only on the following morning that an unidentified Buryat arrived at their lodgings and took them to see a Russian who introduced himself simply as Chervonny. After some careful probing on both sides, the Russian finally identified himself as Boris Shumyatskii (Minister of Foreign Affairs and at that time acting Premier of the FER), and showed them a letter he had received from Makstenek.He said that their mission had been explained by the Consul but he wished to learn more from the Mongols themselves. After the two had obligingly related their story, Shumyatskii promised to summon them again in a few days.

Shumyatskii, as he himself admitted later, knew nothing about these Mongols other than what he had learned from Makstenek's letter. This certainly makes sense if the Mongols were expected in Irutsk, not in Verkhneudinsk. Shumyatskii, however, did not pass this fact on to the Mongols but simply advised them to wait a few days, during which time he probably intended to wire for instructions. Danzan and Choibalsan were evidently pleased at the outcome of this meeting and immediately dispatched a wire to their comrades in Urga saying that they had arrived safely and that "the matter will be (decided) later in Verkhneudinsk."[155]

They returned to their lodgings expecting to hear soon from Shumyatskii, but days passed without any word. They visited the Russian twice with a plea that the Soviets decide quickly whether they intended to help Mongolia. All they received were counsels of patience and reminders that Russian revolutionaries had spent many years before Tsarism was finally toppled. He assured them that the success of the Mongolian revolution was inevitable, but added that it might take years, even generations, before it was concluded.

Three weeks passed since coming to Verkhneudinsk and the two Mongols seemed to be no closer to an answer than when they had arrived. Becoming impatient and even a little angry at Shumyatskii, who persisted in replying to their requests for immediate assistance with lessons in Russian history and exhortations of patience, they finally decided that independent action had to be taken, with or without a Soviet decision. But they would need help. Danzan proposed enlisting Zhamtsarano, and Choibalsan recommended recruiting an old friend of his, the Buryat E. Rinchino.

The Mongols visited Shumyatskii and after politely listening to his counsels of patience reminded him that the situation of their country was perilous and asked if Zhamtsarano and Rinchino could be allowed to collaborate with them. Shumyatskii was startled by the request and asked for their full names and some background information. The two Buryats were duly summoned, and a few days later Rinchino appeared at the rooms of Danzan and

Choibalsan. On the following day the three men visited Shumyatskii, who told them that a decision on their petition was being taken at that very moment, and that they would have their answer in a few days.

On the same day Zhamtsarano arrived in the city. After the four had talked over their plans they composed a second telegram to Urga: "First, business is good. Secondly, comrades to leave next have not arrived. What is the delay? Thirdly, remind you of the importance of bringing the Bogd's present."[156]

The"Bogd's present" was of course a coded reference to a letter with his seal. The sources do not explain who requested this letter or why. It is unlikely that the FER, which had absolutely no need for such a letter, asked for it. Shumyatskii's statement, that a decision on their request was imminent, certainly indicates that he had been in touch with Irkutsk, which may have responsible for the request. It is also possible that the Mongols in Verkhneudinsk decided by themselves that such a letter was necessary (it is instructive that the party members in Urga suspected that Danzan was the real author of the request).

This telegram was received in Urga around July 24. Although a decision taken earlier by the remaining members to wait for a definite answer from the Soviet government meant that the party achieved very little during the intervening three and a half weeks since Danzan and Choibalsan's departure, the revolutionaries did continue to meet at Bodoo's yurt, now moved to the banks of the Tuul' river for reasons of security. But while Danzan and Choibalsan were in Verkhneudinsk waiting impatiently for an answer from Shumyatskii, the MPP members in Urga had been growing increasingly anxious. Days went by after the first telegram and still no news from Verkhneudinsk. It was feared that they might have been arrested by the Chinese, thus imperiling every other member of the party. Discreet inquiries among the lamas, princes, and Russians yielded nothing.

Immediately after receiving the second telegram ten men assembled in Bodoo's yurt to discuss their next moves. Unspecified "comrades," one of whom unquestionably was Bodoo, complained about the request for the Bogd's seal, but there appeared to be no alternative. Zaisan Jam'yan was directed to draft a letter formally requesting aid from Soviet Russia and to take charge of securing the Bogd's seal. More names were drawn for a second delegation to Russia: Bodoo, Dogsom, Sükhbaatar, Losol, and Chagdarjav. Because none of the members of the party had access to the inner circle of the Khutukhtu's court, Da Lama Puntsagdorj, a well-known nationalist, friend of Jam'yan, and luminary in the court, was asked to present their case. Puntsagdorj agreed and on the morning of July 26 took the letter to the palace. It was not until 1:00 or 2:00 the next morning that the party learned the court's answer.

What exactly transpired that day in the Khutukhtu's palace will probably never be known, but according to Puntsagdorj himself the party very nearly did not get the seal at all. Perhaps inspired by the idea of an approach to a foreign power, two more letters requesting assistance were drafted by the lamas, one to the United States and the other to Japan. But the court was reluctant in the extreme to consent to a letter to the Soviets. One Mongolian source asserts that the Bogd Khaan pondered all day and deeply into the night before reaching a decision on this third letter. It was only after consulting three astrologers that the Bogd consented.[157]

The reasons for the ultimate agreement of the court, however, are not too baffling (ignoring for a moment the uncertain influence of the astrologers). Only a month earlier Hsu Shu-cheng had reaffirmed his vow to transform Mongolia into a province of China, and although the recent power struggle in north China had removed the Anfu clique from government, the Mongols had no reason to think that the frontier policies of the new government would be any less exacting than those of its predecessor. The fact that the request itself was a very limited appeal for assistance--probably contemplating no more than diplomatic intervention and possibly money and guns--may have also reassured the court. This request to Soviet Russia read in part:

> Therefore, we request that the circumstances of our desperation be considered and that the necessary assistance and

> protection be rendered. Should you agree to aid us, we ask that you send your answer and (explain) how it seems possible, without war or disorder, through negotiations and review, and according to the exigencies of the moment, to restore the autonomous government. In addition, will you please inform us to what extent it is possible to coordinate your actions and assistance with other powers loyal to you.[158]

It should be stressed that the court did not intend a return to full Chinese suzerainty, despite the use of the term "autonomous." This was made very clear in the preamble of the letter which stated that the Mongols hoped to form an independent state with the Jebtsundamba Khutukhtu as khaan and to nullify the statement in the Kyakhta treaty that Mongolia was part of China. It intended, in other words, to restore full independence.

Bodoo and his friend Chagdarjav, carrying the seal of the party, left Urga probably that very morning (July 27). They reached Troitskosavsk a week later and then departed for Verkhneudinsk. This fact would normally have deserved no more than a footnote were it not for a very interesting, and revealing, event which occurred. While in Troitskosavsk they drafted their own appeal to Soviet Russia, one which reflected a very different political emphasis, and stamped it with the seal of the party:

> We, the representatives of the Mongolian people, have been authorized to declare and request the following. Since the declaration of Mongolian autonomy with the assistance of the Russian Imperial Government, a group of persons has existed among the Mongols which has recognized the destructiveness of the feudal-theocratic system of government (in Mongolia), under which the cultural and social-economic level of the population could not improve.
>
> ...Having worked out a democratic-republican

> platform it began to spread national-revolutionary ideas among the population and decided to appeal to Soviet Russia for assistance in the restoration of Mongolian independence.[159]

The sources are not very helpful in explaining the reason for a second appeal nor have Communist historians labored over the problem. We must look therefore elsewhere, in particular to Bodoo himself, for the answer. Bodoo had persistently argued that the Khutukhtu should be by-passed in favor of a direct party appeal to the Soviets, and fearing perhaps that the arched, conservative language of an appeal from the Bogd Khaan would irritate the Bolsheviks, he decided to supply them with an orthodox revolutionary address. This would certainly be consistent with his personality and political convictions insofar as they are known. The absence of any other signatures suggests that the rest of the party was either ignorant of this document or refused to agree to it. It is likely that Makstenek supported Bodoo in the value of a separate appeal, although there is no reason to believe that the style and idiom did not accurately reflect Bodoo's own political beliefs--whether Chagdarjav shared them is another question.

Immediately after receiving the letter with the Bogd's seal from Puntsagdorj, preparations were made for the trip north. Dendev had to borrow one hundred fifty taels from a monastic treasury, and Sükhbaatar sold his yurt in order to raise money for the trip. Sükhbaatar and Dogsom secretly left Urga on the night of July 30 carrying with them the letter, which was concealed in the handle of a whip. After rendevousing with Losol on the next day they proceeded north posing as merchants. On August 8 Sükhbaatar, Losol, and Dogsom departed by steamship for Verkhneudinsk.

By the evening of August 10, when Sükhbaatar and his companions had reached their destination, there had already occurred a radical change in the composition of the party which was to influence profoundly its history for the next decade. This was the enlistment of Buryats, such as Rinchino, Zhamtsarano, Tsenden-Ish, Ts. Balamso, and others.

Until perhaps March 1921 there were more active Buryat members of the MPP than there were Khalkha, and throughout the 1920s they exercised a disproportionate amount of influence. They should not be regarded as Russian surrogates, for their services to the Mongolian revolution were freely and genuinely given. Some (Rinchino in particular) became indispensable links between the Soviets and Mongols because of their fluency in both Russian and Mongolian and their radical political orientation.

In this constellation of new Buryat recruits, it was Rinchino who was the brightest star. His emerging role as factotum to Shumyatskii in Verkhneudinsk and then to Gapon in Irkutsk enhanced his image within the party itself and increased his value to the Russians. But because neither Soviet nor Mongolian historians have dwelled upon his contributions to the revolution (he was executed during the Stalinist purges), it is difficult to assess the extent of his influence and power. What evidence is available, however, suggests that it was considerable.

## The Soviet Reply

A few days after arriving in Verkhneudinsk all seven Khalkhas met with Shumyatskii. They were told that the Far Eastern Republic was merely a buffer state and could not possibly decide on their request, but a special train, guarded by soldiers, had been arranged to take them to Irkutsk. They were to be accompanied by Rinchino, who had been provided with the necessary instructions regarding their contacts in Irkutsk.

The seven Mongols left for Irkutsk in the company of Rinchino and several other Buryats (Zhamtsarano remained in Verkhneudinsk). They arrived on either August 19 or 20 and were immediately summoned to the office of F.I. Gapon, chief of the newly formed Section of the Eastern Peoples of the Siberian Bureau of the Russian Communist Party (later to be reorganized as the Far Eastern Secretariat of the Comintern) to whom they presented the letter of the Khutukhtu. The Mongols described the intolerable oppression of the Chinese and the princes, and explained their reasons for forming a party. Now, they said, they had come for help.

Gapon, after meditating silently for a while, expressed his personal opinion that the Soviet government would aid them. But first, a document was required from the party explaining its goals, the kind of government it intended to form after receiving assistance, how it planned to fight the Chinese, and what weapons were required. Gapon then proceeded to interrogate the Mongols more closely. He asked if the nobles agreed with the aims of the party to restore independence. The Mongols replied that all but a few did. Gapan wanted to know about their specific military needs and asked if Soviet troops were required. The Mongols answered that they did not need troops, only instructors, and that they would require ten thousand rifles, twenty cannon, and three hundred machine-guns. They assured Gapon that their own troops could expel the Chinese, although they would need 700,000 to 800,000 _yanchaan_ (rubles?) to finance their revolution. When the Mongols asked what the Russians expected in return, Gapon replied that the Soviet government wished nothing more than the restoration of Mongolia's rights.[160]

After the Mongols returned to their quarters Bodoo and Dogsom, the most literate of the seven, were commissioned to compose a new party document. But Gapon's request had reopened an old wound and soon a quarrel broke out between Bodoo on the one hand and Danzan and Losol on the other. Bodoo chided the two for having insisted on the Bogd's seal, thereby delaying and endangering the appeal to Russia. Danzan in turn criticized Bodoo's arrogance, which, he charged, had impeded coordinated work between the two underground groups several months earlier. Bad feeling was so intense that for two days the partisans of Bodoo and those of Danzan refused to eat together or even to walk on the same side of the street.

Communist historians have consistently interpreted this quarrel more broadly as an ideological struggle between two groups: one, the reactionary faction headed by Bodoo and Danzan, which saw the party simply as the representative of the Bogd Khaan; the other, led by Sükhbaatar and Choibalsan, regarded the party as the genuine vanguard of revolutionary Mongolia. The liberal reordering of names, a legacy of Stalinist historical writing, remains uncorrected. What seems to have happened in fact is that the seven men split into two factions, the Consular Hill and the East Urga--in other words, they regrouped into their pre-June 25 alignments. What we do not know, however, is how much this was a debate over the objectives and methods of the party, or to what extent the quarrel was a personal one, fueled by the mutual animosities of Bodoo and Danzan. Certainly the history of Choibalsan, Losol, and Demid, our only source for this episode, describes it as though it were a private feud between these two men.[161]

It was fortunate for the party and for the future of the revolution that Rinchino was present to patch up their differences. Rinchino's efforts were helped by a meeting on August 23 or 24 with Gapon and a certain Pozner, member of the Revolutionary Military Committee (Revvoensovet) of the Fifth Red Army. The Mongols were told that, in accordance with the policy of the Soviet government and the Russian Communist Party to assist the small, oppressed countries of the world, "we shall certainly render assistance in this affair of yours." However, they added, the form of this assistance could not be decided in Irkutsk. They would have to send representatives to Omsk, then capital of Western Siberia, where the objectives of the MPP could be explained and a decision taken on the sort of aid that the Mongols would receive.

The Mongols immediately held a meeting at which they reconciled their differences and drew up a document dividing the seven into three groups and enumerating the duties of each. Danzan, Losol, and Chagdarjav were to negotiate in Omsk the question of "either making Mongolia a sovereign, independent state or obtaining autonomy." Sükhbaatar and Choibalsan were to remain in Irkutsk and serve as a communication link between the delegates to Omsk (and later to Moscow) and those who returned to Urga. They were directed to organize a party press and to train with the Red Army. Of the three groups this was the least important assignment, reflecting the relative youthfulness of Sükhbaatar and Choibalsan and the fact that politics was still in command. The most important duties went to Bodoo and Dogsom, who were to return to Urga and

> ...enlarge the party, increase its strength, recruit army units, send them to specified areas, collect arms, communicate important information (to the delegates in Russia), consider seriously and decide any important matter, post representatives in the country, learn the opinions of the high and low (classes) and conduct secret discussions with them, publish and distribute the party oath and books, lay the foundations and promote the permanent existence of the party and the declaration of its ideology, and openly and secretly prepare its skill and ability.[162]

On the following day "instructions" were drawn up for the Omsk delegates. Danzan and his companions were directed to ask four things of the Soviet government. First, help in establishing relations with foreign countries, including north China and the Kuomintang. Secondly, twenty-four thousand armed Soviet cavalrymen in case the Peking government, aided by foreign powers, should seek to suppress the Kuomintang (!) and the revolutionary movement in Mongolia. Thirdly, a loan of an unspecified amount to the "newly established government" of the party in Mongolia and to the MPP. And finally, after "autonomy" had been restored, the intercession of Soviet Russia with the Peking government in recovering money, property, and weapons confiscated by the Chinese military authorities.[163]

On the basis of these "instructions" a letter was drafted, dated August 29 and addressed to the Mongolian and Tibetan Department of the Section of Eastern Peoples, which was signed by "Bodoo of the People's Party and Dogsom, Representative of Outer Mongolia." The text began with a short description of social conditions in Mongolia, where a hundred hereditary princes and five hundred "deceitful taij" rule the country, enslaving and exploiting the people. It complained that members of the Ikh Shav' were being taxed beyond endurance and that the power of the lamas, who represented only a third of the (male) population, was excessively large. Our People's Party is five hundred-strong, it read, but in alliance with the "party of minor officials," it numbers over a thousand:

> ...for these reasons, we of the People's Party, having received great assistance from Russia, will formally join with (your) designated representatives and, having obtained autonomy by utilizing their military force, will make the Khutukhtu a limited monarch; utilizing their powers, we will adopt measures to deprive most of the hereditary princes of their authority and, once we have extricated ourselves from the hands of others (i.e., the Chinese), as soon as we obtain internal self-rule, we will adopt to the best of our ability the practices of various foreign countries and especially measures to establish a system which serves the people's rights and interests; after we have achieved somewhat improved circumstances and as soon as there is better awareness (among the people), after one or two years there will be further development [in the revolution], and if we then smash the minority of the power-holders we will accomplish the matter with little internal trouble and hardly any criticism abroad; this will expedite the time when there will be long-lasting good results mutually beneficial to the People's Parties of Russia and Mongolia...
>
> Point one: We request from the Soviet government of Russia the necessary open and covert major assistance to the Mongolian People's Party in the quickest possible time as well as facilitation of the restoration of autonomy.[164]

The documents, which must be viewed as a single,

indivisible statement of principles and tactics, plainly manifested the party's commitment to national and social revolution. To a considerable extent they anticipated the subsequent measures which the party took after July 1921, when the Jebtsundamba Khutukhtu was transformed into a limited monarch, the system of hereditary nobility was eliminated, and the khamjlaga and shav' nar were emancipated. The reference to a "newly established government" was premature but did indicate the party's intention to form its own civil administration. While the Mongols made no reference to adopting Marxism-Leninism as their ideology, their social philosophy was sufficiently clear: end the system of hereditary rule, end theocratic government, and end class oppression in Mongolia.

It is not surprising that these documents were not published until after the revolution. Except for the shrill cry of merciless racial war against the Chinese, a cause to which nearly all Mongols were sympathetic, the party could take refuge in and drawn strength from its vaguely worded political aims. A clearer statement of party objectives at this time would have surely ruptured its tenuous alliance with the court and, more importantly, have spawned doubts in the minds of many arats about the desirability of the party's aims. It was for this reason that these and other firebrand declarations issued later during the revolution were either suppressed or permitted a very limited circulation.

There has been some scholarly debate over the stated goal to restore "autonomy." This has frequently been seized upon by Western historians to show that these Mongols were political conservatives who desired no more than the restoration of Chinese suzerainty and, by inference, the preservation of the existing social system. This is a rather difficult problem, for neither the Bogd Khaan's court nor the revolutionaries ever offered a precise definition of "autonomy."

A close examination of the sources suggests, however, that autonomy was generally identified with total independence (and by the court with the restoration of theocracy), although it occasionally implied a woolly and very diluted recognition of some special relationship with China. This is clearly its use here. It is also possible that the revolutionaries placed a slightly different construction on the word than did the Bogd Khan government. Following the receipt of a letter in April 1921 from "party comrades" in Urga stating that, with the expulsion of the *gemins* (Chinese troops) and the restoration of autonomy by von Ungern-Sternberg, the goals of the party had been accomplished, the Central Committee of the MPP replied: "It was never a matter of restoring autonomy in its former shape. On the contrary, in our first compact (i.e., the party oath adopted on June 25, 1920) we decided that it was necessary to take political rule into our own hands and to give freedom to the people."[165]

These documents have an additional interest since they outlined the strategy of the party for revolution in Mongolia, a strategy which was to dominate the thinking of the Mongols for the remainder of the year. According to this plan, which may or may not have been conceived with the counsel of the Soviets in Irkutsk, the geographical pivot of the revolution was to be Urga, not Kyakhta as eventually developed. Bodoo and Dogsom, the senior and probably best connected of the seven (with the exception of Danzan, whose skills were needed for the critical task of eliciting aid from the Soviet government), were directed to return to the city and begin the work of building up the party, organizing an army, and agitating among the people. Once Danzan had secured a binding Soviet agreement to help the party, he along with the other Khalkhas and Buryats still in Russia were to rejoin their colleagues in the capital, where money and guns from Soviet Russia were to be transferred. But events turned out differently.

# CHAPTER VII

## THE SOVIETS--RELUCTANT ALLIES, 1920

After these seven young Mongols and their Buryat allies had split into three groups, another drama was unfolding several hundred miles away which was to alter the course of the revolution and Mongolian history. This was the appearance of Baron Ungern-Sternberg. Until Now Mongolia had not been directly touched by the Russian revolution or civil war. There were refugees, to be sure, and occasional rumors of invasion, but the Mongols in general had not yet experienced the terrors of events in Siberia. When Ungern crossed the frontier in the early part of October with his Asiatic Division, however, he brought the Russian civil war with him. But more importantly--and this is decisive for understanding the Mongolian revolution--his invasion provoked Soviet intervention and ensured the victory of that very political order which he was so determined to prevent.

### Ungern-Sternberg in Mongolia

Baron Roman von Ungern-Sternberg (1882-1921), from a distinguished family in the Baltic region, began his military service in the navy, but tiring of inactivity travelled to eastern Siberia, where he served in various Cossack units. He was a troublesome officer. His temper and exaggerated sense of pride led to quarrels, even duels, with his fellow officers and eventually forced him to relinquish his commission in the Imperial Army. The outbreak of the World War rescued him from genteel oblivion and provided the ideal outlet for a man of Ungern's temperament and military talents. He advanced quickly and by 1920 had risen to the rank of lieutenant-general.[166]

Eyewitness accounts are totally consistent in

describing Ungern as pathologically brutal--qualities in which he surpassed even other Cossacks--and émigré accounts of his brief sojourn in Urga from February to May 1921 are filled with horrifying tales of his mindless cruelty. His sadism rightfully earned him the epithet, the "Mad Baron."

There have been various explanations for Ungern's invasion of Mongolia: that he was responding to an invitation from the Bogd Khaan, or that he was escaping prosecution by the Russian administration in Manchuria. Neither of these is likely, however. Most Soviet historians argue that Ungern was under secret instructions from Semenov to form an anti-Bolshevik front in northern Mongolia. In January 1920 Semenov had organized a government in Chita which claimed to represent Siberia east of Lake Baikal. But his grip over the area was weakening under the combined assaults of partisan forces and army units of the Far Eastern Republic, particularly after the Japanese at Gongota Station in mid-July agreed to evacuate their troops from the Transbaikal and Priamur regions. The Gongota Treaty had stipulated that neither the FER nor Japan were to be held responsible for the activities of partisan units, which operated independently and at their own risk. Soviet historians believe, therefore, that Semenov's announcement claiming that Ungern had split off from the White Russian command and declared the status of partisan for himself and his men was a ruse, designed to save the Japanese possible embarrassment in the future.

There are several objections to this theory. Ungern was by temperament insubordinate and erratic, and it would certainly not have been out of character for him to end his association with Semenov and to strike out on his own (the fact that Ungern continued to correspond with his former commander does not necessarily prove that he was still subject to Semenov). There was no compelling reason, moreover, to mask Ungern's operations as "partisan" in order to avoid embarrassing the Japanese. If Semenov, who was fighting openly under the umbrella of the Japanese Expeditionary Army in Siberia, did not need to claim partisan status for himself, it was even less necessary for Ungern, who was hundreds of miles away in the forgotten wilderness of Outer Mongolia.

And finally, Ungern's activities for the next several months--he did not open that "second front" until eight months later, concentrating instead on securing his own hold over Mongolia--reflected personal ambition more than coordinated action with Semenov in Manchuria.

It is more likely that Ungern's Mongolian adventure was not the product of design at all, but rather was the result of Soviet pursuit across the Mongolian border, after which events took an independent and unforeseen course. Unrelenting harassment by partisan units had taken a heavy toll on Ungern's troops, and he was being pursued by a detachment of troops of the Far Eastern Republic. It was probably during or after his escape across the border that plans took shape for his visionary pan-Buddhist, anti-Bolshevik confederation of Asian states to be centered at Urga.

Ungern, with a force of perhaps a thousand men, including Russians, Buryats, Central Asians, and Japanese, entered Mongolia in early October 1920.[167] He advanced south toward the center of the San Beise banner (present-day Choibalsan), where he was aided by local officials in recruiting Mongols to replenish his units. From there he moved west along the Kerulen river toward Urga, picking up possibly another two hundred Mongols on the way. He endeavored to arouse Mongolian support by claiming that his purpose was the liberation of Mongolia from the Chinese and the restoration of the Bogd Khaan to his rightful throne. Even the Khutukhtu responded to Ungern's message and secretly communicated with him. Ungern's seige of Urga, lasting from October 26 to November 7, finally had to be lifted because of stiff Chinese resistance, large number of casualties, and lack of ammunition. He then withdrew into the Tsetsen Khan aimag, where he set about repairing his losses by pillaging Chinese shops and conscripting young Mongols.

The troubles of the inhabitants of Urga, however, were only beginning. Discipline among the Chinese troops under the command of Ch'u Ch'i-hsiang and his deputy Kao Tsai-t'ien had quickly eroded. Although the quality of military forces of Republican China varied considerably from region to region, Chinese soldiers were generally troublesome and unmanageable, and the conditions of their service in Mongolia--a region hundreds of miles from home where both natives and climate were uniformly inhospitable--could only have undermined morale. These troops, moreover, had not been paid for several months. Ungern's attack ignited this simmering discontent. Homes belonging to Russians and other Europeans, including the Russian Consulate, were plundered and many Russians were arrested; some were killed by marauding soldiers, others were executed *in camera* by the Chinese authorities (it is impossible to determine the extent of complicity of senior Chinese authorities in reprisals against the Russians and Mongols, or to what extent they were simply unable to control their own troops). The ferocity of the pogrom reminded observers of the Boxer xenophobia two decades earlier.[168]

The Mongols also had difficulty finding refuge from Chinese vengeance. In Urga and its vicinity livestock, horses, clothing, food, forage, yurts, and virtually anything remotely useful to the soldiers were taken from the arats. What could not be moved was burned. The city was placed under martial law and a curfew and ban against public meetings was imposed. Mongols on the streets were harassed, some were shot. The monastery of Dambadarjaa just outside Urga was looted by soldiers and several of its lamas were murdered on the pretext that they had harbored Ungern. By the time the fury of the Chinese had spent itself, several dozen people were dead and hundreds of livestock were stolen.[169]

To the consternation of the Mongolian population, the Bogd Khaan and some of his attendants were placed under guard--for their own protection, it was announced--in an empty building near the High Commission. Several leading nobles, including Da Lama Puntsagdorj, Namsrai Wang (former Minister of Justice of the Bogd Khaan Government in 1912), Damdinsüren (who died in captivity), and Magsarjav, were arrested and imprisoned. As early as late August the Chinese had known vaguely of a plot involving Orlov, the Urga nobles, and the Khutukhtu to restore independence and of a mission to Russia (which they incorrectly believed had been sent to Semenov). They undoubtedly suspected that there was a link between Ungern's presence and this conspiracy.[170] These clumsy maneuvers could not have played more into Ungern's hands.

Ch'en I left for Urga shortly after his appointment on September 8 as pacification commissioner (he was forced to linger en route because of Ungern's attack), arriving in the first half of November. Ch'en immediately tried to check the growing disaffection among the Mongols for the Chinese administration in Urga. The Khutukhtu was released from detention and returned to his palace, although sentries were posted at its gates. Ch'in-wang Puntsagtseren was installed as the new Urga deputy, and a staff of well-known church and lay princes was appointed to assist him.

Ch'en also realized that the restoration of morale and discipline among the troops was vital, especially in view of the probable return of the Russian "bandits." Even before arriving in Urga, Ch'en had sent a month's pay to the troops, and during the next two months he paid more back wages with money borrowed from Chinese banks in Urga. Unrest continued to spread through the ranks, however, and became so serious that Ch'en I and others feared that the garrison would not fight the Russians at all.

Another intractable problem facing Ch'en was the unwillingness of Ch'u Ch'i-hsiang, a former lieutenant of Hsu Shu-cheng, to relinquish supreme authority to Ch'en. The sources also imply that there was a split in the military leadership itself, probably between Ch'u, who was associated with Hsu's frontier defense administration, and Kao Tsai-t'ien, who was from Suiyuan. This may partially explain why a satisfactory plan of defense for Urga was never organized. Some measures, however, were taken: Chinese merchants and artisans were mobilized to augment the garrison, and squads of soldiers were positioned at various strategic spots in the nearby hills.

Ungern was thrifty with his use of the month and a half respite following the retreat from Urga. Conscription was ordered in the banners of the Tüsheet Khan and Tsetsen Khan aimags--these new recruits were formed into a regiment under Luvsantseveen Tergüün (taij of the first degree) and the Buryat Zhambalon--and a make-shift provisional government was organized under Ungern, to which were appointed some banner officials from the Tsetsen Khan aimag. Ungern now had a force of perhaps five thousand men,[171] and proclaiming his intention of liberating the Khutukhtu from Chinese imprisonment he advanced on Urga.

Ungern made his move in late January, when he attacked a large detachment of Chinese troops in the region of Bayangol along the Urga-Kyakhta tract. This activity convinced the Chinese command that the main thrust of the attack could be expected from the north. Chinese officers were persuaded of this by the fact that Ungern's first assault three months earlier had come from that direction. The south, they believed foolishly as events were to show, was protected by the Bogd uul mountains and was therefore left virtually undefended. Before the main offensive was launched, a small group of men under the Bargut Luvsan (Luvsantseveen?) and the Tibetan Saj Lama made a daring raid into the city itself and rescued the Bogd Khaan and his consort, who were removed to the nearby Manzshiryn monastery for safety. In the meantime Ungern stormed Urga from the east and south, and by February 3-4 the Chinese inhabitants of the city, soldiers and civilians alike, were in panicked flight.

What followed was a horrible carnage of Chinese, who were chased and ruthlessly slaughtered by Ungern's troops. One eye-witness has described the terrifying sight of a mass of desperate men, fleeing north as fast as they could, plundering and killing as they ran.[172] Their pursuers, especially the Mongols, mercilessly slayed every Chinese whom they caught. Hundreds, possibly thousands of Chinese died that month, if not by a bullet or sword, then by the unforgiving Mongolian winter.

Ungern's seizure of Urga also sounded the death knell for the Chinese administration in western Mongolia. Alarmed by the news of Ungern's second assault on Urga, the Chinese in Khovd had carried out a pogrom of Russians on (lunar) New Year's eve (February 8). Some Russians fled into the steppe, where many died of exposure, and others went into hiding in the city. The Chinese population quickly departed the city on March 25, however, when they learned that a Cossack unit under the command of Esaul Kaigorodov was approaching.

The transfer of Chinese authority to the Russians in Uliastai was more orderly. By March the Chinese realized the hopelessness of their position and an agreement was reached with the Russian residents allowing them to leave the town unmolested. They left for Ku-ch'eng in Sinkiang in the second half of that month, although their caravan was pillaged by a White Guard band no more than forty miles outside the town.[173]

Ungern could now begin his grandiose plan for the restoration of monarchism in Asia. He met with Puntsagtseren, who had enjoyed a very brief stint as the Urga Deputy, and his staff to acquaint them with his objectives and to propose that the Bogd Khaan and his consort be brought back to Urga, where they would once again preside over the "autonomous government." After the corpses had been removed and the city tied up, the Bogd Khaan ceremoniously returned to Urga in the latter part of February. A grateful king rewarded Ungern and his lieutenants for their services in expelling the Chinese and restoring his throne: the rank of chin-wang was bestowed on Ungern, Rezhukin, Naidanjav, Zhambalon, and Luvsantseveen, while the Khutukhtu signaled Ungern's special contributions by conferring on him the title of khan and declaring Ungern to be the reincarnation of the Fifth Jebtsundamba Khutukhtu. The five ministries of the previous "autonomous government" was revived under the prime ministership of the Jalkhanz Khutukhtu.

Despite the restoration of the Mongolian government, real power resided exclusively in Ungern. His command over the army was complete and his hold on the minds of the Mongols--who believed him to be an avenging reincarnation of the God of War--was so total that the court and government had no choice but to submit to his will. Ungern cautiously removed himself to the background, however, ruling through the agency of the Bogd Khaan's government and his lieutenant, Luvsantseveen, who was appointed head of the all-important Ministry of Finance.

Ungern's behavior during the occupation could hardly have been expected to instill confidence or affection for him among the population. A Bureau of Political Investigation, headed by Ungern's second in command, the notorious Sepailov, began to search for Bolshevik sympathizers with a frightening zealotry. This was the "White Terror," the loyalists' reply to the"Red Terror" in Urga at the beginning of 1920; among those who died were Kucherenko, Gembarzhevskii, Tsybyktarov, and Cherepanov. But the net was cast so wide that the innocent and guilty alike were ensnared, and the hunt continued unchecked for so long that even White émigrés began slipping out of the city.

Ungern's honeymoon with the Mongols was similarly shortlived, for he proved to be not the liberator the Mongols had hoped, but only another oppressor. If the Mongols were shocked by his brutality, they were anguished by the increased conscription of Mongolian youths and the requisitions of livestock and other property, all in preparation for the day when he would move against Soviet Russia. Witte, the former Financial Adviser to the Bogd Khaan Government, was instructed to find three million taels to maintain this army.[174] "Requisitions," a term used to dignify White Guard looting, and military conscription for a war of doubtful benefit to the Mongols, pushed the arats deeper into poverty and forced many of them to retire ever farther into the steppe (it was now, Communist historians maintain, that the "revolutionary situation" in Mongolia began).

## Mongolian Revolutionaries in Urga, Irkutsk, and Moscow

When the Mongolian revolutionaries broke up into three groups in late August, there was no intimation of the radical changes which had occurred in the party during the month and a half of their absence. After Bodoo and Dogsom reached Urga in mid-September they discovered that the party was in a shambles, that some of its members had been imprisoned by the Chinese while others were in hiding, and that a large reward had been offered by Chinese authorities for each of the seven revolutionaries who went to Russia. It is in fact surprising that the mission to Russia, known to so many people both inside and outside the court, remained such a well-kept secret for as long as it did. But once the Chinese had caught the scent, they were tireless in tracking it down. Jigmiddorj and Jam'yan, who had served as links between the court and the party, were arrested and tortured. Eventually the entire history of the party and the details of the mission to Soviet Russia were extracted, and the Chinese immediately posted a reward of a thousand dollars apiece for the seven men. There was a second wave of arrests, apparently occurring after the Chinese learned of Ungern's approach. The authorities, believing that this force was responding to the request of the court for help against the Chinese, arrested several prominent lay and church princes, including the Khutukhtu himself.[175]

The future of the party seemed bleak indeed. Its members in Urga were gradually losing contact with the Russian revolutionaries, who were forced into hiding after Ungern's occupation of the city. Nor was the Khutukhtu's court or nobles residing in Urga eager to continue their association with the party once the Chinese were alerted to its existence. By the time Bodoo and Dogsom arrived in Urga the situation had changed completely, and both men were confused as to their next step. Under such circumstances it was impossible to fulfill the earlier plans to build the party and organize an army, and the longer they remained in the city, the greater was their danger. Bodoo, therefore, left immediately for the east. According to Bodoo's later explanation, he intended to cross the Minzinskii mountain range into Russia but was forced to join Ungern's army, which he encountered on his path moving west. Rather than escape, he decided to take advantage of this opportunity to discover Ungern's plans.[176]

Although Communist historians have repeatedly accused Bodoo of betraying the revolution for more limited, nationalistic aims by siding with Ungern, we should remember that Bodoo was not a seer, and neither he nor anyone else knew what kind of assistance, if any, could be expected from the Soviets --or when. He understood only that the party organization in Urga had been mauled, that the Chinese were more powerfully entrenched than ever, and that

Ungern had offered himself as Mongolia's salvation.

Dogsom tried to accompany Bodoo in flight but was forced to return to Urga. Shortly afterwards, he met with Dugarjav, and the two of them agreed that, because of the arrests and intensive Chinese surveillance, any kind of constructive party work in the city not only would be futile but exceptionally hazardous. Therefore, Dogsom and his wife, Dugarjav, and Altangerel pitched their tents in the Chinggelt mountains, close to Urga, in order to keep abreast of events. Just before retiring into the hills Dogsom sent a telegram to Irkutsk:

> We (Bodoo and Dogsom) arrived safely. Right now the situation in Urga has become extremely difficult. Most of the party members have been arrested by Chinese soldiers. Although I have spoken with several of the remaining comrades, it has become extremely dangerous to do party work. Therefore, Bodoo has gone east to the Tsetsen Khan aimag in order to seek an ally (Ungern?). I, Dogsom, am staying here and shall spy out the situation, keep in touch with the party comrades, and do party work. Although I shall try to send you reports, I do not know whether or not I can hide in Urga. I shall explain the situation later by letter.[177]

They remained in the mountains for several weeks, but increased Chinese patrols eventually forced them to separate. Dogsom and Dugarjav went to the Manzshiryn monastery but soon afterwards split up again (Dogsom went to Darigangga, and Dugarjav went east but was mobilized into Ungern's army); Altangerel departed for Erdene zuu monastery. Thus, by mid-November the party in Urga had virtually ceased to exist. The future of the revolution now depended on the resourcefulness and resolution of those who were waiting in Soviet Russia.

Sükhbaatar and Choibalsan were eager to begin their work in Irkutsk. At their request, they were enrolled in the officer's school of the Fifth Red Army and assigned to classes corresponding to their military experience. After a few days, however, Sükhbaatar became seriously ill and was forced to abandon his training; he recovered, thanks to the ministrations of a Red Army doctor and the nursing of Choibalsan.

During this time they were also mastering the symbols and lore of the Bolshevik revolution. In September Sükhbaatar addressed a regional conference of the Russian Communist Party as a representative of the MPP. Greeting them in the name of the arats of Mongolia he said: "The appeal of your party has reached the cattleherders of the empty steppe of Mongolia, who suffer from the three-fold enslavement of lamas and princes, Chinese militarists, and world capital. The Communist revolution has sparked a revolutionary world fire in the East. The masses of the East are rising...."

They also became acquainted with the staff of the Buryat-language newspaper _Dawn_, published by the Fifth Red Army, which agreed to help them produce a revolutionary paper for Outer Mongolia. With its assistance and some help from the Comintern, a new paper, _Truth of Mongolia_ (_Mongolyn Ünen_), was organized, its first issue appearing on November 10, 1920. This was less a newspaper than a political pamphlet, and its strident ideological tone suggests that Sükhbaatar received not only technical but considerable editorial assistance as well. The paper criticized the selfishness of the princes and lamas, and among other things called for the transference of power to the people and the nationalization of all property. It should be added that only six issues of the paper ever appeared, and there is no evidence that copies circulated widely, if at all, in Khalkha Mongolia.[178]

Although Sükhbaatar and Choibalsan had begun their work in Irkutsk with great confidence, their morale plummeted to the lowest possible point after receiving Dogsom's report that the organization of the MPP in Urga had collapsed. Not only did communication with the capital end soon after that, but, with the exception of one rather uninformative wire from Danzan and Chagdarjav in mid-September, nothing more was heard from the delegates in Moscow. Gapon told Sükhbaatar of increasing Chinese oppression in Mongolia and of rumors that a White band had invaded Mongolia, a fact, he noted, which could only complicate the Mongolian situation. They continually badgered Gapon for more information about their comrades in Moscow and Urga, but Gapon replied that he knew as little as they did. Their circumstances were not made any more agreeable by the scarcity of food in the city, the result of a terrible famine in Siberia, or by their social isolation (the Buryats, who had been so eager to help earlier, had quickly melted away, much to the anger of the two Khalkhas). Sükhbaatar, Choibalsan, and Losol (who had returned from Omsk to Irkutsk) had even taken to quarreling among themselves.[179]

When Gapon told the Mongols, probably on October 31 or November 1, that a White Guard prince Baron Ungern was laying siege to the Chinese garrison at Urga, it could not have come at a time when they were more demoralized. They told Gapon that assistance was required immediately, and although his reply has not been recorded, he may have advised them that a formal request to the Soviet government would be helpful. The letter, dated November 2, was addressed to the Soviet Commissar of Foreign Affairs and the Mongolian-Tibetan Department of the Comintern:

> Because a White army has entered Mongolia and begun fighting the Chinese it is the opinion of us representatives that this will in the end bring suffering to our Mongolia and is contrary to the (interests) of the Soviet government. Moreover, we do not believe at all that the great affair of our nation (i.e., the liberation of Mongolia from the Chinese) has been accomplished by the refugee troops of Semenov. Because we Mongols have already come to the Soviet government with a request for assistance and protection, we beg therefore that troops be sent immediiately into our Mongolia to liquidate the soldiers of Semenov and to free (it) from Chinese hands. Will you please have mercy on the suffering of our people and help.

The letter went on to warn that if help were delayed, the "evil philosophy" of the Whites would spread throughout the country and permit the White Guards to conspire with Mongolian reactionaries. If Russia sent its troops, the Mongols would assemble their own forces, for whom weapons were also requested.[180] Reference to Mongolian "forces" was of course intended to give a false impression, but the three men were desperate and perhaps believed, as they had when they met with Sorokovikov in Urga earlier, that they must put on a bold front in order to coax the Russians to action. There is no record of a Soviet reply. A telegram was simultaneously dispatched to Danzan urging him to complete speedily his negotiations in Moscow.

They could not know, however, that the Soviets after weeks of uncertainty were very close to reaching a decision on this very question. Earlier Danzan, Losol, Chagdarjav, and Rinchino had met several times with Soviet authorities in Omsk, to whom they explained their objectives and requirements. They were told that the Omsk government was not empowered to make a decision on such an important matter and that the Mongols would have to proceed to Moscow, where their work and aims must be explained again. This was the same message they had received in Verkhneudinsk and Irkutsk.

They arrived in Moscow, probably in the second half of September or early October. Danzan and Chagdarjav sent a telegram to Irkutsk with the message: "We have arrived safely. How are you doing? We have arrived in Moscow and are meeting with the authorities." According to Danzan and Chagdarjav themselves in a statement made later, they met "repeatedly" with various officials, including those of the Comintern, and explained their reason for coming to Moscow. (Although no documents have been found in Soviet archives to tell us with whom the Mongols consulted in Moscow, most Communist historians write that they were received by the Commissar of Foreign Affairs G.V. Chicherin, Commander of the Red Army S.S. Kamenev, and by V.I. Lenin himself.) But the Mongols, given no clear answer, were forced to wait.

One day, around November 10, they were unexpectedly summoned to a meeting with representatives of the Comintern and Communist Party, and told that the Soviet government had decided to supply them with all the guns they required, the exact amount of which could be fixed later. It was necessary for them to return quickly to the border and there begin preparations for their "work." The oppression of the Chinese militarists and White Guards was increasing, they were told, and the Mongols were advised to agitate among the frontier population and to enlarge the party beyond its present membership of "five hundred." A large army would also have to be formed. The Russians did add an important qualification. Since the Mongols had taken upon their own shoulders responsibility for this revolution, it was necessary that they expel the Chinese by themselves. If the Whites should invade Soviet territory, then of course the Red Army could be dispatched into Mongolia to destroy them; otherwise, it would be "inappropriate" to send Soviet troops across the border. Danzan and Chagdarjav promptly sent off a telegram to Irkutsk: "We have met with the high authorities of Moscow and now have completely and successfully accomplished our objectives. Shall be returning soon. Convey this information to the Urga comrades."[181]

## Soviet Policy Toward China and Mongolia, 1917-20

After keeping the Mongols dangling for a month or more in Moscow, why had the Soviets so suddenly promised them an unlimited supply of guns and money and urged them to return immediately to the frontier, where they were to kindle the fires of revolution? The answer must be sought many hundreds of miles away, in Mongolia itself. Ungern had appeared, almost out of nowhere, at the gates of Urga and laid siege to the city for two weeks from October 26 to November 7. This event could not but have disturbed the Soviet government. The ink on an armistic agreement signed with the Poles was hardly dry, and the overwhelming bulk of Soviet troops and military equipment was still on the western front, where they had been concentrated for service in the campaign. Siberian partisans in the meantime had their hands full with Semenov in the Transbaikal region. If Ungern were to seize Mongolia, he could transform it into an anti-Soviet front which could pose a serious threat to Siberia east of Irkutsk and perhaps the whole of Siberia as well. The Moscow government could not possibly allow Mongolia to become another White Guard sanctuary and springboard for military activities as Manchuria had been and continued to be. There was no choice but to act quickly and decisively.

On November 6, 1920 the headquarters of the Fifth Red Army in Irkutsk received an order to prepare a military expedition against Ungern. The order stated that Ungern had seized Urga and that his units were now moving eastward. The Red Army was directed to "concentrate quickly the 104th Brigade in the region of Troitskosavsk with a sufficient amount of artillery and cavalry, thereupon to cross the Mongolian border and attack the detachment of Baron Ungern with the aim of smashing and destroying it."[182]

On November 11, at almost the very moment the Soviets delivered their reply to Danzan in Moscow, the government of Soviet Russia sent a note to Peking claiming that the Chinese military command in Mongolia, unable to deal with this White Guard force, had appealed to the governments of Soviet Russia and the Far Eastern Republic to help them combat the marauders. The note stated that Soviet troops were being sent into Mongolia to deal with the White Guards, and that "as soon as the White Guardist gangs in Mongolia are annihilated, the Soviet troops will regard their task as accomplished and will leave Chinese territory (my emphasis) immediately."[183]

Ironically, this note was sent four days after Ungern had already lifted the siege, but considering the state of communications in Siberia at this time, it is very improbable that the Soviets could have known this. Nevertheless, when Moscow did learn that Ungern's assault had been repulsed, a second note dated November 28 was sent to Peking:

> ...we consider it necessary to report to the Chinese government that the Russian Republic, placing the inviolability of foreign territory above all else, finds it possible to delay the sending of its military force into the territory of Mongolia, being convinced that the

> Chinese government will immediately take energetic measures for the complete and rapid liquidation of the indicated robber bands which are hostile to Russia.[184]

It has frequently been argued that this Soviet offer of aid was merely a pretext to disguise Moscow's real objective, the seizure of Mongolia, and since the Chinese government had never authorized its officials to request Soviet intervention, it is thought by many writers that this "appeal" from the Chinese military authorities in Mongolia was a fabrication.

It is more likely, however, that the Soviets were genuinely troubled by Ungern's presence in Mongolia, a fact which is supported not only by the logic of the fragile Soviet position in eastern Siberia but by the rescission of this November 11 offer after Ungern had been beaten off. Although as late as November 2 the senior spokesman of the Soviet Commissariat of Foreign Affairs for the Far East V. Vilenskii was still insisting that Soviet Russia would not intervene against Ungern, when the Soviets learned, erroneously, that Ungern had in fact occupied Urga, they were forced to abandon their Olympian detachment for a more active role in deciding Mongolia's fate.

The authenticity of the "appeal" of the Chinese military authorities is rather perplexing. It is not impossible of course that the Soviet government manufactured the appeal. On the other hand, there is no convincing reason why it should have done so, especially at a time when Moscow was exceedingly anxious to receive diplomatic recognition from China and when the artifice could be so easily exposed. It seems illogical, moreover, that the Soviets would risk diplomatic embarrassment or, worse yet, a military confrontation with Japan by producing a bogus appeal--and then just as suddenly withdrawing it.

According to Soviet archives, on October 27 a representative of the Chinese "high official" (presumably the Kyakhta Deputy High Commissioner) informed the Chief of the Border Region of the Far Eastern Republic that Ungern had inflicted considerable losses on the Urga garrison, and because it was impossible for Chinese to cope with this attack the Chinese government had no objection to troops of Soviet Russia and the FER entering Mongolia and fighting alongside Chinese forces against Ungern.[185] The date of October 27 is puzzling, for this was only one day after the assault on Urga began. Nevertheless, it is entirely possible that a Chinese representative had met with Russian frontier officials and that these Russian officials had misinterpreted, or elected to misinterpret, these discussions as an appeal for Soviet intervention.

For several weeks the Soviets had been unable to reach a decision on the Mongolian request, and it was only after Ungern attacked Urga and threatened to convert Mongolia into a White Guard stronghold that the Bolsheviks agreed to help the Mongols. Why had it taken them so long to decide? Why had the Soviets failed earlier to intervene on the side of the Mongols against the Chinese? And why did this assistance, promised to the MPP in November 1920, not materialize until mid-February of the next year? To answer these questions we must examine the entire background of early Sino-Soviet relations and their impact on Mongolia.

Lenin, despite his recognition of the important contribution which the "bourgeois," anti-colonial revolutionary movement in Asia could make to world revolution, had been unwilling to abandon the fundamental Marxist faith in the necessity of a socialist revolution in the industrially advanced West. Even for a few years after the Russian revolution he continued to be guided by the belief that socialism could not take root in Russia with its backward economic system unless it was accompanied by a revolution in one of the more developed countries, especially Germany. The tenacity with which he held on to this conviction seemed justified by the striking social unrest in Europe at this time.

Indeed, so certain were Lenin and others of the imminence of European revolution that a new Communist International (Comintern) was founded in 1919, and in the days following revolutions did break out in Hungary and Bavaria. Enthusiasm and confidence among the Bolsheviks were at no time greater than in the summer of 1920, when the Red Army marched into Poland. Delegates to the Second Congress of the Comintern (July 19 to August 7) were euphoric over the successes of the military campaign and were thoroughly committed to its victorious conclusion. It was precisely at this moment, when the attention of the Russians was riveted on Poland, that delegates of the MPP arrived in Verkhneudinsk.

But the expected uprising of Polish workers did not occur, and the Red Army was driven back. The Soviet government was forced to conclude an armistice in October 1920, certainly a bitter pill for the Russians to swallow, although it did bring much needed peace to the western front. October brought the Soviet government new military security on other fronts as well. In the south Wrangel's Black Sea assault was decisively routed, and in the east the Japanese finally evacuated the Transbaikal region. The end of hopes for a European revolution and the urgency of repairing the damage wrought by three years of revolution and civil war had a marvelously sobering effect on Soviet leaders. By the end of 1920, as many scholars have noted, the Soviets were showing a new pragmatism and spirit of accommodation in their relations with the West. Economic and diplomatic relations were seriously, if reluctantly, sought and Soviet thinking with regard to domestic and foreign policies was now guided by the recognition that economic reconstruction was an unavoidable condition for the continued survival of the Soviet state. The Kronstadt rebellion demonstrated, as nothing else could, that internal needs had to be given priority. The abandonment of War Communism for the New Economic Policy in March 1921 was the domestic corollary of this new pragmatism in foreign policy.

Although Lenin had not underestimated the potential for revolution in the East, it was only when the prospect of revolution in Europe receded that he gave this question more earnest thought. The emphasis nevertheless continued to be on the progressive role which wars of national liberation against Western colonialism could play in the world revolutionary movement. Lenin's most important pronouncement on this subject was made in his "Theses on the National and Colonial Question" before the

July-August congress of the Comintern in 1921. Here he argued that Soviet Russia must support not only proletarian-communist movements in the West, but bourgeois-democratic movements in Asia as well, for without external help from revolution in Asia, revolution in Europe could not succeed. Proletarian aid, moreover, would permit these countries to by-pass the capitalist stage of development.

But as Soviets began to restore the old Tsarist frontiers, Lenin's lofty oratory of aiding wars of "national liberation" and supporting "bourgeois-democratic" forces in "anti-colonial" movements imperceptibly took on a special "Russian" quality. The countries where Bolshevik theorists worked most ardently to apply Lenin's "Theses" were those on which the security of Soviet Russia most depended: Persia, Afghanistan, Turkey, Armenia, and China.

When the commentaries of these theorists are stripped of their rhetorical bark, the message was clear enough. Indigenous political forces, irrespective of their social philosophy, which were ready to assert an independent foreign policy and had a realistic chance of taking and holding power were to receive Comintern support. The sympathy of these nationalist forces to Communism was less important than their resolve to govern independently of the West. The best insurance for the survival of the world revolution--that is, the Soviet state--was to girdle Russia with anti-Western governments. This line was formally adopted at the Fourth Comintern Congress in 1922, when the policy of the "united front" (in colonial countries this meant the alliance of communist parties with nationalist movements) became the common program for all members of the Communist International.

Thus, as one prominent historian of Russia has observed, by March 1921 Soviet foreign policy in the East as well as in the West had become conservative and cautious.[186] Lenin himself noted this publicly and privately on several occasions. In a report of February 2, 1920 for example he stated that Soviet policy in the East must be "still more cautious and patient, for here we are dealing with nations that are much more backward..."[187] Lenin had to restrain the radicalism of Sultan-Galiev, who in 1919 advocated the formation of an Eastern Red Army and a bold program to revolutionize the East. In a note scribbled on a June 4, 1920 telegram from Trotsky to the Commissariat of Foreign Affairs Lenin wrote: "In the East we must apply ourselves to political and educative work...while counseling every possible caution against steps calculated or bound to entail military support from us."[188]

Soviet policy was consistent and deliberate. Both nationalist and communist movements in Asia were to be supported, depending on which could be used to greater effect as a lever against the West. It has often been observed that there was a duality in Bolshevik policy: while on the one hand the Soviet government negotiated with existing, recognized governments, on the other the Comintern surrepticiously labored to overthrow them. The conclusion of one scholar, that there was no such duality in Soviet policy in the Middle East since the twin purposes of revolution and national security were served by the Soviet program of supporting nationalist governments, is equally applicable to China and Mongolia.[189]

In Turkey, Persia, and Afghanistan, and in their policy toward Mongolia as well, the Bolsheviks generally preferred to deal with an established government rather than with a communist party, whose future was often problematical at best. In Turkey the discovery by summer 1920 that Kemal Pasha's nationalist movement was enjoying enormous popularity, in contrast to the languishing state of the Turkish Communist Party, resulted in Soviet overtures to the Kemalists and eventually to political and material support--despite the Kemalist suppression of the Turkish Communists in 1922 and 1925.

The establishment of a British protectorate over Persia in 1919 had forced the Soviet government to abandon its hitherto moderate line toward Teheran and induced the Persian Communist Party to take an uncompromising revolutionary stand. When the Teheran government began to pull away from Great Britain after the Soviet attack on Denikin's fleet on the southern shores of the Caspian Sea in May 1920, however, diplomatic negotiations ensued between the two governments and in February 1921 a treaty, which included an important provision against the interference of any third country (Great Britain) in Persian affairs, was signed. Only then were Soviet troops removed from Persian soil and Comintern support for the Persian Communist and other separatist movements pared in favor of strengthening normal relations with Teheran. The Soviet government also established links with the young nationalist Amir of Afghanistan, despite his continued aid to the Basmachi rebels. In February and March 1921 the Soviet government concluded treaties all three countries.

Soviet Russia was keen to establish relations with China for the same reasons that it sought relations with its other Asian neighbors. There was of course the general diplomatic offensive waged in the East to counter Western influence, but China, the largest country in Asia and sharing the longest border with Russia, was a special prize. There were also special problems, both symbolic and real, between Russia and China which required attention: the Chinese Eastern Railway, the activity of White Russians in China, and the Boxer Indemnity. Moreover, it was vital for eastern Siberia, whose economy was devasted by the civil war, to reestablish commercial links with Manchuria (Chinese exports to Russia in 1920 were only twenty-four percent of what they had been in 1916).

For its part, the Anfu government certainly did not lack problems requiring consultation with the Soviets. The Chinese were demanding reparations for losses suffered by Chinese citizens in Russia during the civil war. There was concern over the large number of Chinese serving in the Red Army and it was feared that they were being indoctrinated in Bolshevism (diplomatic protection was also sought for them). The Chinese also wanted to see curbs placed on the White Russians, who as in the case of Ungern for example were often as destructive to the peace of northeastern China as they were to Russia.

The Anfu government equally had reasons for wishing to postpone official negotiations with Moscow. Some problems, such as Outer Mongolia and the Chinese Eastern Railway, had been resolved unilaterally and in violation of previous treaties with the old Tsarist government. To open diplomatic negotiations with Russia would unavoidably lead to the reopening of these issues. In 1918 the Peking government had decided moreover to act uniformly with the Allies and not to recognize Soviet Russia. The Chinese "declaration of war" against Germany, making it a belligerent of sorts in the World War, tied China even more closely to the Western powers. And finally, China's diplomatic efforts in 1919 were focused on the peace conference in Paris, where the Chinese anxiously hoped to recover Shantung taken from them first by the Germans and then by the Japanese. There was no urgency to talk with Moscow.

The frothy tide of Chinese nationalism, however, forced Peking to review its thinking about Russia. The indifference of the Allies at Paris to China's insistence on the recovery of Shantung aroused the intellectuals and merchants against the West. The Karakhan Manifesto, issued in July 1919 but not reported in the Chinese press until March 1920, could not have been more timely. The declaration denounced Western imperialism in Asia and repudiated all Tsarist treaties with and concerning China. The offer to return the Chinese Eastern Railway to China without compensation, a concession later denied by Moscow, was particularly attractive. The Soviet gesture was a refreshing contrast to the behavior of the Allies, and newspapers and public organizations in China began demanding that the government reconsider its position toward Russia.

Between April and June 1920 the Peking government, intrigued by Karakhan's offer and under pressure, was making quiet approaches to the Bolsheviks. Fan Ch'i-kuang, who had served earlier in Mongolia, was secretly sent to Vladivostok to meet Soviet representatives and discuss the specifics of the Manifesto. There was a meeting of Soviet and Chinese representatives in Copenhagen in April. In that same month the Russian press reported the arrival of a "Chinese and Mongolian military-diplomatic mission" in Verkhneudinsk. And in June the Peking government sent a commission of three foreign advisers, including B.L. Simpson (Putnam Weale), to the Far Eastern Republic on a fact-finding tour.[190]

The most important contacts between the Soviets and China were the missions of I.L. Yurin and Chang Ssu-lin. The Far Eastern Republic had declared its desire to establish relations with China and for this purpose sent a delegation to Peking headed by Yurin. Although he arrived in Peking in August 1920, several months elapsed before serious negotiations really began (in mid-December) because of doubts in the minds of Chinese government officials regarding Yurin's authority to speak on behalf of regions in eastern Siberia other than the small area controlled by the Verkhneudinsk government. Talks were suspended a month later when Peking presented the FER with an enormous list of claims for losses incurred by Chinese citizens in Russia during the civil war. Negotiations did not resume until the spring of 1921.

The mission of Chang Ssu-lin was even more disappointing to Moscow. Chang had been sent by Hsu Shu-cheng's Frontier Defense Office to the Far Eastern Republic as a "military representative" to take advantage, in his words, of the remarkable opportunity presented by the "state letter" (i.e., the Karakhan Manifesto) and to investigate the circumstances of Chinese citizens living in Irkutsk. Chang had also been instructed to assess the situation of the FER and to determine whether it would be in the interest of China to establish diplomatic relations with it. But soon after arriving Chang realized that Moscow was in fact dictating the FER's foreign policy, and without waiting for authorization from Peking he left in late August for European Russia.[191]

The Soviet government was suspicious of Chang's credentials and very reluctant to treat with him. In early July a note was sent to the Chinese Foreign Ministry asking whether Chang was empowered to conduct "negotiations for the restoration of diplomatic and commercial relations" on behalf of the Peking government. North China was at that moment in the throes of a brief civil war and the Chinese Foreign Ministry did not reply. The Russians were clearly under a misapprehension, for they thought that Chang was the chief of a diplomatic mission (a claim which Chang had apparently arrogated to himself) and it was on that basis that he was accepted without waiting for confirmation from Peking. Chang was warmly received and even invited to the home of Karakhan, a courtesy which made a special impression on Chang. In the meantime, talks went on in the

Commissariat of Foreign Affairs. The Russians were anxious to receive Chinese diplomatic recognition and on several occasions Karakhan pressed Chang to wire his government inquiring whether a "preliminary" treaty of friendship might not be signed.

Chang, obviously impressed by the advantages of such a treaty, made this point repeatedly in his dispatches to Peking. On September 23, however, the Chinese Foreign Ministry finally replied with a terse message: "Affairs within the Ministry (require) personal discussion. Hope (you) will return immediately." The Russians at first pleaded with him to stay, arguing that there were yet other matters which needed to be discussed. But when they discovered in mid-October that Chang was merely a representative of the now dismantled Frontier Defense Office and had never been authorized to go to Moscow, they were angry. Karakhan sent him a note bitterly pointing out their surprise at learning of his duplicity. Chang had no alternative but to return to Peking. Before leaving, though, he was received by Lenin on November 2 (nine days before the Soviet offer of assistance to China in the defeat of Ungern) and was given an appeal addressed to the government of the Republic of China reaffirming the July 25, 1919 Manifesto and expressing the desire of the Soviet government for diplomatic relations.[192]

It is ironic that on September 23, the very day Chang Ssu-lin was ordered home, a presidential order was issued in Peking declaring that Tsarist diplomats in China would no longer be treated as the legitimate representatives of Russia (Boxer Indemnity payments had already ceased since August 1). Later in the month Russian extraterritorial rights in China were also abolished, and in February 1921 the (White) Russian civil administration in Harbin was closed down and a Chinese superintendent appointed to govern the city.

While the Soviets may have been encouraged by this step, which appeared to demonstrate China's new flexibility over the Russian question, their cup was far from running over: the September 23 order also stated that the Peking government's attitude toward the internal conflict in Russia would continue to be guided by that of the Allies. It is difficult to resist the observation that shortly after this the Comintern helped to organize the Chinese Communist Party and committed itself to helping the Kuomintang.

From 1921 to 1945 Soviet policy with respect to Mongolia, like that of its Tsarist predecessor, was undeviatingly faithful to the principle that Mongolia was part of China, but also like its predecessor the Soviet government refused to tolerate more than nominal Chinese suzerainty over the country. The Soviet position toward Mongolia between 1917 and 1921, however, was much less clear. The evidence suggests that Mongolia was never thought about seriously, if at all, by either Bolshevik theorists, or Comintern officials, or Soviet diplomats. Nor did Lenin pay much attention to Mongolia. The few scattered references in his collected works, used simply for the purpose of illustrating Tsarist imperialism, are invariably coupled with the names of other Asian countries.

If Lenin and other Bolshevik thinkers were ready to acknowledge the possibility of only a "bourgeois" revolution in such comparatively advanced Asian countries as Turkey, India, and China, how much less hope must they have held out for a country like Mongolia with a pastoral economy and a small and overwhelmingly illiterate population? In the words of one speaker before the 1922 Congress of the Toilers of the Far East, "As long as the basic economy of Mongolia is cattle-raising distinguished by patriarchal tribal features, to preach Communism and the proletarian revolution is ridiculous."[193]

Lenin voiced very similar views to the Mongolian delegates in November 1921. When asked whether the MPP should become a communist party, he advised against it saying that a communist party was a party of the proletariat. "There is still much work for the revolutionaries to do in state, economic, and cultural construction before a proletarian mass is created from herdsman elements."[194] References to Mongolia are absent in Soviet and Comintern statements on Asia, though this changed after the establishment of a new revolutionary government in Urga in the summer of 1921. Another reason for the general silence was probably that, unlike China, India, Persia and other Asian states which were in the process of "decolonialization," Mongolia since the seventeenth century had been subject to China, itself one of the "oppressed" countries of Asia.

The failure of the Soviet government in the early period to develop a policy toward Mongolia resulted in a number of inconsistencies and contradictory statements from the Commissariat of Foreign Affairs itself. The earliest Soviet declaration on Mongolia in Russian or Chinese sources is a private conversation in January 1918 between a secretary of the Chinese Legation in Petrograd and Deputy Commissar of Foreign Affairs Polivanov. When asked to explain the position of the Soviet government toward Mongolia, Polivanov answered:

> The Mongolian rustics are ignorant and closely resemble (the people of) the ancient autocratic state (of Chinggis Khan). Naturally in this century they are incapable of being independent and governing themselves. The best plan would be for the people of the Republic of China to civilize and educate them, and after the autocracy (of the Bogd Khaan) has been overthrown, to allow them again to become completely independent.[195]

Although we must allow perhaps for a special Chinese construction of this statement, it is nevertheless clear that Polivanov was recommending a period of tutelage for Mongolia during which China would implement a program of modernization in preparation for eventual independence. The point of interest here is that while he was prepared to allow China a very active presence in Mongolia, there was no suggestion of a Russian role. In mid-1919, however, this same Ministry issued a declaration stating that Mongolia was independent of either Petrograd or Peking, a policy enunciated again by V. Vilenskii in *Izvestiya* in November 1920. And yet, in the November 10, 1920 telegram to Peking stating that Soviet troops were being sent into Mongolia, Mongolia was referred to as part of Chinese territory.

Even though Lenin had given the MPP and its work his blessing, Soviet support for the Mongolian revolution between November 1920 and February 1921 was still equivocal, primarily because of Moscow's overriding commitment to establishing full diplomatic relations with the Peking government. Chinese intractability to Russian diplomatic overtures, the refusal of the Peking government to budge from its alliance with the West, and the occupation of Mongolia by a White Guard Army weakened this commitment and persuaded the Soviet government to agree to aid Mongolian nationalist forces against China. The Russians were determined to defend their frontiers against anti-Soviet forces, and Mongolia was geographically too important to ignore, a point which Lenin himself signaled in a conversation with Danzan and Chagdarjav in November 1920: "(Lenin) pointed out Mongolia's role as a buffer country between the two struggling worlds, East and West, and noted that the only correct attitude for the toilers of their country to take would be to struggle for their own political and economic independence."[196] But after Ungern had taken Urga in early February, Soviet support for the Mongols was pushed to a new, and higher, stage.

That the Soviets were unwilling to act precipitately in Mongolia, and indeed in the Far East generally, may be explained by other factors. The Red Army was exhausted after bitter fighting in Poland. In Siberia the Soviet advance had stopped after reaching Irkutsk in late 1919, not only for fear of provoking hostilities with Japan but because of the enfeebled state of Soviet troops. The Revolutionary Military Council of the Eastern Front reported for the period December 1919 to January 1920: "Red Army troops of the 28th Brigade have completed a difficult passage through famine-stricken steppes. Poorly clothed, half-starved, and exhausted...(sic) An epidemic has broken out. Up to fifty percent of the Akmolinsk regiment has fallen ill."[197] In March 1921 I.N. Smirnov, Chairman of the Siberian Revolutionary Committee, complained in a secret telegram to Lenin that the army of the FER was "unclothed and hungry."[198] The Red Army was in a similar state. Only one army, the Fifth Red Army, was left on the eastern front, and by the time of Ungern's first appearance in Mongolia many of its more experienced units had either been demobilized, or sent west to fight in Poland, or assigned to the labor front to help repair the badly damaged Siberian economy.[199]

Siberia was in chaos. Tens of thousands of farms were destroyed; the Trans-Siberian Railroad was in a woeful condition with over twelve thousand rolling stock and fourteen hundred steam engines out of service; western Siberia was suffering from a terrible typhus epidemic; and food was short everywhere. Siberia was hardly given an opportunity to recover when in late February 1920, in preparation for war with Poland, Lenin ordered that everything possible had to be transported rapidly from Siberia and the Urals to the western front.[200]

The presence of a Japanese army in the Russian Far East was another factor which constrained Soviet freedom of action. Over the protests of some radicals who wished to see the Red Army continue its advance beyond Irkutsk and the Russian Far East sovietized, the Politburo of the Central Committee decided in February 1920 that a buffer state had to be formed in eastern Siberia. Leon Trotsky, Chairman of the Military Revolutionary Council, wrote that month:

> The clash of our regular troops with the Japanese will serve as a pretext for rabid chauvinist agitation by the Japanese and will turn the scales in favor of the advocates of sending out further occupation forces...Beware of the snares of the Japanese interventionists.[201]

The Far Eastern Republic, formed on April 6, 1920 with its provisional capital at Verkhneudinsk, during its early life controlled no more than the region between Lake Baikal and Verkhneudinsk. This situation changed with the agreement of the Japanese in mid-July to evacuate the Transbaikal and Priamur regions and to the formationof a non-communist buffer state in which other armies or governments (the Japanese clearly had Soviet Russia in mind) would not interfere. The areas were evacuated by the Japanese army in mid-October 1920 and in its wake the White Guards also pulled out. Soon afterwards a conference of representatives of various organizations, assemblies, and regional governments in eastern Siberia was held and declared that rule over the Russian Far East was to be transferred to a provisional government in Chita.

To be sure, the Japanese had returned eastward back into Manchuria, but their designs were still obscure and the possibility that they might return, if provided with a suitable pretext, could never be excluded. The Moscow government, therefore, had to act cautiously. A remark by Lenin in December 1920 shows how aware the Russians were of the Japanese danger: "We cannot have a war with Japan and must do everything to try not only to postpone war with Japan but, if possible, to avoid it."[202] It was impossible for the Moscow government to anticipate how the Japanese would react to a Soviet expeditionary army into Outer Mongolia or to open support for Mongolian nationalists only a month or so after the Japanese had left the Transbaikal region.

## The Revolution Mired

Danzan, Chagdarjav, and Rinchino returned from Moscow to Irkutsk between November 15 and 17 with an undisclosed amount of money and a limited number of weapons. The Buryats, who a little earlier had been so invisible, suddenly reappeared when news leaked out that the Moscow delegation had been successful, and a general meeting was held on November 17 to discuss the future of the party.

Communist and other writers have described this meeting as one of the milestones of the history of the party when the members of the MPP, reunited after several months, resolved on a carefully deliberated course of action to intensify the national-liberation and anti-feudal revolution. Our only account of this conference informs us that, in view of the suppression of the party in Urga and the fighting between the Chinese and White Guards there, it was decided to shift the epicenter of the revolution from Urga, as was the original plan, to the northern frontier zone centering around Kyakhta. The party would have to be rebuilt, soldiers recruited, and the remaining party members in Urga summoned north. In accordance with this plan,

Sükhbaatar and Choibalsan, along with some Buryats, were sent on ahead to Kyakhta, and Danzan, Losol, and Chagdarjav were left in Irkutsk to continue discussions with the Red Army concerning material assistance to the party and to keep abreast of the White Guard situation in Mongolia (Rinchino stayed in Irkutsk until April working on the party newspaper and serving as the representative of the MPP to the Comintern).[203]

In ascribing such a high degree of clarity and purpose to this conference, however, our source was influenced probably more by the actual course which the revolution subsequently took than by the proceedings of the meeting itself (it is important to note that no records of this conference were ever kept). A study of the few available contemporary documents and an analysis of the party's activities between the second half of November 1920 and early February 1921 indicate that there was considerable aimlessness and confusion among its members, and that the Mongols in fact continued to regard Urga as the staging ground of the revolution. Despite Dogsom's gloomy communications, the precise state of the party apparatus in Urga was still unknown, and an unsigned telegram which arrived from Urga about the same time as the conference asking that weapons be sent to Mongolia via Khövsgöl lake and an army readied must have renewed their faith in the vitality of the party organization in the capital. Moreover, the White Guards had been beaten off from Urga, and the Mongols probably thought that once again they had only to contend with the Chinese.

The inactivity of the party during the following two months was best reflected in the movements of Sükhbaatar and Choibalsan. Leaving their colleagues in Irkutsk, they departed for Verkhneudinsk disguised as Chinese workers. At Verkhneudinsk they hired a cart and arrived in Troitskosavsk on November 22 in the company of the Buryat Balamso. Although the sources--documents and memoir literature--reveal nothing of their activities from November 22 to the middle part of January, we are informed by most histories that these two men immediately engaged in a vigorous effort to recruit a partisan army and to agitate among the Mongolian frontier pickets and banners to the east and west of Kyakhta. The admittedly meagre and contradictory evidence, however, suggests that these activities did not occur until late January or early February.

Indeed, the very silence of the sources obliges us to conclude that very little was achieved during these two and a half months. This emerges clearly from an undated letter sent by Sükhbaatar and Choibalsan to Urga while they were in Kyakhta:

> Concerning the reason for submitting (this letter), after reaching Kyakhta on the 18th day (sic) of November, we planned to begin our intended work. However, when the money which we were to receive from Tsentrosoyuz did not materialize, it was impossible (for us) to go. Despite the repeated telegrams which were sent (explaining) these circumstances, there has been no reply. Therefore, the two of us have not known what to do. Although we have remained here perplexed without anything to do, we have met with Puntsag, whom our party posted here...Esteemed wise comrades, we hope that this (letter will prompt) you to ponder deeply on appropriate measures to be taken and to implement this affair (i.e., the uprising against the Chinese) without postponing or abandoning it.[204]

Not only does the letter show how bewildered Sükhbaatar and Choibalsan were in Kyakhta, but the fact that the pair was asking for instructions from Urga implies that the Mongolian revolutionaries in Russia still regarded the capital as the heart of the revolution. The phrase, "it was impossible to go," is intriguing and suggests that the two Khalkhas were supposed to travel on to Urga and that the stay in Kyakhta was originally planned only as a pause.

A letter then arrived in Kyakhta from unnamed party members in Urga advising them in rather cryptic terms against seeking aid from Soviet Russia and that Danzan and the others should be recalled to Kyakhta, where this question (of foreign assistance) could be discussed more thoroughly. "Not one of our party has gone over to the White Russians...(sic) For the time being there is nothing for our party to do except to await the outcome of the battle between the two sides (White Guard and Chinese). If in the meantime we meddle in this matter, there will be no benefit other than the suffering (caused) by stepping in between two enemies."[205]

All work in Urga and Kyakhta was thus in suspension and it was only in Irkutsk that the party may still have been active, although even this activity was probably very limited. For the next two and a half months the Mongols waited for a break to occur. That break was to be Ungern's seizure of Urga. In the meantime, however, the revolution was mired.

Sükhbaatar and Choibalsan stayed with Makstenek in Troitskosavsk biding their time. Probably frustrated by the tedium they and their new Buryat companion I.I. Vasil'ev (Badam) decided in mid-January to leave Troitskosavsk and cross the border, but a telegram from Losol and Chagdarjav stating that they would soon be arriving forced them to postpone the trip. The pair arrived five days later, leaving Danzan in Irkutsk to continue thrashing out a program of military assistance to the party. It is surely no accident that their return to the Mongolian border coincided with alarming reports of a fresh and larger Ungernist army in eastern Mongolia. According to the memoirs of Balamso, Danzan and the others in Irkutsk had decided that more serious attention had to be given to the building up of the party and that a conference should be held for that purpose in the coming spring at Gegeetiin (Saruult) datsan in Soviet Buryatia to elect a central committee.[206] These instructions were probably relayed to Troitskosavsk by Losol and Chagdarjav.

The Mongols remained in Troitskosavsk for another week, during which time they met with Makstenek and outlined their plans to cross the border to the adjoining banners and border pickets and recruit members for the party. Makstenek approved the plan but enjoined them to avoid the pickets east of Kyakhta (that is, the territory adjoining the FER) and to confine themselves to the region west of the town (the teritory bordering Soviet Russia). He explained that, with Chinese soldiers and spies continuously passing through the Far Eastern Republic, the work of the MPP might come to Peking's attention. There was probably a more important reason for this warning. Yurin was at that moment meeting with Chinese authorities in Peking, and Makstenek may have feared that if the connection of the FER with the Mongolian People's Party were known, it might prejudice those negotiations. The Mongols agreed, and around January 20 Sükhbaatar, Choibalsan, Losol, Chagdarjav, Vasil'ev and Balamso rode west. Losol and Vasil'ev were dropped off en route and the rest went on to Gegeetiin datsan, where they established a temporary headquarters.[207]

From Gegeetiin datsan Choibalsan and Chagdarjav visited the banner of Sum'yaa Beise in the vicinity of present-day Tsagaannuur. Sum'yaa, a commoner from the Ili region of Sinkiang, had led over three hundred Ööld and/or Chahar familes (sources differ) to Mongolia at the time of the Chinese revolution in 1911 and was allowed to form a special banner along the border to the north of Urga. He had acquired the rank of beise for his military services to the Bogd Khaan Government. The strategic position of his banner and Sum'yaa's well known anti-Chinese feelings made him an obvious ally of the party. This explains why Choibalsan in his conversation with Sum'yaa sought to tap his patriotic instincts and sense of fealty to the Bejeweled Throne.

This pattern in which the revolutionaries claimed legitimacy by referring to themselves as representatives of the Bogd Khaan and describing their objectives as the defense of religion and race and the restoration of the Khutukhtu's throne was to be repeated over and over again during the next few months. There was no attempt to appeal to class solidarity, and only infrequently did they allude to the democratic or social aims of the party. This was, after all, a war of independence first and foremost. Sum'yaa and his younger brother Demberel were persuaded by the exhortations of Choibalsan--Demberel so much that he immediately joined the MPP.

Danzan accompanied by S. Borisov, head of the Mongolian-Tibetan Department of the Far Eastern Secretariat, and Tseden-Ish arrived in Gegeetiin datsan about the first part of February. During the past three months Danzan had met several times with representatives of the Russian Communist Party, the Soviet government, and the Red Army before the Russians had finally agreed to furnish the Mongols with rifles, cartridges, and artillery shells (to be delivered via the border village of Naushki, a few miles west of Kyakhta) in preparation for an armed uprising in Mongolia.[208] According to this decision, probably taken at a plenary session of the Far Eastern Secretariat in Irkutsk on February 10 (six days after the fall of Urga to Ungern), the "struggle of the Mongolian people for liberation and independence" was to be aided with money, guns, and military instructors.[209]

Although the Moscow government had agreed in November 1920 to help the revolutionaries even by the very early part of February there was still no sign that the Soviets intended to translate this promise into material assistance, with the exception of some money and weapons which Danzan brought back with him from Moscow. Danzan, and presumably Rinchino, approached the Soviet authorities in Irkutsk several times but without receiving a firm reply. Indeed, all the evidence points to the fact that the Soviet government had changed its mind. Ungern had been driven back from Urga with heavy losses and the Chinese again appeared to be firmly in control. The Mongolian crisis had passed, the order for Soviet troops to cross the Mongolian border was countermanded, and aid to the Mongolian revolutionaries was suspended.

This state of affairs could not last for long. Soviet hopes for Chinese diplomatic recognition faded with the departure of Chang Ssu-lin and the refusal of the Peking government to appoint a consul in Moscow or to accept Soviet representation in China. Moreover, on December 31 the Soviet government received a curt reply from the Peking government to its November notes regarding Russian troops in Mongolia, which made it very clear that the Chinese would not tolerate Soviet intervention in Mongolia under any circumstance.

But now the worst had happened. The Urga garrison had fallen to Ungern and Chinese troops were in flight, and the Peking government, unwilling to allow coordinated action with Soviet troops against Ungern, had proven itself incapable of dealing with the emergency by itself. Moscow would have to find an independent solution. On February 8 orders were issued by the Command Staff of the Fifth Red Army and the Eastern Siberian Military District for certain units, then engaged in repairing the Trans-Siberian Railroad, to reinforce the defenses of Troitskosavsk immediately.[210] Two days later the Far Eastern Secretariat of the Comintern in Irkutsk formally agreed to help the Mongols in their revolution.

# CHAPTER VIII

## VICTORY OF THE REVOLUTION, 1921

The presence of Sükhbaatar and his fellow revolutionaries at Gegeetiin datsan, venue of the planned party conference, suggests that the accent was on political organization rather than on military buildup, and that the Mongols believed the eventual reckoning would come later, at Urga, and then be settled by guns. Possibly in a rough sort of way they were following the Bolshevik model by stressing political organization and agitation in preparation for an armed seizure of power. But in one stroke Ungern had changed the entire situation. The center of the Chinese occupation was now Kyakhta, only a few miles away, and with the new promise of Soviet equipment prospects never looked brighter for ending the Chinese hold over Mongolia.

### The Revolution Begins

Preparations had to be made quickly. Danzan left for the Daichin Wang banner to the southeast of Kyakhta, probably in order to spread the message of national revolution. Choibalsan and Chagdarjav, disguised as lamas, went to Urga to contact the remaining members of the party and to assess the situation of the party organization in the capital. But, as they discovered, with so many members of the party including Bodoo now in Ungern's service, the party in Urga had virtually ceased to exist.

They met secretly with Bodoo and Dendev, who acquainted them with what had happened since they were last in Urga and in particular with the ferocity of Ungern's repressions. They urged Choibalsan to pass a warning on to Kyakhta that the Whites intended to conscript Mongols into their army and to continue the war against the Soviets. Bodoo for unexplained reasons did not accompany them back north. Instead, Choibalsan took Sükhbaatar's family out of the city, posing as attendants of the Erdene Shanzudba.

After learning of Urga's fall Sükhbaatar left Gegeetiin datsan with some others and returned to Troitskosavsk with the intention of setting the revolution in motion immediately. On February 16 there was a meeting of the party members in Kyakhta, attended by Sükhbaatar, Losol, Borisov, Tseden-Ish, Zhamtsarano, L. Demberel and perhaps others. The importance of this conference cannot be stressed too greatly, for it was both a milestone and turning point in the history of the revolution. Since the merger of the two underground groups in June 1920 the work of the party had moved at a very irregular tempo, with quick bursts of great energy followed by prolonged lulls of inactivity. Indeed, the minuscule size of the party and the poverty of its real accomplishments oblige us to use the word "revolution" in a very limited sense.

But the meeting of February 16 changed that. This conference in effect resolved on creating a national revolution out of a conspiracy of expatriates and their Buryat allies (it was a sign of the times that only two of the six persons recorded as having been present at the meeting were Khalkha Mongols). A formal resolution was passed to recruit a partisan army, to expel the Chinese, and to occupy the northern region. Because the nearby banners of Daichin Wang and Akhai Kung were occupied by White soldiers, it was noted that recruits had to be drawn from the Mongolian police at Kyakhta Maimaicheng (under the command of Puntsag and a certain Dar'jav), the banners of Erdene Wang and Sum'yaa Beise, and the frontier pickets east and west of Kyakhta. Sükhbaatar, the obvious choice, was appointed commander of a partisan army yet to be formed.[211]

On the following night Puntsag with fifteen of his men collected their clothes and horses and quietly departed for Troitskosavsk, where they rendevoused with Sükhbaatar. Two flags, yellow (Buddhist) and red, were made and inscribed with the words "Let us promote the power of the People's Party." And on February 19 this small detachment, which became the nucleus of the partisan army and the forerunner of the present national army of the

Mongolian People's Republic, left for the Khyaraan frontier picket to the east of Kyakhta.

At this same time Sükhbaatar, using as his base in Kyakhta the home of the Buryat Bimbaev (a well known translator and compiler of a Russian-Mongolian dictionary), was travelling daily to the Erdene Wang banner and the frontier pickets east of Kyakhta recruiting partisans, despite Makstenek's earlier injunction to avoid the region adjoining the Far Eastern Republic. He posed as a representative of both the Bogd Khaan and the People's Party, the formation of which, Sükhbaatar carefully explained, the Khutukhtu himself had approved, and announced that the task immediately before the Mongols was the expulsion of the Chinese from Kyakhta.

Sükhbaatar made important converts in the chief of the Khyaraan frontier picket Damdinsüren, a former officer of the Erdene Wang banner Belegsaikhan Kung (another of the non-hereditary nobles), and an Inner Mongolian from the Gorlos banner who had fought with Togtokh in Inner Mongolia the lama Khasbaatar.

No sooner had Puntsag's unit, numbering around twenty men, left Kyakhta, than skirmishes began with Chinese patrols perhaps three times its size. The fighting, centering primarily in the Khyaraan area, continued for less than a week and sometime between February 23 and 25 the partisans were pushed across the border of the FER by a larger Chinese force. To the consternation of the Mongols they were arrested by a Russian border patrol, disarmed, and charged with illegally crossing the frontier. Puntsag and his men were badly shaken and word was sent immediately to Sükhbaatar. Soon, two letters arrived, one from Sükhbaatar ordering Puntsag and his troops to pass through Russian territory to a place called Altan at the confluence of the Selenge and Orkhon rivers, and the other to the Russian commander instructing him to return the guns and horses of the Mongols.[212]

Sükhbaatar had probably decided to transfer them to Altan because Soviet arms were expected there, and because the authorities of the FER were sensitive to the anti-Chinese activities of the MPP immediately across its border and fearful of the possible complications they could create in relations with China and Japan. At roughly the same time, Sükhbaatar ordered Vasil'ev to leave for the Sum'yaa Beise banner, where sixty-five partisan recruits had been assembled by Sum'yaa, and then to move to Altan.

## The Kyakhta Conference

The mood of the Mongolian revolutionaries in Kyakhta was optimistic. Although caught off-balance by Ungern's occupation of Urga and the subsequent flight of Chinese northward, the new pledge of Soviet aid was a rejuvenating tonic and badly needed incentive to a more effective organization of the party. Of first importance was the formation of a partisan force to clear the Kyakhta region of the remaining Chinese troops now concentrated there. Secondly, the party, hitherto a comparatively amorphous organization totally ill-adapted to the needs of national revolution, needed better structuring and clearer ideological definition. A conference in Kyakhta in early March, celebrated in 1924 as the first congress of the Mongolian People's Revolutionary Party, was to address itself to both questions.

After Sükhbaatar returned to Troitskosavsk in mid-February from Gegeetiin datsan, there had been a series of consultations with Danzan, Belegsaikhan, Zhamtsarano, the Buryat G.I. Danchinov (who worked in the Far Eastern Secretariat), and some others over the implications of Ungern's occupation of Urga. It was concluded that the original plan to build a strong base in the northern region, from which representatives would be invited to a party conference later in the spring, had to be scrapped in favor of an immediate assembly attended by whoever was on hand. The conference met secretly from March 1-3.[213] Eighteen persons, including the Comintern representative S.S. Borisov and members of the MPP living in Troitskosavsk, as well as recent recruits to the partisan army (generously referred to in the stenographic reports as "representatives of the people's army and various banners") were present at its first session.

Danzan, who was elected to chair the sessions of March 1 and 2, opened the meeting by presenting an agenda of topics to be considered by the assembly during the next three days: how the party was to deal with the current situation, the formation of a staff command headquarters, and the problem of acquainting the masses with the party's philosophy. Danzan then reported on the results of the MPP delegation to Soviet Russia, after which he introduced the first item of the agenda for general discussion. This subject apparently dominated the meeting for the entire day and the assembly did not break up until 11:00 that night.

The sources are very uninformative regarding the day's meeting. We are told only that Danzan endorsed the following objectives of the Mongolian revolution: eliminating disorder in the country, defending the Yellow Faith, and securing Mongolia's independence. He moved that the conference recognize Soviet Russia as the only reliable ally of the Mongolian revolution.

The second mission, attended by twenty-six persons, convened on the afternoon of March 2. Danzan's earlier motion was approved by the delegates. The conference also resolved to organize an army command staff of five persons: Sükhbaatar (chief of staff), Belegsaikhan and Danzan (secretaries), and two Russians nominated by the Red Army. Concerning the final item on the agenda, the assembly agreed to appoint Danzan and Sükhbaatar to supervise the work of acquainting the Mongolian population with the party's credo and recruiting new members into the MPP.

The final session, which opened at 12:00 on the afternoon of March 3, elected Sükhbaatar as its chairman and Zhamtsarano as the deputy chairman. The meeting began with a speech from Danzan warning that as the danger from the Chinese receded, there was a new threat emerging from the White Guards and the Mongolian princes who had allied with them:

> Now, our Mongolian People's Revolutionary Party (sic) is presented with a two-fold objective: the complete liquidation of Chinese rule, the complete separation of Mongolia from the White Russians, and the establishment of a democratic government which unites the people. (This will be

> accomplished) by relying on Soviet Russia. I call upon this assembly to issue a decision aimed at granting national freedom to the masses of Mongolia and establishing a people's government.

Following Danzan's address the assembly unanimously approved a motion that a telegram be sent to the Executive Committee of the Comintern "in order to strengthen friendship." The assembly then "unanimously" approved a document composed by Ts. Zhamtsarano and called the "Proclamation of the Mongolian People's Party to the People of Outer Mongolia."[214] This is a rather curious document, which on careful examination reveals a great deal about the party and its objectives. The "Proclamation" was in fact divided into two parts, an introduction and the text itself, and the difference in tone and content between the two is remarkable.

The first part of the introduction was an orthodox Marxist-Leninist diagnosis of the World War and an exegesis of Communist philosophy. It bristled with neologisms, such as "proletariat" (proletari ard), "capitalism" (kapitalyn ajil), "money-monopoly" (möngö zoosyg yamagt erkhlekh) and other expressions and concepts surely incomprehensible to most of the assembly. The second part treated of the situation in Mongolia and Tibet and called not only for a war of national liberation but of social and political emancipation.

The text of the "Proclamation," by contrast, was a comparatively restrained document filled with the traditional formulae regularly met in the bureaucratic language of the Mongols. It contained no surprises, no unfamiliar precepts or revolutionary appeals.

> Because this is the time when the various tribes and nations of the world are all taking the right to promote their respective race and system, following the will of Heaven and in accordance with the seasons the arats of the many banners and shav' throughout our country are in agreement and have decided sincerely and

> resolutely to take possession of their own land and rivers and (to end) suffering and bring happiness to the people. We are united by an unshakable faith to work without concern for our own lives and property, to open the great road of progress, to restore the government that was destroyed, to reconnect what was cut, and to reassemble what was destroyed. We have organized the Mongolian People's Party and proclaim to the people of our Mongolian race the principles of our party.

But perhaps the carefully worded party manifesto, entitled the "Ten Principles," which was appended to the "Proclamation," is even more interesting for it was the clearest statement yet of the party's philosophy and aims. Article two was the most pertinent in this respect: "Therefore, the aim of the Mongolian People's Party is to unite all the Mongolian peoples (Ündesten) in the future and form a state. At the present time, we aspire to free (ourselves) from the reactionary rule of China and to restore the autonomous Outer Mongolian state which has just been destroyed."

But what the "Ten Principles" left unsaid was how the party contemplated accomplishing its aim and what role it envisaged for the Khutukhtu and hereditary princes. Nevertheless, the careful reader was left in no doubt that this party represented a serious threat to the old ways. It was obvious that the MPP intended to assume power once the Chinese and Ungernists had been expelled and that its philosophy of government was derived from unfamiliar and iconoclastic principles which challenged the old order:

> Our People's Party will examine what will become of such questions as external and internal government (policy), religious beliefs, long established Mongolian customs and way of life, the present world situation, and the future. We will resolve them in conformity with the long-term well-being and progress of the Mongolian

> nation. However, if we consider it appropriate to stop those things which are not beneficial to the masses, which are harmful or not in accordance with the current times, or which are dying or already backward, then we will if possible alleviate them; otherwise we will not refrain from liquidating them by (using) harsh measures.[215]

After the conference had approved the "Proclamation" Makstenek, representing the Commissariat of Foreign Affairs, greeted the assembly on behalf of his government and promised that the Soviet state would provide "uninterrupted assistance to deliver the (Mongolian) people from foreign and domestic reactionaries." Sükhbaatar, as chairman of the assembly, thanked Makstenek for this pledge of Soviet aid and declared: "I am fully confident that with the moral and material support and assistance of the Soviet Russian government, the Mongolian People's Party can be victorious over the foreign and domestic enemies, and that the Mongolian masses will in the near future enter the road of progress and join the brotherhood (evtei ger bül) of labor." Before the conference ended, a central committee of four persons was elected: Danzan (chairman), Losol and Dambadorj (members), and one placed reserved for a representative of the Comintern.

The "Proclamation" and its "Ten Principles" have been the subject of some controversy among Communist writers almost from the moment they were written. In its first issue the organ of the Far Eastern Secretariat Narody dal'nego vostoka criticized the "Proclamation" for being "suffused to a considerable degree with nationalism and vague notions of human wealth."[216] Nationalism referred, of course, to the preeminence given to the struggle for independence and the inclusion of a pan-Mongolian statement (a regular claim in MPP programs until 1925). Kallinikov, a well known Soviet commentator on Mongolian affairs during the 1920s, described the "Principles" as "distingushed by great moderation and only slightly touching upon questions of restructuring the internal (social) relations."[217]

But "revolutionariness" depends largely on the

norms you accept, and Leninist principles, which were intended for application chiefly in Europe, were not pertinent to Mongolia. The accent on national identity may have troubled Communist writers, but Marxist internationalism was also wholly irrelevant to the Mongolian situation. Our touchstone must not be the politics of Europe or Russia, but rather the degree to which the Mongolian revolutionaries were challenging the existing social and political system of their own country.

One must also remember that, in its public declarations, the extremist objectives of the party were either camouflaged or suppressed altogether. Hence, while the relatively innocuous text of the "Proclamation" was immediately printed and distributed in several thousand copies, it was not until later in the year after these revolutionaries had occupied Urga that its introduction was published.[218] According to one source, there was even an argument at the conference over whether the party should call itself a "revolutionary party" (boshgyg khalakh nam). The assembly decided against it for "tactical" reasons.[219]

One part of the "Ten Principles" which has attracted some scholarly attention is article three, which states that the Mongols would not refuse to participate in a federated China made up of several autonomous regions. It is unlikely, however, that this concession to Chinese suzerainty was the idea of the Mongols. More likely, it originated with the Russians, who probably advised the Mongols that the Soviet government would not support total Mongolian independence. It is instructive that the tone of this article is grudging, even truculent, and probably was a formula worked out with a great deal of difficulty.[220]

The party conference in March was a major development in the history of the party. Its delegates, many of whom probably had not heard of the party one month before, now claimed the right to govern Mongolia in its name. The formation of a central committee and a general staff were major institutional refinements, which not only made good sense administratively but may have contributed to a general feeling that these Mongols were now "serious" revolutionaries. There is no evidence that the conference was manipulated by Moscow, although Borisov, Makstenek, and Danchinov were certainly helpful in its organization. The stenographic reports, incomplete as they are, leave one with the impression that it was the Mongols themselves who guided the sessions and that problems were debated uninhibitedly.

Ten days after the conference the Central Committee called a general meeting in Troitskosavsk presided over by Dambadorj in the absence of Danzan and attended by nineteen members of the party. This meeting resolved to form a provisional government of seven men under the chairmanship of Chagdarjav; also included were Sükhbaatar, Sum'yaa Beise, Belegsaikhan, Bodoo (who had apparently just returned from Urga), Choibalsan, and a representative from Uryankhai. In the public announcement of this decision published in the party newspaper in April, it was declared that although the Bogd Khaan had been restored to the Bejeweled Throne, power resided with Ungern. Therefore, the people have taken up arms, the announcement claimed, to liberate Mongolia from the tyranny of the Chinese and White Russians. The aim of this government was not only to rid Mongolia of the foreigners but to "give necessary attention to promoting the power of the masses." Leaving no one in doubt about the democratic aims of the party, the newspaper declared that this provisional government was instructed to organize a congress of representatives of the people for the election of a regular government and the adoption of a national constitution.[221]

## Kyakhta Liberated

Immediately after the MPP conference the Mongols addressed themselves to their most pressing problem, the liberation of Kyakhta. The area around Kyakhta had been thrown into confusion since the arrival of Chinese refugees, and the local arats were being molested and occasionally killed by marauding bands of Chinese troops. In a resolution passed by the Central Committee on March 6 it was decided to occupy Kyakhta, although it was also noted that the number of partisans had to be increased through both voluntary recruitment and conscription, and that weapons and military instructors must be procured from Soviet Russia.

The problem of enlarging the size of the partisan army was in fact a serious one, and the party quickly discovered that voluntary recruitment was insufficient. The living conditions of the partisans at Altan, already arduous, were aggravated by the winter cold and serious shortages of tents and food. This necessitated frequent trips to Troitskosavsk, where supplies could be purchased, and requisitions from the local arats, whose attitude toward this has not been recorded. Although the official Mongolian histories relate that the arats responded enthusiastically to the appeal of the MPP to enlist in the partisan army, the reminiscences of the partisans themselves are rather more ambivalent. There were those who were eager to join the battle against the Chinese; but equally there were others who refused or fled, or those who enlisted under duress. One should not infer from this, however, that the Mongols were either reconciled to Chinese occupation or suspicious of the party. In a great many cases parents and wives were the ones who put up the strongest resistance to the party's recruitment campaign.

By the time of the march on Kyakhta, the partisan force numbered about four hundred men drawn from the frontier pickets east of Kyakhta and the Erdene Wang and Sum'yaa Beise banners. They were organized into four regiments under the command of Puntsag, Khasbaatar, and Sum'yaa Beise (there was also a machine-gun unit commanded by Ch. Damdinsüren).

In March the Soviets began to contribute more seriously to the revolution by supplying the Mongols with weapons and military advisers (the total number of whom probably never exceeded twenty before May), who helped in preparing the Mongols for their attack on Kyakhta. D.I. Kosich, for example, a member of the Military Revolutionary Council of the Fifth Red Army, advised Sükhbaatar on a strategy of taking Kyakhta from the Chinese. And the partisans were instructed briefly but intensively by Russian advisers in the throwing of grenades and in artillery and machine-gunnery.

Nor was the political education of the partisans

ignored. The Far Eastern Secretariat sent some Russians form the political department of the Fifth Red Army to Altan, where they trained Choibalsan and Dambadorj--both of whom were fluent in Russian as a result of several years of study in Siberia--as "political commissars." The two Mongols are reported to have worked earnestly to indoctrinate the partisans in the objectives of the revolution.[222] A staff command of the partisan army, officially named the Partisan Army of the People's Party, was formed about March 13. The Russian Lyatte, assisted by Baraid and Litvintsov, was appointed chief of staff (included in the Staff Command were Commander-in-chief Sükhbaatar, Deputy Commander-in-chief Sum'yaa Beise, and Belegsaikhan and Tseden-Ish).[223]

At about the same time a supply of weapons (rifles, grenades, ammunition, and swords) had secretly reached Altan along a disused commercial tract through the frontier village of Naushki. Although the Soviets were to send more arms later, the total amount of material aid received from the Russians during the entire course of the revolution was negligible, never enough even to outfit a force which by July numbered no more than seven hundred men. The Mongolian partisans were forced to find their guns elsewhere, mainly from Chinese troops whom they captured or killed.

On March 15 the Central Committee and Staff Command met to work out a detailed plan for the capture of Kyakhta. The conference was of one mind on the need to expel the Chinese but differed regarding tactics. Danzan, Chairman of the Central Committee, was apprehensive of taking Kyakhta by force in view of the superior number of Chinese troops and suggested instead that the Chinese be removed through negotiation.

Danzan has been criticized by contemporary Communist historians for advancing a "policy of capitulation." There were in fact sound reasons for hesitating to take on the Chinese. There were between two thousand and twenty-five hundred Chinese troops in the area, outnumbering the Mongols by at least five or six times.[224] The Mongolian soldiers, moreover, were ill-equipped and ill-trained. The wisdom of Danzan's doubts was confirmed during the fighting itself, when the Mongols were compelled to retreat after exhausting their ammunition. Had it not been for timely assistance from the Russians, the Partisan Army would have been forced to lift its siege altogether. Although some historians have written that Danzan's proposal was rejected by the Central Committee, the fact that an unsuccessful attempt was made on March 15 to persuade the Chinese commander to surrender peacefully suggests that his proposal was accepted, either wholly or in part.

On the night of March 17 Sükhbaatar led his partisans toward Kyakhta. The heavy frost and a snowstorm made this short journey a difficult one, but by dawn Mongolian troops were in position and launched their attack from the northwest on Soviet territory. Rumors had reached the Chinese in the town that a Mongolian army, five thousand-strong under the command of White officers, was approaching from the south. Ch'u Ch'i-hsiang, therefore, set up a forward line of defense outside the town leaving only a token force in the garrison. The Mongols, attacking unexpectedly from the rear, were able to drive forward quickly, but the hurried return of Ch'u's reinforcements now put the partisans under pressure. The Mongols eventually ran out of ammunition and withdrew. Zhamtsarano in Troitskosavsk quickly obtained a cartload of ammunition and a cannon from the FER, which by the end of the day was set up on the heights overlooking the town. The tide of battle soon turned in favor of the Mongols and by nightfall Kyakhta was theirs.[225]

The battle, bravely and hard fought by both sides, ended in victory for the Mongols, who lost only seven men. Their victory was considerably aided by the appalling conditions inside the Chinese garrison, however. The troops of Ch'u Ch'i-hsiang were poorly clothed, short of ammunition, and by now totally demoralized (Ch'en had reported to Peking that the troops who escaped from Urga to Kyakhta had not shown the slightest will to fight). Kyakhta Maimaicheng was in a chaotic state. Just as in Urga the Chinese soldiers, who had suffered so terribly during the last two months, in a frenzy killed several dozen Russians and Mongols in the town.[226] The plundering of the town and its inhabitants, begun by Chinese soldiers, was continued by some of the Mongolian partisans after Kyakhta was taken. It was only through draconian measures taken by Sükhbaatar that the partisans were brought under discipline. But this was not the end of the town's sufferings. Kyakhta Maimaicheng soon caught on fire and burned to the ground. Only a few buildings remained standing after the blaze was extinguished.

Reports of the fate of the Chinese troops who fled Kyakhta are vague and contradictory. Establishing their numbers is an additional problem, as not only troops but merchants and other private citizens escaped as well. While the details are not known, the general picture of the flight is fairly clear. Many Chinese fled south along the Kyakhta-Urga tract pursued by Mongolian partisans who were under orders to destroy them. The chase was abandoned on approaching Urga but taken up again by Ungern. One group was caught by Ungernists at a place called Ulaan khad, around thirty miles west of Urga, where it was almost totally wiped out. Those who survived were reformed as a cavalry regiment in Ungern's army. Other groups of Chinese fled toward Kukuhot or Kalgan also pursued by Ungern's units.[227]

There is no way of knowing how many escaped or how many died. Most of the refugees from Kyakhta, numbering perhaps six thousand--including Ch'en I, Li Yuan, Ch'u Ch'i-hsiang, and other Chinese civil and military officials--fled to the Far Eastern Republic, where they were fed and housed and then returned to China.[228] Ch'en I, like San-to, became a casualty of his Mongolian service. He was blamed for the defeats at Urga and Kyakhta and deprived of his office.

March 18, the day of Kyakhta's fall, has been established in Communist historiography as the beginning of the "anti-imperialist and anti-feudal revolution" and the birthday of the Mongolian People's Army. It was also the end of an era reaching back to the seventeenth century and the threshold of another when the Mongols found a new patron to guide them into the twentieth century. The old model was Ch'ing, the new model was Soviet. China was never again to enjoy the influence it had in the past. For the Mongols, the taking of

Kyakhta was a psychological, military, and political triumph. No longer were they an impotent band of political malcontents hidden away in a frontier village of Siberia, but were now a revolutionary army which had indisputably proven its mettle in open combat with the enemy.

The Mongolian Provisional Government immediately moved to Kyakhta Maimaicheng. The city had been devastated by fire, and perhaps to salute its new future, both physically and symbolically, it was renamed Altan bulag ("Golden Spring"). Until now this government of six men had operated more like a committee in which the responsibilities of its members were imprecisely defined. This was changed on March 24, when three ministries (housed in yurts) were organized: Internal Affairs under Belegsaikhan, Army under Sükhbaatar, and Finance under Chagdarjav (who continued to serve as chairman of the government).

The new government now controlled an area stretching about sixty miles from east to west and thirty miles to the south. A "Proclamation from the Mongolian People's Provisional Government to the People, Lamas, and Princes of All Mongolia" was issued announcing the formation of a government, the expulsion of the Chinese, and the transference of supreme power into the hands of the Mongolian people. The crimes of the White Russians were catalogued and a promise was made to drive them out. But this was not all. "The Outer Mongolian People's Government, in accordance with the (proper) time, will summon the representatives of the masses of all Mongolia and convene a congress. This mighty affair of our race will be discussed and an independent permanent government of the Mongolian people will be elected. Let us prepare for this."[229]

## The People's Party Aims for Domination

The MPP conference in Kyakhta, the establishment of a people's government, and the liberation of Kyakhta renewed the confidence of the Mongolian revolutionaries in their movement and the inevitability of its victory. This change of attitude was reflected very plainly in their correspondence with the Bogd Khaan Government in Urga during the latter part of March and April. No longer were the revolutionaries deferential or solicitous. Their letters manifested a new assertiveness, even impudence, which was not missed by the Khutukhtu's court. The party's boldness can be seen also in the growing willingness--as much through omission as admission--to declare publicly the revolutionary program of the party. If in February the revolutionaries had posed as champions of the Khutukhtu and the old regime, by the latter part of March there were fewer references to the Lamaist patriarch and more public pledges to liberate the people from the tyranny of their feudal princes. The tone of these letters and declarations had become so forthright and acerbic that both the Urga establishment and the border population must have been very clear about the social aims of the party. The lamas and nobles of Urga were accused of failing to provide proper leadership for the people and, by inference, of being responsible for the present difficulties of the country.

Although the Khutukhtu's court did not deign to answer these communications, a letter was received, signed simply by the "comrades in Urga"and written possibly--although by no means certainly--under compulsion, which was clearly intended as the court's reply. It pointed out that the original objectives of the party had been to implement the terms of the Tripartite Treaty, to elevate the Bogd Lama as sovereign of Mongolia, to restore the autonomous government, and in particular to venerate the Yellow Faith and preserve the traditional ways. Although these ends had now been achieved, party members in Kyakhta were espousing objectives "completely different from (those which) we first discussed." The letter warned that international wars were invariably the result of attempts to alter the traditional ways and concluded with an ultimatum that they cease propounding their heterodox ideas and return to Urga.

On April 30 the party replied with what was their clearest analysis yet of the social situation in Mongolia. It was written in the stiff bureaucratic manner of the Ch'ing period but with a message so withering as to overpower its polished style. Autonomy was a fiction, the letter stated, and it was Ungern, not the Bogd Khaan, who governed in Urga. The "comrades" were chided for speciously arguing that chaos resulted from attempts to change the old ways. On the contrary, "doing away with the old and making use of the new has become the way of the world." The people perfectly understood that it was the "improprieties and filthiness" of the avaricious princes and lamas which were to blame for the present tribulations of Mongolia. Their organization was called a people's party to signal the resolution of its members to work for the common good. The people knew very well which government, Kyakhta or Urga, worked on their behalf.[230]

Further communication ended. Indeed, further communication was purposeless. The contest was now to focus on capturing the hearts and minds of the people, in particular those living in the northern part of Mongolia. From March to May there was a spirited campaign of propaganda conducted by both sides. The party saturated the zone with leaflets summoning the people to take up arms and explaining the objectives of the party, the reason for allying with Soviet Russia, and why war with the White Guards was unavoidable. Although the struggle against the Whites continued to be emphasized, every reader knew that Mongolia could expect a new order once peace was restored.

The Bogd Khaan government was not idle either. It barraged the banners to the north of Urga with warnings that the ideology of the revolutionaries would eventually destroy the state and tear away at the very foundations of the Yellow Faith, not to mention the suffering which it would inevitably inflict. In mid-April, for example, a letter was sent to the troops in the eastern border complaining about the "Red Mongols:" "The Bolsheviks have succeeded in convincing a few Mongols in the Tüsheet Khan aimag...It is necessary to be wary of them. Truly, they are persons with an infection worse than the plague."[231] Apprehensive of the effectiveness of the party's revolutionary propaganda in the north, the court even staged an exorcistic ceremony in Urga, attended by the Jebtsundamba Khutukhtu himself, which tried to cast a spell over the MPP.

The People's Party began moving to the west in

its search for allies and to assert the authority of the provisional government over a larger part of Mongolia. In the latter half of March a letter was sent to the league assemblies of the two Dörvöd aimags announcing the impending arrival of representatives "to establish order and protect the Mongolian population of the northwest border region." The league officers were directed to abolish torture, to attend carefully to the needs of the people, to familiarize themselves with the past declarations of the the party, and to mobilize a large number of lamas and arats for military service against the Whites. In the first part of April Khasbaatar and Dambadorj were appointed commissioners to western Mongolia with instructions to form an army against the Whites. Siren Shoizhelov (Natsov), a Buryat who represented the Far Eastern Secretariat, accompanied them as an adviser.

At the same time Chagdarjav was sent to the Darkhat people of Khövsgöl and to Uryankhai with instructions to acquaint the population of these areas with the aims of the party and to form partisan units. He was accompanied by the Buryat I.V. Chenkirov, who like Natsov was also an agent of the Far Eastern Secretariat. In mid-April shortly before his departure Chagdarjav had been "freed" from his duties as head of the government and minister of finance. Bodoo was appointed chairman of the government while continuing to supervise foreign affairs, and Losol was appointed minister of finance.

We are not told by the sources why Chagdarjav, head of the revolutionary government, should have been sent on such an obscure and in many respects irrelevant assignment. But the fact that his leadership could be so casually dispensed with surely is testimony to his unimportance in the party. Conversely, it marks the reemergence of Bodoo as a leader of the revolution.

March was a very active month for the Mongolian People's Party. The political and social targets of the revolution had been defined and announced in the party manifesto. A provisional government had been organized and, after the fall of the Kyakhta garrison, transferred to Mongolian territory. And party representatives were sent to various regions of the country to assume vice-regency powers on behalf of the party and government.

March was important too for the increasingly close and lively relations of the MPP with the Comintern. Although the Far Eastern Secretariat had regularly been in contact with the party through its unofficial representative S.S. Borisov, the Comintern never publicly recognized a relationship with the MPP and even privately the general tone of its interest and involvement was pitched quite low. On March 6, immediately after the party conference and in the flush of confidence in the party's future, the Central Committee and Command Staff of the Partisan Army drew up an appeal to the Far Eastern Secretariat requesting that it be admitted into the Comintern.

It was not until the end of March that the petition was approved, but the MPP was accepted only as an associate member with the right of deliberation (but not voting). The decision of the Comintern to accept the party on such a limited basis, denying it full membership, reflects to a great extent the skepticism, and even indifference, of its leadership toward the likelihood of authentic revolution in such a backward country.

Even before the qualified admission of the MPP into the Comintern, the counsel of Borisov must have been heard attentively, although the sources do not disclose the degree of his actual influence on party decisions. But a plenary session of the MPP from March 29 to 31, attended by representatives of the Far Eastern Secretariat, was to bring the party at least officially more tightly within the discipline of the Comintern. In addition to discussing the the immediate objectives of the revolution and the organizational and ideological aims of the MPP, this meeting resolved that the MPP would both in theory and in practice follow the advice and instructions of the Comintern. It appears that in practice, however, the influence of Comintern representatives was more limited than this resolution suggests. Not three weeks later, on April 19, these representatives were accused by the provisional government of exceeding their authority by interfering in the work of government departments over which they had no jurisdiction: "The differences of opinion between officials of our government and officials of the department of the Comintern have hindered the policy of the government and must be stopped immediately." The session demanded the recall of those Comintern agents who had been recently attached to the MPP.[232] Apparently Borisov was recalled and replaced by Rinchino.

The acceptance of the MPP into the Communist International, albeit on qualified terms, was more than simply a gesture. It was the first public recognition that there was a formal association between the party and Soviet Russia and must be regarded as a watershed in the development of Soviet policy toward Mongolia. Until March the Russians had been content to regard Mongolia as essentially a Chinese problem and were exceedingly reluctant to prejudice their relations with Peking by visibly supporting a nationalist faction whose avowed aim was to create an independent Mongolia. The delegates of the MPP to Soviet Russia in 1920 had in general been kept at arm's length and placed in the care of junior Soviet officials, most of whom were Buryats. But the decision to include the MPP in the Comintern was evidence of the new importance which the Soviet government attached to the MPP and of its irrevocable commitment to an independent Mongolia. This new turn in Soviet thinking was reflected in a communication from Moscow to Wellington Koo, Chinese Minister in London, in late May: "If China does not wish to abandon Mongolia, it should immediately contact this party and cooperate with it in opposing the Khutukhtu."[233] The Soviets were, in effect, telling China that it could no longer presume to act independently in Mongolia. Henceforth, Peking must work with the MPP, and with Soviet Russia.

But even as the Mongols, with help from the Comintern, were preparing for their party conference in Kyakhta, the Soviets were making a final bid to seek an independent solution to the Mongolian problem with the Chinese. Soon after arriving in Kyakhta, Ch'en I was approached by Makstenek, acting on behalf of the Soviet government, with a suggestion that Soviet troops be permitted to operate in Mongolia up to a distance of twenty miles south of the border in order to observe Ungern's movements. Makstenek promised to withdraw these troops as soon as the danger from Ungern had passed.

Ch'en consulted with Li Yuan and other senior Chinese officials in the town. It was their opinion that, in view of the generous Soviet aid both to Chinese officials and people who had fled Urga, they should agree to a "mutual-protection zone" of eight miles in which Russian troops would be permitted free movement (Soviet archives contain a letter from Chinese authorities in Kyakhta dated February 18 or 19 "requesting" the entry of Soviet troops into such a zone[234]). According to Ch'en I's account, the Kyakhta Deputy High Commission soon afterwards received another letter proposing that a joint Soviet-Chinese expedition be undertaken against the White Guards and that Peking allow the Soviet government to "take on the responsibility of assisting China in recovering Urga."[235]

It is possible that this second letter indicated a change of mind on the part of the Soviets. On the other hand, it is strange that the Russians would have contented themselves with an eight-mile zone when it had consistently been Moscow's aim to destroy every White Guard band on the frontier. A proposal for a joint Russo-Chinese expedition against White Guards in Mongolia had been made earlier, in November 1920, and similar proposals were made to Peking for joint action in Sinkiang and Manchuria. Perhaps Makstenek misunderstood his instructions, or perhaps he had not explained them clearly enough to Ch'en I, requiring a second clarification.

In any case, Ch'en wired his government explaining the situation and the "new" Soviet proposal. On March 3 the Cabinet Secretariat replied: permission was given for a mutual-protection zone of eight miles but the Peking government refused to countenance the use of Soviet troops to recover Urga, as it would be "injurious to the national entity and to Chinese sovereignty."[236]

## Soviet Troops in Mongolia

Between March and May there were further refinements in the organizational structure of the government, party, and army with the addition of new departments, many of which had Russian advisers. In May a Political Education Department was formed under Danzan in the Ministry of Army (with a Russian adviser). In April a commission was created to formulate plans for the organization of cooperatives. In April or May the Mongolian Telegraph Agency (MONTA), in obvious imitation of the Russian Telegraph Agency (ROSTA) was founded. And in April a Revolutionary Military Council, again modeled on the Soviet Revolutionary Military Council, was formed and included Sükhbaatar, Choibalsan (now deputy commander-in-chief), and the Russian P.I. Litvintsov.

Plans for the democratization of Mongolia and the further development of the machinery of the party and provisional government had to be deferred, however, until the more pressing question of who ruled Mongolia was answered. Ungern had never concealed the fact that his ultimate target was Soviet Siberia, and his energetic campaign to mobilize the Mongols and requisition materiel for this expedition was well known in Kyakhta. On March 16, two days before Kyakhta was besieged, the MPP sent an appeal to the Soviet government "urgently requesting (it) to assist immediately the People's Provisional Government of Mongolia with measures aimed at ending the outrages and plunderings of the Russian White Guards and cleansing all Mongolian territory of the White Guard bands..."[237] The wording of the appeal was rather vague and the form of assistance required was not specified. Curiously, this appeal was not published in Soviet newspapers as was the practice, nor is there any record of a Soviet response.

According to reconnaisance information of the Staff Headquarters of the Fifth Red Army in May, Ungern's total force numbered between ten and eleven thousand men, although only about half was under his immediate command. The rest were distributed among different White Guard units stretching from the Onon and Kerulen rivers in the east to Uryankhai in the west. Even this figure misrepresents the real strength of the White army in Mongolia. Ungern's brutal discipline and his practice of compulsory conscription meant that an intolerably large proportion of these troops was inadequately trained and highly unreliable.

The Soviets, whose strategy was to concentrate all their forces first against Ungern and then against other White units operating in western Mongolia, had positioned a Soviet-FER-Mongolian army numbering about ten thousand men in the vicinity of Kyakhta. The 35th Division of the Fifth Red Army (seventy-five hundred men) formed the backbone of this force. In addition, there were Russian partisan detachments, units of the People's Revolutionary Army of the FER, and around seven hundred Mongolian partisans, whose numbers had been doubled as a result of an order conscripting all Mongolian males (excluding lamas living permanently in monasteries) over the age of nineteen. There was also a Kalmuck International Brigade of eighteen men--during the following months two more groups were sent, bringing the total number to around one hundred--sent by Moscow to serve as instructors and officers in the Mongolian Partisan Army.

One must certainly wonder why Ungern was so foolhardy as to attack a force perhaps twice the size of his own--an expedition which, at least in retrospect, was doomed to failure. Soviet historians believe that the renewed White military activities in Manchuria and the Maritime Region at the very moment of Ungern's expedition north was no coincidence and is incontrovertible evidence that Ungern was working under Semenov's instructions.

According to Ungern's own testimony at his interrogation, however, he had at first hoped to draw the Red Army into Mongolia, probably reasoning that his popularity among the Mongols, his familiarity with the terrain and its suitability for cavalry warfare would give him the edge. But the expected invasion did not materialize and Ungern began to fear that the inactivity of his Russian and Mongolian troops in Urga, as well as their growing restiveness, would lead to the dissolution of his army. It was for these reasons, Ungern explained, that he ordered the attack.[238] The protest of Ungern, who undoubtedly knew that he would be executed and therefore had little reason to perjure himself, that he had acted alone seems of the two to be more creditable.

The Baron planned to launch a three-pronged assault against Soviet Siberia: the main force under his personal command would advance on Kyakhta and from there into the Transbaikal region; a second unit under Colonel Kazagrandi was to move through Modon khöl toward Irkutsk; and a third force, a detachment of Yenesei Cossacks commanded by Ataman Kazantsev, was to advance through Uryankhai in the direction of Minusinsk and Krasnoyarsk.

Military activities began during the last ten days of May and continued until June 13-14, although the decisive fighting did not occur until the last few days of this period. It developed, although this had not been foreseen, that Red Mongols fought mainly White Mongols, and Red Russians fought White Russians. The Mongolian partisans held Altan bulag, against which Ungern sent his "Chahars" (that is, Inner Mongolians) under Bayar Kung, a sometime confederate of Togtokh, the well-known Inner Mongolian "bandit." The bulk of Ungern's troops by-passed Altan bulag and attacked Kyakhta from the southeast. His army was routed, however, and forced to retreat back into Mongolia.

Less than two weeks after this defeat a joint Russian-Mongolian expeditionary army crossed the border to destroy the White Guards. Western and Chinese writers have described this expedition as an "invasion" designed first and foremost to install a puppet Mongolian regime in Urga. The American historian G.G.S. Murphy has argued this perhaps the most forcefully: "The most striking piece of evidence, however, for the belief that the threat of Ungern-Sternberg's troops was not the real reason for Red intervention in Mongolia was that they had in fact already been destroyed before the decision to invade Outer Mongolia was taken."[239]

When was the decision taken to send troops into Mongolia and what were the genuine aims of that expedition? Even while military activities around Kyakhta were only beginning a meeting of representatives of the Far Eastern Republic, the Revolutionary Military Council of the Fifth Red Army, and the Far Eastern Bureau of the Central Committee of the Russian Communist Party was held on June 1. This conference:

> ...formulated the political tasks connected with rendering military aid to the Mongolian people. It was stressed that the Mongolian operation was more important as a means of opposing Chang Tso-lin and supporting the revolutionary strata of China and Mongolia. The goal of the operation is the complete defeat of Ungern and his expulsion from Urga and the border region, and the establishment of national Mongolian rule.[240]

This resolution, therefore, established the three essential objectives of the expedition: first, to eliminate Ungern and his entire army; secondly, to set up a Mongolian revolutionary government; and thirdly, to block an invasion of Mongolia by Chang Tso-lin.

The formal decision to dispatch an expeditionary army was taken on June 14, when S.S. Kamenev, commander of the armed forces of Soviet Russia, directed the Revolutionary Military Council of the Fifth Red Army to pursue Ungern into Mongolia. A session of the Politburo two days later, chaired by Lenin, confirmed the decision. Soviet troops were directed to "support unconditionally the program of self-determination and national liberation of Mongolia ...(sic)"[241] On June 15 the Commissar of Foreign Affairs Chicherin, with more hypocrisy than candor, sent a declaration to the government of China announcing that Russian troops were being sent across the border of Mongolia to fight the common enemy of both the Russian and Chinese people "in order to defend the rights of China." Chicherin promised, moreover, that "Russian troops will evacuate Mongolia as soon as their task is completed."[242]

Russia, having just concluded a war with Poland and a campaign against Denikin, not to mention six destructive years of war with Germany revolution, and civil conflict, was simply too economically crippled to maintain a large army at Kyakhta for any length of time. Ungern's capture of Urga in February forced the Siberian Revolutionary Council to review its military preparedness. Recognizing that the cavalry of the Fifth Red Army and the army of the Far Eastern Republic were inadequate to deal with Ungern, the 35th Siberian Infantry Division, then working on the labor front, was reactivated and transferred to the Baikal area, and a large number of reservists was called up.[243] Had Ungern not attacked Russia but waited patiently in Urga, the Soviet government sooner or later would have been forced to take the initiative. Consequently, from the moment the decision to call up reserves was taken (probably in March-April), the logic of the situation required that the Soviets drive deeply into Mongolia to clear out the Ungernists once and for all. Since 1918 White Guards had been free to harass eastern Siberia from their sanctuaries in either Manchuria or, to a much lesser extent, Mongolia. Ungern may have been defeated at Kyakhta in June, but in the natural course of things he could have reformed his army in preparation for another, perhaps more successful, offensive later. Nor could the possibility be excluded that all future anti-Soviet military operations might be launched from Mongolia now that the Chinese were increasingly interdicting Manchuria to the Whites. The chain of reasoning had reached its irreducible limit. Soviet troops, while still assembled, had to be used to obliterate Ungern's army before it had an opportunity to regroup.

The decision to send troops into Mongolia, rather than the result of a single meeting of Soviet authorities in Moscow, evolved gradually out of the changing military and political situation in Mongolia and Russia after February 1920. The immediate and primary objective of this expedition was the total destruction of Ungern. The decision to help plant a nationalist pro-Soviet government in Urga was a development of the same reasoning. As far as the Soviets were concerned, it was not enough simply to destroy the Whites and then retire back into Russia. Mongolia had to be made as secure as possible from occupation by potentially hostile organizations in the future. The various warlord governments in Peking and the Bogd Khaan Government in Urga had in this respect proven their incapacity or unreliability.

During the lull of several days following Ungern's defeat, Soviet forces on the border were reassembled and supplies gathered for the impending assault. There were meetings between Soviet and Mongolian authorities to discuss strategy, logistics, and a number of related questions. On June 28 the main expeditionary army under the overall command of K.A. Neiman advanced across the frontier into Mongolia, although some Soviet units had crossed the border no later than June 8 in pursuit of retreating Ungernists. The expeditionary army, totalled around ten thousand men with cannon, armored cars and four airplanes, advanced on Urga, though the summer heat, absence of roads, and mountainous terrain retarded its progress.

On July 6, in spite of the pleas, threats, and incantations of the Khutukhtu's court, the first Russian and Mongolian troops entered the city, according to eyewitnesses to a joyous reception from the inhabitants. The Mongolian revolutionaries speedily went to work to take over the reins of power. On July 9 a letter was handed to the Bogd Khaan's court accusing the officials of the old government of deceiving the Bogd Khaan and the people and of committing acts injurious to the Yellow Faith. Now, it said, power had been placed in the hands of the people. "The disorder which reigns presently is as much due to the shortcomings of the leaders as to the fact that the existing laws and situation do not correspond any longer to the spirit of the times. Everything, therefore, except religion, will be subject to gradual change."[244] On July 10 the Central Committee of the MPP issued a resolution declaring the formation of a new government headed by Bodoo with the Jebtsundamba Khutukhtu as a limited monarch. On July 11, celebrated as independence day in the Mongolian People's Republic, the Khutukhtu was ceremoniously installed on the throne of Mongolia.

With Ungern's ignominious flight back into Mongolia, his army began to crumble. Well-known Mongolian leaders, such as Magsarjav, the Jalkhanz Khutukhtu, and others, hastily put as much room as they could between themselves and the General, and various White detachments began to act with a degree of independence unthinkable before May. All this only helped to excite Ungern to greater paranoia and desperation. In late July he made a final attempt to restore the situation. Apparently acting on information that a Japanese army was marching into the Far Eastern Republic he led his troops again across the border toward Verkhneudinsk, but was blocked by the Soviets and forced to retreat once more. The career of von Ungern-Sternberg, god of war and reincarnation of the dauntless Geser Khan, ended shabbily. He was seized by his own Mongolian troops, trussed up, and left on the steppe. Ungern later in the year was brought to trial and executed by the Soviet government.

As the pace of fighting in the Tüsheet Khan aimag was slowing, the war shifted to western Mongolia, where White units under Kaigorodov, Kazantsev, and Bakich, perhaps around four thousand in all, were operating. Khasbaatar, Dambadorj, and Natsov had formed a Western Mongolian Regional People's Revolutionary Government in July under the Dörvöd Dalai Khan Tümendelgerjav--the formation of an independent administration was probably thought necessary because of the power of regional sentiments in the west--and armed units were organized under the command of Khasbaatar. In the meantime, Magsarjav had quietly decided to throw in his lot with Red forces. On July 21 he massacred the White Russians in Uliastai. By the end of the year the White armies in western Mongolia had been either destroyed or expelled.

Despite the Soviet pledge to remove its troops once Mongolia had been liberated from the White Guards, it was not until 1925 that an announcement was made declaring their complete withdrawal. On July 12, the day following the formation of a new government in Urga, the Mongols had appealed to Soviet Russia "not to remove units of the Soviet army from the borders of Mongolia until the moment of the final liquidation of the threat from the common enemy." Almost a month later, on August 10, the Soviet government formally replied agreeing to this.[245]

Although most contemporary observers believed, and many historians continue to believe, that the Russians maintained a large garrison in Mongolia from 1921 to 1925, the evidence indicates that there was no more than a handful of Soviet troops, mainly Kalmuck advisers.[246] We are informed by most

Western writers that the presence of these Soviet troops was required to protect the revolutionary government in Urga from the intrigues and insurrections of Mongolian malcontents and to impress the Soviet stamp deeply upon Mongolia. In fact, Soviet troops, or more precisely the impression of Soviet troops, remained in Mongolia in order to deter the Chinese from launching a military expedition to recover the country.

Ever since receiving news of Ungern's seizure of Urga the Peking government had shown the very same inertia, confusion, and incredible naivité that that characterized its behavior toward Mongolia in 1918 and 1919. Government ministries continued to correspond and investigate inconclusively, while all China waited for a warlord to deliver the frontier back to China. There was a debate within the government regarding the best way of tackling the Mongolian problem. All the ministries were agreed that nothing short of a military expedition would suffice, but some believed--and the President of China Hsu Shih-ch'ang was the most insistent on this point--that China was powerless by itself to defeat the Whites. Because the behavior of Soviet Russia, which after all was locked in a death struggle with the White Guards, toward China contrasted favorably with that of the Whites, it was felt that the Soviet proposal of a joint expedition made by Makstenek in February should be accepted. Other agencies, in particular the Foreign Ministry, made various objections to this, the most important of which was their profound conviction that the Soviets, once invited into Mongolia, would use this as a lever for other demands.[247]

As always, events moved too quickly for the ponderous machinery of the Chinese government to react. First Urga, then Kyakhta, and finally all Mongolia were lost. Chang Tso-lin, the warlord of Manchuria, had agreed to his appointment on May 30 as commander of a Mongolian expedition. The promise of the central government to donate three million dollars from the national treasury was undoubtedly helpful in persuading Chang to make this "patriotic sacrifice," as he called it. Although it has often been suggested that Chang never seriously entertained the idea of sending an expedition to Mongolia, a recent study shows, however, that he did intend to send an army of thirty thousand men to Urga but that the occupation of Urga by Red forces in July and new developments in the see-saw struggle for power between the northern warlords in China forced him to postpone, and eventually to abandon his plans.[248]

The appointment of Chang Tso-lin to recapture Urga emboldened the Chinese government to take a more intransigent position toward a Soviet proposal for a tripartite conference to discuss Mongolia's relationship with China. The Chinese argued, as they had always argued, that Mongolia was a part of China. Hence, the Peking government would not recognize the right of a Soviet army to cross the "Chinese" frontier, nor would it agree to allow Mongolia to become a subject for international negotiations. Yurin tried unsuccessfully to raise the question with the Chinese Foreign Ministry in late July-early August. The matter, the Chinese replied, was now in the hands of Chang Tso-lin.

The question of Mongolia continued to plague Sino-Soviet relations and helped to foul the climate of discussions between the Peking government and the Soviet and FER missions of Yurin, Paikes, and Joffe. It was only in 1924 that Karakhan was able to conclude a treaty with China according to which Soviet Russia recognized Outer Mongolia as an integral part of China and agreed to withdraw Russian troops. But the failure of the treaty to define Mongolia's relationship with China more precisely meant that Mongolia was in fact completely independent of China. The chasm separating the fiction of Mongolia's international status and its reality was bridged only in 1946, when the Nationalist government of China recognized the full sovereignty of the Mongolian People's Republic. Chiang Kai-shek was to withdraw this recognition a few years later.

# CONCLUSION

Did Mongolia, in its relationship with China and Russia (and to a lesser extent with Japan) during the decade from 1911 to 1921 find itself between the "hammer and the anvil?" This certainly has been the conclusion of Western writers, and even the Mongolian Minister of Internal Affairs Tserenchimed is alleged to have used this metaphor in conversation with Korostovetz. It is true, of course, that the geographical position of Outer Mongolia, its military and political vulnerability, did seriously reduce the scope of its activities in foreign affairs. But one must be warned against the temptations of settling for geopolitical solutions, despite their neatness and symmetry, to explain Mongolia's position in Asia. Equally, one must avoid simplifying, and thereby distorting, the political situation of the Mongols as a choice between being ruled by one of two equally undesirable masters. In practice, the Mongols had a great deal more room to maneuver in, and the alternatives were not so harsh, as this formula of a hammer and anvil seems to imply.

Seventeenth to nineteenth century Mongolian sources, written in a direct, chronicle-like fashion, are not especially helpful in clarifying the world view of the Mongols. To understand their political instincts, we must look to the pattern of their relationship with China and Russia as it has evolved since the seventeenth century. In general, their behavior reflected a tribal psychology of seeking fleeting and narrowly aimed military alliances, in return for which the Mongols were prepared, if necessary, to submit to their patron. But for the Mongols, submission--and this is the key element of the affair--was merely an expedient calculated to elicit a commitment of aid. It was never expected to result in a challenge to their internal sovereignty. For the Russians and the

Manchus, however, submission was more of a political than a military act. It was a solemn covenant, the cornerstone of the entire arrangement.

Although the evidence is admittedly thin on this point, it does seem clear that every collision of the Eastern Mongols with one of their neighbors in the last three centuries has in its essential features been a mirror image of each of the others. One of the Altyn Khans submitted to Russia in the 1630s out of fear of Ligden Khan. The Khalkhas submitted to China in 1691 (some to Russia) following an Oirat invasion. And some princes, including the Jebtsundamba Khutukhtu, proposed taking the oath of allegiance to the Tsar in the mid-eighteenth century at the time of the Chingunjav revolt. All were desperate bids for military assistance and there is no evidence that the Mongols understood the consequences of such pledges.

This logic certainly governed their thinking in 1911, when the Khalkhas saw no contradiction between accepting a Russian protectorate and proclaiming, and insisting on, their full independence and sovereignty. In 1919 the Mongols were prepared to "submit" once again to China, but only on terms that guaranteed their absolute sovereignty in internal affairs. And in 1920, after Hsu Shu-cheng had reminded the Mongols of the reality of Chinese rule, a few Khalkhas turned once more to Russia with an appeal for help (there was no suggestion of submission this time, perhaps because the Soviets had not demanded this as a precondition). Russia's contribution to the Mongolian revolution, it was surely believed, would be limited to military aid--the implementation of social reforms did not require foreign help.

Although Russians were included in the Mongolian revolutionary organization after March, they were employed primarily as military advisers, and in this sphere their influence must have been considerable. This should not trouble us too greatly, for the frontier peoples since the time of the Hsiung-nu have regularly imported the most advanced technology (in the largest sense of the word) of their neighbors, especially China, through prisoners and refugees.

The evidence strongly suggests, however, that the

overall impact of these Russians (excluding the Buryats) on the internal political decisions of the MPP must have been rather modest, although this may not have been for want of trying. In April 1921 the Mongolian provisional government demanded the recall of Comintern agents who had recently been attached to the MPP. A month earlier the government passed a resolution prohibiting all disagreements between officers of the Mongolian and Russian armies and directing them to work in a spirit of harmony and mutual assistance. And when Shumyatskii visited Urga in the fall of 1921, he repeatedly warned the Russian advisers that their responsibility was solely to instruct the Mongols, not to interfere in their internal affairs.[249] This suggests, on the assumption that there is no smoke without fire, that differences between the Russians and Mongols continued at least until the end of 1921, if not longer.

It should be added that the role of the Buryats and Kalmucks in the party, which was very important indeed almost from its inception to the late 1920s, cannot be indiscriminately lumped with "Russian imperialism." These men were, first and foremost, Mongols. The complaint of a Kalmuck commander who was sent to western Mongolia in 1921, that he was constantly referred to by the arats as a "Russian gentleman" and his exclamation "but I'm a Mongol," is a telling example of the intensity of their nationalism. A closer study of the activities of the Buryats and Kalmucks in Mongolia during the 1920s, I suspect, would probably show that they behaved more as Mongols than as Soviet agents.

With each new crisis in the unsettled period of the seventeenth and eighteenth centuries the Mongols' allegiance swung in a pendular movement from Russia to China and back again. In this respect, therefore, the analogy of the hammer and anvil--if by that we mean that the Mongols felt obliged to seek an accomodation with one of their two neighbors--is not altogether inaccurate. It would be well to remember, however, that except for relatively minor border clashes in the second half of the seventeenth century Mongolia never had an adversary relationship with Russia. Indeed, the Mongols regularly relied on the Russians for military assistance when they needed it.

It would also be well to remember that the motives for turning to Russia in 1911 and 1921, although not substantially different from earlier periods, were nevertheless much broader. On both occasions the aim was not simply to defend Mongolia but to change Mongolia, and Russia was sought because it had both the technology and financial resources to help in this transformation. It is doubtful that the Mongols wanted the Russians to direct this process--this is certainly one lesson of the Bogd Khaan years. If this analysis of Mongolian thinking is correct, it would indicate that the sovietization of Mongolia, which was most pronounced during the Stalinist era between 1928 and the mid-1950s, was carried out with considerably less than total unanimity within the Mongolian People's Revolutionary Party.

The question of whether the dispatch of Soviet troops into Mongolia in June 1921 was an expedition, or an invasion, has provoked a great deal of controversy. For most Western and all Chinese historians, the victory of the Mongolian revolution was in fact the successful conclusion of a long-standing Tsarist objective to bring Mongolia within the mantle of the Russian empire. But the historical sources are sufficiently obscure on this point to allow Communist historians to argue with equal conviction that Soviet Russia was moved only by the highest principles of international revolutionary solidarity. Both arguments, however, are weakened by rigid preconceptions of the nature of Soviet foreign policy, and a closer, more dispassionate study of the period tells a very different story.

Since the mid-nineteenth century the Russians, when formulating their foreign policy for Asia, had placed a very low priority on Mongolia, not only because they were hobbled by the suspicions and rivalries of other great powers in East Asia, but because of the importance which Petersburg traditionally ascribed to relations with China. After 1917 Soviet Russia's diplomatic isolation and China's stature in Asia, not to mention a variety of problems that pestered relations between the two, increased the importance of receiving full diplomatic recognition from China. This was the first factor which inhibited Russia from acting arbitrarily in Mongolia.

The second was the crippled state of the Russian economy after so many years of revolution and civil war and the urgency of putting soldiers of the Red Army to work repairing the railroad and industries of Siberia. Since serious reconstruction could not begin until the Siberian borders were stabilized and secure, the Soviets were quick to respond to Ungern's invasion of Mongolia with an announcement in November 1920 of their intention to send Red Army units across the frontier to deal with the Whites. And they were equally quick to withdraw that declaration when it appeared that the Chinese were able to settle the Ungern problem unassisted.

However much Red Army troops were required on the labor front, China's proven incapacity after February-March 1921 to subdue Ungern and its categorical refusal to accept Moscow's offer of help forced the Soviets into independent action in Mongolia in order to ensure the integrity of their borders and the survival of the new Soviet state. From this point onward, the progression of logic was irresistible. If China could not guarantee Mongolia's buffer role, then the Mongols themselves must--the obvious candidate was the Mongolian revolutionaries, whose loyalty to and dependence on Soviet Russia was clear. Although it is possible--the sources are not at all helpful on this point--that the Russians in deciding to help the Mongols were at least partially fired by a vision of a revolutionary future for Mongolia (this was unquestionably true of the Buryats), the Moscow government was surely persuaded more by strategic than by ideological goals.

Although the Soviets in June 1921 had promised to evacuate Red troops from Mongolia as soon as the "common enemy" had been expelled, the Moscow government did not announce their final evacuation until 1925. If Peking had accepted the Soviet proposal of independent or joint military action in either November 1920 or late February 1921 would the Russians have found a pretext to keep their forces in Mongolia? For the reasons which have been outlined above and discussed more thoroughly in the last two chapters of this study, it is probable that the Soviets would have honored that promise. This, of course, can never be tested for the Chinese did not take the gamble. It is revealing, however, that at the request of Chinese authorities at Tarbagatai in northern Sinkiang--an area which, it is important to note, had earlier been a target of Tsarist expansion--Soviet units entered Sinkiang between May and July 1921, cleared the region of White troops under Bakich, and then retired back into Soviet Russia. The evidence suggests that the Russians would have done the same in Mongolia. Had the Chinese understood this, Mongolia might be a province of China today.

## FOOTNOTES

1. Chang Mu, p. 194.

2. Gur'ev, Politicheskie otnosheniya, pp. 5-6; Baranov, p. 17.

3. For example, Gol'man and Slesarchuk, "Russkie arkhivnye materialy," p. 175; and Yano Jin'ichi, pp. 26-37.

4. Farquhar, "The Ch'ing Administration," pp. 315-16.

5. Przheval'skii, p. 80.

6. Maiskii, Mongoliya, p. 172, has suggested the first figure; the second comes from a report in the newspaper News of the Capital (Niislel khüreenii sonin bichig), cited in Sürenkhorloo, p. 9. The general dimensions of Maikii's estimate are supported by other published statistics. See in particular Natsagdorj, Ar Mongold, pp. 27, 55; and Svechnikov, Russkie, p. 40.

7. Gilmour, Among the Mongols, p. 238; Przheval'skii, p. 50; Piassetsky, vol. 1, p. 14.

8. Pozdneyev, Mongolia, vol. 1, p. 31.

9. This and the next two quotes are from Gur'ev, Politicheskie otnosheniya, pp. 14-18, passim.

10. This estimate of the size of the Russian population in Outer Mongolia during the late Ch'ing is based on Svechnikov, Russkie, p. 148; Bennigsen, p. 16; Obruchev, Ot Kyakhty, p. 30; Kendall, p. 284. For trading figures see Bogolepov and Sobelev, pp. 161, 309-25; Moskovskaya torgovaya ekspeditsiya, pp. 5-16; Obruchev, "Bol'she vnimaniya," p. 125; Rupen, "Outer Mongolian Nationalism," appendix 7a.

11. Hsieh Pin, p. 46.

12. Ta-ch'ing, vol. 2, p. 1011; Jamsran, p. 97.

13. Popov, p. 4.

14. Shirendev, Mongoliya, p. 71.

15. Dendev, pp. 2-3.

16. IBZI, ser. III, vol. 1.1, no. 269, pp. 328-29.

17. *Ibid.*, ser. III, vol. 1,1, no. 269, p. 329, fn. 3. "Approaching negotiations" was a reference to the 1881 Petersburg Treaty, which was due to be renewed that year.
18. *Ibid.*, ser. III, vol. 1.1, no. 269, p. 329, fn. 3.
19. *Ibid.*, ser. III, vol. 1.1, no. 329, p. 405.
20. *Ibid.*, ser. III, vol. 1.1, no. 329, p. 406, fn. 2, no. 366, p. 448.
21. *Ibid.*, ser. III, vol. 1.1, no. 416, pp. 494-95, vol. 1.2, no. 459, p. 575; Wu Hsiang-hsiang, p. 248.
22. *IBZI*, ser. III, vol. 1.2, no. 607, p. 729, no. 670, pp. 783-84.
23. Ch'en Ch'ung-tsu, pien 1, p. 7.
24. Ch'en Lu, pp. 181, 184-85; Shirendev, *Mongoliya*, p. 76; Sandag, *Mongolyn*, pp. 151-52.
25. Burdukov, pp. 55-56, 76-79; Ch'en Ch'ung-tsu, pien 1, p. 29; Sandag, *Mongolyn*, p. 291; Puntsagnorov, p. 40.
26. Sandag, *Mongolyn*, pp. 280-81.
27. Korostovetz, pp. 152-53.
28. *IBZI*, ser. I, vol. 2, no. 57, p. 45.
29. These biographical sketches are based on Navaannamjil, p. 187; Korostovetz, p. 154; P-ii, p. 14; Perry-Ayscough and Otter-Barry, p. 116; Sandag, *Mongolyn*, p. 237; Abrikossow, p. 176.
30. Dendev, p. 81; Sandag, *Mongolyn*, p. 283; *BNMAUT*, vol. 2, p. 510.
31. Nasanbaljir, "Jibzandamba khutagtyn," p. 152.
32. Tsedev, *Ikh shav'*, pp. 49-50.
33. *Ibid.*, pp. 40, 46.
34. This sketch is based on the memoirs of the Dilowa Khutukhtu, cited in Lattimore, *Nationalism*, p. 49; Burdukov, *V staroi*, p. 109; Bulstrode, p. 176; Andrews, p. 68.
35. Korostovetz, p. 162.
36. *BNMAUT*, vol. 2, p. 459.
37. The best translation of these telegrams may be found in Salomon, "China's Policy," pp. 82-89.
38. Korostovetz, p. 127.
39. Wu Hsiang-hsiang, p. 252.
40. This discussions of the negotiations in Urga is based on Korostovetz, pp. 170-71; and *Sbornik*, nos. 5-6, pp. 4-5.

41. Korostovetz, p. 216; Dendev, p. 82.
42. Korostovetz, p. 256.
43. *Ibid.*, p. 234.
44. *Sbornik*, no. 45, pp. 45-46.
45. Korostovetz, pp. 220-24; Burdukov, *V staroi*, p. 99.
46. *The China Yearbook: 1916*, p. 579; Puntsagnorov, p. 60; P-ii, p. 15; Damdinsüren, pp. 64-65; Popov, pp. 18, 41.
47. *Sbornik*, no. 26, p. 31.
48. *Ibid.*, no. 31, pp. 34-35.
49. Hsu Shu-hsi, pp. 355-56; *Sbornik*, no. 72, p. 63.
50. *Sbornik*, no. 72, p. 63.
51. Li Yü-shu, *Wai Meng-ku ch'e-chih*, pp. 24-25.
52. Korostovetz, p. 276; Popov, pp. 37-38; Sandag, "Avtonomit yum uu," p. 21.
53. Shirendev, *Istoriya*, p. 93.
54. See Isono, "The Bogro's Letter;" also *IBZI*, ser. I, vol. 1, no. 46, p. 39, fn. 2, no. 46, pp. 41-42; Popov, pp. 53, 58-59.
55. Dendev, pp. 90-91; *IBZI*, ser. I, vol. 1, no. 142, p. 125.
56. Records of these negotiations may be found in *IBZI*, ser. I, vol. 1-3, 6.2 *passim*.
57. *IBZI*, ser. I, vol. 5, no. 447, p. 272.
58. The following account of the Tripartite Conference is based principally on the dairy of Ch'en Lu, pp. 16-32; also on Pi Kuei-fang, pp. 28-32; Ch'en Ch'ung-tsu, pien 1, p. 23-52; *IBZI*, ser. II, vols. 6.1-7.2, *passim*.
59. Sandag, *Mongolyn*, p. 301.
60. *IBZI*, ser. II, vol. 7.2, no. 712, p. 699.
61. Friters, *Outer Mongolia*, p. 112.
62. Korostovetz, p. 225.
63. *Ibid.*, p. 158.
64. Ligüü, p. 12.
65. *Ibid.*, p. 8; Korostovetz, p. 93; Puntsagnorov, p. 89.
66. Korostovetz, p. 158.
67. Grumm-Grzhimailo, vol. 3, pp. 662-64; Penskii, p. 168.
68. Zlatkin, *MNR*, p. 100.
69. Maiksii, *Mongoliya*, p. 277.
70. For more on Kozin see Maiskii, *ibid.*, pp. 227-28; Puntsagnorov, p. 114; Friters, *Outer*

Mongolia, p. 111; Dendev, p. 98; Zlatkin, MNR, pp. 74, 97; Kallinikov, Revolyutsionnaya, p. 68.

71. IBZI, ser. II, vol. 8.2, no. 683, p. 635, fn. 2; Burdukov, V staroi, p. 391; Shirendev, Mongoliya, pp. 113-17; Maiskii, Mongoliya, p. 185; Kallinikov, Revolyutsionnaya, p. 58.

72. Bobrik, pp. 53-54; Korostovetz, p. 264.

73. Korostovetz, pp. 155-56, 235; Shirendev, Mongoliya, p. 141; and Istoriya, pp. 82-83; IBZI, ser. I, vol. 2, no. 148, p. 149; Puntsagnorov, pp. 132-133; Bat-Ochir, Dashjamts, pp. 13, 18-23.

74. Rinchin, in his historical novel Üüriin tuyaa, pp. 336-42, gives a fascinating account of Khanddorj's death reconstructed from conversations with people who attended him that night.

75. Ch'en Lu, p. 72; BNMAUT, vol. 2, p. 530; Jagchid, p. 97, fn. 2.

76. IBZI, ser. II, vol. 8.2, no. 899, p. 792, fn. 2. The following account of the Bavuujav affair is based on Ch'en Lu, pp. 70-104.

77. This account of investiture is based on Ch'en Lu, pp. 69-144; BNMAUT, vol. 2, pp. 526-27, 536-37; Dendev, pp. 138-39; IBZI, ser. II, vol. 8.1, no. 178, p. 161, no. 202, p. 181.

78. Ch'en Lu, p. 105.

79. Ibid., p. 97.

80. COKHSL: WMK, no. 14, p. 162, no. 21, p. 164.

81. Ibid., no. 26, p. 166.

82. Ibid., no. 66, p. 183, no. 73, p. 187.

83. Ibid., no. 65, p. 183.

84. Ibid., no. 73, p. 189.

85. Ibid., no. 100, p. 215, no. 103, p. 217, no. 105, pp. 217-18.

86. Ibid., no. 111, pp. 220-21.

87. B. Shumyatskii, "Desyatiletie mongol'skogo oktyabrya," in Vostochno-sibirskaya pravda (March 30, 1931), p. 72, cited in Kungurov and Sorokovikov, p. 44.

88. COKHSL:WMK, no. 111, p. 221.

89. Puntsagnorov, p. 162.;

90. COKHSL: WMK, no. 69, p. 67.

91. Ibid., no. 8, p. 160.

92. Istoriya Tuvy, vol. 2, pp. 65-66; Shoizhelov, Tuvinskaya, pp. 36-40; Iezuitov, pp. 47-48.

93. Ch'en Ch'ung-tsu, pien 2, pp. 114-31.

94. COKHSL: WMK, no. 240, p. 296.

95. *Ibid.*, no. 35, p. 325.

96. *Ibid.*, no. 1, p. 305, no. 5, p. 308. For an account of the tragic death of the Sain Noyon Khan see DamdinsÜren, pp. 82-83.

97. *COKHSL: WMK*, no. 102, p. 376; *BNMAUT*, vol. 3, p. 58; Puntsagnorov, p. 55; Kallinikov, *Natsional'no*, p. 35; Shirendev, *Istoriya*, p. 106; and *Mongoliya*, p. 171; Tsibikov, p. 55; Shoizhelov, "Natsional'no," p. 209.

98. Shirendev, *Mongoliya*, p. 174; *COKHSL: WMK*, no. 111, pp. 386-87.

99. Valliant, "Japanese," p. 18.

100. Puntsagnorov, pp. 170-71; Shirendev, *Istoriya*, p. 148.

101. Kallinikov, "U istokov," pt. 1, p. 61; *COKHSL: WMK*, no. 159, p. 415.

102. *COKHSL: WMK*, no. 159, p. 415, no. 170, p. 419.

103. *Ibid.*, no. 256, p. 464.

104. *Ibid.*, appendix 1, p. 26; Serebrennikov, p. 62; Grumm-Grzhimailo, vol. 2, p. 764; Kallinikov, *Natsional'no*, p. 36.

105. Popov, p. 25.

106. Burdukov, *V staroi*, p. 115.

107. Tserendorj, *Niislel*, pp. 11-13, 21-22.

108. Korostovetz, p. 226; *BNMAUT*, vol. 2, p. 551.

109. Natsagdorj, *Manjiin*, p. 273.

110. Bobrik, p. 38, noted in 1913 that it was impossible to be certain of the region's loyalty to Urga, and Burdukov, *V staroi*, p. 116, observed that by 1914 a large number of lay and church princes wished to return to China.

111. Burdukov, *V staroi*, p. 117.

112. *Ibid.*, pp. 142-43.

113. *COKHSL: WMK*, no. 203, p. 435, no. 154, pp. 411-13.

114. *Ibid.*, no. 253, pp. 461-62.

115. For the Chinese text of the draft articles, including the subsequent revisions made by the Peking government, see *ibid.*, no. 367, pp. 538-53. Russian and Mongolian historians refer to sixty-four articles, a figure which is probably based on the Mongolian-language text in Dendev, pp. 146-72. Dendev's sixty-fourth article provides for the right of all Inner Mongolian and Bargut refugees who fled to Outer Mongolia after 1911 to return to their

homes without fear of punishment. Such a provision had been included in the exchange of notes between China and Russia following the signing of the Kyakhta treaty in June 1915. Most or all of these refugees, moreover, had already taken advantage of the amnesty. Therefore, since this sixty-fourth article is probably spurious, I shall follow the Chinese text.

116. Ibid., no. 377, p. 567; for the text see ibid., no. 378, pp. 567-68.

117. Ibid., no. 352, p. 516.

118. Ibid., no. 372, p. 561, no. 377, pp. 566-67, no. 386, pp. 573-74.

119. The text of Hsu's proposals may be found in ibid., no. 108, pp. 380-84.

120. Ibid., no. 404, pp. 584-85.

121. Historians are by no means agreed on the number of Chinese troops in Mongolia at this time, some giving as high a figure as fifteen thousand. My estimate is based on ibid., no. 397, pp. 580-81; and a report in Sovetskaya Sibir' (November 17, 1920) cited in Shirendev, Mongoliya, p. 220.

122. COKHSL: WMK, no. 387, pp. 574-76.

123. Ibid., no. 387, pp. 574-76, no. 420, pp. 592-93, no. 412, p. 588.

124. Ibid., no. 404, p. 584, no. 48, pp. 586-87.

125. Ibid., no. 414, p. 589; BNMAUT, vol. 3, p. 64; Shirendev, Istoriya, p. 112; Lattimore, Nationalism, p. 120.

126. The following account, which differs somewhat (mainly in chronology) from the standard description of events given by Russian and Mongolian historians, is based on COKHSL: WMK, pp. 589-97; Puntsagnorov, p. 205; Dendev, pp. 175-76; D. Sükhbaataryn tukhai, pp. 71-72; Ch'en Ch'ung-tsu, pien 3, p. 4; Bat-Ochir, Dashjamts, pp. 31-32; Navaannamjil, p. 225.

127. Ch'en Ch'ung-tsu, pien 3, p. 11; Shirendev, Istoriya, p. 114; Puntsagnorov, p. 202; Bat-Ochir, Dashjamts, p. 34.

128. Chang Hsing-t'ang, pp. 130, 135; Ch'en Ch'ung-tsu, pien 3, pp. 12-13; BNMAUT, vol. 3, p. 65; Bat-Ochir, Dashjamts, p. 34.

129. Hsu Tao-lin, Hsu Shu-cheng, pp. 262-66; Ch'en Ch'ung-tsu, pien 3, pp. 13-14; Tserendorj, p. 28.

130. Zlatkin, Ocherki, p. 102; Puntsagnorov, p. 205. Chinese merchants estimated the total damage to private and public buildings in Khovd in 1912 at 415,690 taels (COKHSL: WMK, no. 129, pp. 138-56). This figure does not include losses of merchandise, livestock, and so forth.

131. Liu Shou-lin, p. 475.

132. Ch'en I informed Peking that the "nobles of the four aimags" (that is, the upper house) had approved abolition, although the "officials of the Tüsheet Khan aimag who worked in the Bogd Khaan Government" (that is, the lower house) refused. Ch'en explained that these men had been given lavish titles and ranks by the Khutukhtu and were put up to their resistance by the lamas. COKHSL: WMK, no. 414, p. 589.

133. This biographical sketch is based on Choibalsan, Losol, Demid, vol. 1, p. 54; Tudev, p. 200; Bat-Ochir, Dashjamts, p. 51, fn. 18; Kallinikov, "U istokov," pt. 1, p. 75.

134. Genkin, pp. 79-80; Danzan's comment in Choibalsan, Losol, Demid, vol. 1, pp. 183-85.

135. Bawden, The Modern History, p. 254.

136. This account is from Choibalsan, "Sükhbaatar bol," pp. 387-88.

137. Choibalsan, Losol, Demid, vol. 1, p. 55.

138. Onon, pp. 194-95; Shirendev, Mongoliya, pp. 194-95; Kungurov, Sorokovikov, pp. 32-34.

139. Lattimore, Nationalism, p. 67.

140. See Kallinikov, "U istokov," pt. 1, pp. 76-78.

141. The relatively late appearance of Sükhbaatar is confirmed by the Mongolian historian Natsagdorj in his biography of Sükhbaatar, where he writes that Dogsom, Danzan, Dendev, and Jam'yan presented a secret letter to the Russian envoy before "joining" Sükhbaatar. See Lattimore, Nationalism, p. 125.

142. Inchinnorov, "Tüükhen," p. 89, fn. 2.

143. D. Sükhbaataryn tukhai, p. 35; Mongol ardyn juramt, p. 294.

144. Natsagdorj's biography of Sükhbaatar, D. Sükhbaataryn namtar (Ulan Bator, 1943), has been translated in Lattimore, Nationalism. This biography has since been superceded by the study of Bat-Ochir and Dashjamts.

145. On the early activity of the East Urga Group

see Shirendev, Mongoliya, pp. 195-96; Bat-Ochir, Dashmats, p. 36-42; Choibalsan, Losol, Demid, vol. 1, pp. 82-83; Mongol ardyn juramt, p. 276; Internatsionalch, p. 148.

146. Darevskaya, "Stepan," pp. 87-89, 94; Kungurov, Sorokovikov, pp. 75-76; Kapitsa, Ivanenko, p. 15; Kheifets, Sovetskaya Rossiya, p. 432.

147. Dash, Mongol, pp. 84-85.

148. Choibalsan, Losol, Demid, vol. 1, pp. 63-69.

149. Our main source for this meeting is a semi-stenographic report in ibid., vol. 1, pp. 90-98.

150. Mongol ardyn juramt, p. 301.

151. Choibalsan, Losol, Demid, vol. 1, p. 98; Kungurov, Sorokovikov, p. 84.

152. Text of the oath may be found in Mongol Ardyn Khuv'sgalt, vol. 1, pp. 7-8 . For an account of the meeting see Choibalsan, Losol, Demid, vol. 1, pp. 99-104.

153. Choibalsan, Losol, Demid, vol. 1, pp. 147-48; D. Sükhbaataryn tukhai, pp. 74-85.

154. Choibalsan, Losol, Demid, vol. 1, pp. 107-08; D. Sükhbaataryn tukhai, p. 302; Bat-Ochir, Dashjamts, p. 49.

155. Choibalsan, Losol, Demid, vol. 1, pp. 119-20.

156. Ibid., vol. 1, p. 142.

157. Rinchen, p. 373. Although his book is an historical novel, the author claims that this anecdote is based on fact.

158. Shirendev, Mongoliya, p. 203.

159. Yudin, pp. 110-11.

160. Choibalsan, Losol, Demid, vol. 1, pp. 172-83.

161. Ibid., vol. 1, pp. 183-85.

162. The text of the document may be found in Mongol ardyn khuv'sgalt, vol. 1, pp. 10-11.

163. BNMAUT, vol. 3, p. 80.

164. The complete Mongolian text is in Choibalsan, Losol, Demid, vol. 1, pp. 187-93. This translation is from Brown and Onon, pp. 81-82.

165. Kungurov, Sorokovikov, p. 137.

166. Eudin, North, p. 463; Alioshin, pp. 185-87; Serebrennikov, pp. 69-71; Ossendowskii, Beasts, p. 238.

167. While estimates as high as six thousand have been given for Ungern's force at this time, my figure is based on Ungern's own testimony at his trial. See Kislov, p. 15; and Tsibikov, p. 64.

168. Ch'en Ch'ung-tsu, pien 3, pp. 38-39; Serebrennikov, pp. 73-76; Alioshin, pp. 168-69; Forbath, pp.165-73; *The China Yearbook: 1921-22*, p. 647.

169. These figures are impressionistic, based on my reading of Russian émigré literature and Mongolian sources.

170. Choibalsan, Losol, Demid, vol. 2, pp. 62-63; Damdinsüren, pp. 66; Ch'en Ch'ung-tsu, pien 3, p. 33.

171. Dendev, p. 193; Shirendev, *Mongoliya*, p. 221. Again, this figure comes from Ungern's own testimony at his trial; see Tsibikov, p. 80.

172. Forbath, pp. 186-87.

173. Burdukov, "V zapadnoi," p. 38; and *V staroi*, pp. 176-77, 187; Serebrennikov, pp. 103-06, 144; *COKHSL: TPPF, WMK*, no. 113, p. 64, no. 125, p. 76, no. 87, p. 48; Ossendowski, *Beasts*, pp. 109, 160-70, 186.

174. Haslund, *Men*, p. 68; Tsibikov, p. 82; Ossendowski, *Beasts*, p. 234; Serebrennikov, pp. 80-81; Darevskaya, "Stepan," p. 91; Shirendev, *Mongoliya*, pp. 224-25, 244.

175. This reconstruction of events is an attempt to reconcile the conflicting evidence regarding who was arrested and when. See Ch'en Ch'ung-tsu, pien 3, p. 35; *Mongol ardyn juramt*, p. 277; *Internatsionalch*, p. 90; Choibalsan, Losol, Demid, vol. 1, p. 203.

176. Choibalsan, Losol, Demid, vol. 2, pp. 96-97.

177. *Ibid.*, vol. 1, pp. 229-30.

178. *Dash*, *Ardyn*, pp. 26-27; Balkhaajav, p. 6; *Istoricheskii*, p. 32. Some of these articles have been reprinted in *Mongol ardyn khuv'sgalt*, vol. 1, pp. 12-27.

179. Choibalsan, Losol, Demid, vol. 1, pp. 230-35.

180. *Ibid.*, vol. 1, pp. 239-41.

181. *Ibid.*, vol. 1, pp. 242, 244-48.

182. *Sovetsko-mongol'skie otnosheniya, 1921-1974*, vol. 1, p. 464.

183. Eudin, North, pp. 200-01.

184. *Dokumenty*, vol. 3, no. 172, p. 324.

185. Kheifets, *Sovetskaya Rossiya*, p. 446.

186. Carr, vol. 3, p. 257.

187. Lazitch, Drachkovitch, vol. 1, p. 382.

188. Meijer, vol. 2, no. 209, p. 556.

189. See Kapur, Soviet Russia and Asia,1917-1923.
190. COKHSL: IPCS, no. 35, pp. 18-19; Kheifets, Sovetskaya Rossiya, p. 395; Dokumenty, vol. 2, no. 331, pp. 498-99; Pollard, p. 131-32.
191. COKHSL: IPCS, no. 504, pp. 331-32.
192. Ibid., no. 173, pp. 114-15, no. 405, p. 247, no. 441, p. 271, no. 504, pp. 331-32; Kapitsa, pp. 52-60; Dokumenty, vol. 3, no. 109, pp. 213-16.
193. Eudin, North, pp. 228-29.
194. Lenin, vol. 44, pp. 232-33.
195. Chung-O kuan-hsi shih-liao: O cheng-pien yü i-pan chiao-she, vol. 1, no. 126, p. 270.
196. Eudin, North, p. 203.
197. Shereshevskii, Razgrom, p. 57.
198. Meijer, vol. 2, no. 669, pp. 401-03.
199. Kislov, pp. 23-26.
200. Shereshevskii, Razgrom, p. 56; Persits, Dal'nevostochnaya, p. 28.
201. Meijer, vol. 2, no. 465, pp. 51-53.
202. Shereshevskii, Razgrom, p. 50.
203. Choibalsan, Losol, Demid, vol. 1, pp. 248-51.
204. D. Sükhbaatar, no. 18, pp. 37-38.
205. Bat-Ochir, "Niislel,", p. 18.
206. Internatsionalch, pp. 62-63.
207. Ibid., p. 63; Choibalsan, Losol, Demid, vol. 1, pp. 258-61. That Sükhbaatar did not start agitating amongst the frontier pickets and banners on the border until late January 1921, not mid-December 1920 as most historians believe, is supported by other evidence. For example, a border pass issued to Sükhbaatar by the chief of the frontier detachment of the Far Eastern Republic, explaining that he was on "secret and urgent business" and giving him the right of unhindered movement across the border, is dated "_____ 20, 1921." For the document see D. Sükhbaatar, no. 78, p. 114. The editors B. Shirendev and Sh. Natsagdorj have identified the missing month as January, which is indeed the month possible.
208. Mongol ardyn juramt, p. 61; Choibalsan, Losol, Demid, vol. 1, p. 281; Oni vstrechalis', pp. 18-19.
209. Dash, Ardyn, p. 119; Istoricheskii, p. 217;
210. Sovetsko-mongol'skie otnosheniya, 1921-1974, vol. 1, no. 1, p. 2.
211. Mongol ardyn juramt, pp. 248-49; D.

Sükhbaataryn tukhai, pp. 84-86.

212. Bat-Ochir, Dashjamts, pp. 74-75; Kallinikov, "Vooruzhennaya," p. 87; Mongol ardyn armiin, pp. 8-9; Choibalsan, Losol, Demid, vol. 2, pp. 10-11. According to a Chinese source these "Mongolian bandits" numbered "over a hundred or a thousand." Ch'en Ch'ung-tsu, pien 3, p. 52.

213. Oni vstrechalis', pp. 18-22. The main sources for this conference are two similar, but by no means identical, stenographic reports, one in Russian and the other in Mongolian, published under the title Mongol ardyn khuv'sgalt namyn negdügeer ikh khural.

214. For the text of the "Proclamation" and its introduction, see ibid., pp. 16-33.

215. This translation is from Brown, Onon, p. 108. For the full text of the "Ten Principles" see Mongol ardyn khuv'sgalt namyn negdügeer, pp. 27-31.

216. Cited in Shirendev, Istoriya, p. 193.

217. Kallinikov, Natsional'no, p. 75.

218. Dash, Ardyn, p. 157.

219. Ibid., p. 49.

220. L. Berlin, who worked in the Soviet People's Commissariat of Foreign Affairs and dealt with the Mongolian delegation to Moscow in November 1921, candidly wrote that while the Soviet government was committed to the principle of Mongolian autonomy under Chinese suzerainty, "the Mongols, hating the Chinese for the historical past in Mongolia, will not accept even the suzerainty of China, insisting on complete independence." "Avtonomnaya," p. 5.

221. D. Sükhbaatar, no. 80, pp. 118-20.

222. Mongol ardyn juramt, p. 350; Dash, Ardyn, pp. 102, 105-06; Oni vstrechalis', p. 23; Internatsionalch, p. 74.

223. Dash, "Janjin," p. 94; D. Sükhbaataryn tukhai, p. 33; Shirendev, Istoriya, p. 205; Bat-Ochir, Dashjamts, p. 86.

224. A variety of figures have been given for the size of the Chinese garrison at Kyakhta, the most popular of which is ten thousand. According to a report of the Red Army dated March 16, however, there were only twenty-five hundred men in the garrison. See Tsibikov, p. 94. Other

contemporary estimates give a somewhat smaller figure. See in particular D. Sükhbaatar, no. 115, p. 165; Dash, Ardyn, p. 108, fn. 3; and COKHSL: TPPF,WMK, no. 29, pp. 13-14.

225. Shirendev, Mongoliya, pp. 281-82; and Istoriya, pp. 209-11; Bat-Ochir, Dashjamts, p. 88; Ch'en Ch'ung-tsu, pien 3, pp. 52-53; Mongol ardyn juramt, p. 74; D. Sükhbaataryn tukhai, pp. 253-54.

226. Choibalsan, Losol, Demid, pp. 169-72; Shirendev, Mongoliya, p. 285; Kallinikov, "Vooruzhennaya," p. 94; Tsibikov, p. 96.

227. Mongol ardyn armiin, pp. 17-18; Sanjdorj, "Olnoo,", p. 129; Shirendev, Istoriya, pp. 215-17; Tsedev, "Mongol," p. 150; Ossendowski, "With Baron Ungern," p. 616.

228. Shirendev, Istoriya, p. 214; COKHSL: TPPF, WMK, no. 54, p. 26, no. 331, p. 195; Persits, Dal'nevostochnaya, p. 255.

229. Text in Choibalsan, Losol, Demid, vol. 2, pp. 156-60.

230. These letters in ibid., vol. 2, pp. 175-81.

231. Dash, Ardyn, p. 120.

232. D. Sükhbaatar, no. 72, p. 70.

233. COKHSL: TPPF,WMK, no. 127, p. 78.

234. Kheifets, Sovetskaya diplomatiya, p. 24, gives the first date; Kapitsa, p. 65, gives the second.

235. COKHSL: TPPF,WMK, no. 15, pp.7-8.

236. Ibid., no. 17, p. 9.

237. This appeal may be found in Dokumenty, vol. 4, p. 780, fn. 43.There is some ambiguity regarding the appeal. In addition to the March 16 request, Soviet and Mongolian historians refer even more frequently to a second appeal of April 10. It is clear from the journal of the Mongolian provisional government, however, that there was only one appeal. April 10 was probably the day the Soviet government in Moscow received it. See Sanjdorj, p. 129. It is also worth pointing out that the journal states this appeal was for help against both Chinese "bandits" and White soldiers. Clearly, the Mongols envisaged Soviet assistance in the taking of the Kyakhta garrison.

238. Tsibikov, p. 109.

239. Murphy, p. 10.

240. Kheifets, Sovetskaya diplomatiya, p. 94

241. *Ibid.*, p. 27.
242. *Dokumenty*, vol. 4, no. 122, pp. 179-80.
243. Kislov, pp. 26, 31.
244. Nasanbaljir, *Revolyutsionnye*, pp. 22-23.
245. *Sovetsko-mongol'skie otnosheniya, 1921-1966*, no. 2, p. 8; *Dokumenty*, vol. 4, no. 178, pp. 259-60.
246. According to Kislov, p. 92, by the end of 1921 all Soviet troops, except a single infantry regiment, had returned to Russia. This infantry regiment may have been the Kalmuck International Brigade, which remained in Mongolia until 1925. For more on this brigade see *S internatsional'noi missiei*. M. Harrison, p. 206, who visited Urga in 1922, and the American Consul in Kalgan S. Sokobin, who visited Urga in 1921 and 1922, have also remarked on the paucity of Russian soldiers whom they saw. (Conversation with Sokobin, September 15, 1975.)
247. See *COKHSL: TPPF,WMK*, pp. 11-38, *passim*.
248. McCormack, *Chang Tso-lin*, p. 55.
249. Tseden, "D. Sükhbaatar," p. 59; Dash, *Ardyn*, p. 47.

# BIBLIOGRAPHY

Abbreviations:

IBZI: Die Internationalen Beziehungen im Zeitalter des Imperialismus

BNMAUT--Bügd nairamdakh Mongol ard ulsyn tüükh

COKHSL: WMK--Chung-O kuan-hsi shih-liao: Wai Meng-ku

COKHSL: TPPF,WMK--Chung-O kuan-hsi shih-liao: Tung-pei pien-fang, Wai Meng-ku

Abrikossow, Dmitrii I. Revelations of a Russian Diplomat. Seattle, 1964.

Aberle, David F. Chahar and Dagor Mongol Bureaucratic Administration, 1912-1945. New Haven, 1962.

Alioshin, Dmitri. Asian Odyssey. London, 1940.

Andrews, Roy C. Across Mongolian Plains. New York, 1921.

Baldo, B. "Lenin i pobeda mongol'skoi revolyutsii," V.I. Lenin i mezhdunarodnoe kommunisticheskoe dvizhenie. Moscow, 1970, pp. 153-74.

Balkhaajav, Ts. "D. Sükhbaatar bol MAKhN, ardyn töriig üüsgen baiguulagch" *(D. Sükhbaatar, founder of the MPRP and the Mongolian state)*, MAKhN tüükhiin asuudal, no. 8 (1973), pp. 5-15.

Ballis, William B. "The Mongolian People's Republic since World War II," in Richard F. Staar, ed., Aspects of Modern Communism, Columbia, 1968, pp. 289-317.

-----. "The Political Evolution of a Soviet Satellite: The MPR," Western Political Quarterly, vol. 9,2 (June 1956), pp. 293-328.

Baranov, A.M. Khalkha. Aimak tsetsen khana. Harbin, 1919.

Barkman, C.D. "The Return of the Torguts from Russia to China," Journal of Oriental Studies, vol. II,1 (January 1955), pp. 89-115.

Bat-Ochir, L. "Niislel khüreen dakh' khuv'sgalchdyn üil ajillagaanaas" *(On the activity of the revolutionaries in Urga)*, Shinjlekh ukhaan akademiin medee, no. 1 (1976), pp. 16-24.

Bat-Ochir, L. and D. Dashjamts. Damdiny Sukhe-Bator.

Biografiya. Moscow, 1971; Mongolian-language edition: D. Sükhbaataryn namtar *(Biography of D. Sükhbaatar)*, Ulan Bator, 1965.

Bawden C.R. trans. "A Contemporary Mongolian Account of the Period of Autonomy," The Mongolia Society Bulletin, vol. IX,1 (Spring 1970).

-----. "An Event in the Life of the Eighth Jebtsundamba Khutukhtu," Asiatische Forschungen, vol. 17, Wiesbaden, 1966, pp. 9-19.

-----. The Modern History of Mongolia, New York, 1968.

-----. The Mongolian Chronicle Altan Tobci, Wiesbaden, 1955.

Bell, John. A Journey from St. Petersburg to Peking, 1719-22. Edinburg, 1965.

Bennigsen, A.P. Neskol'ko dannykh o sovremmenoi Mongolii. St. Petersburg, 1912.

Berlin, L.E. "Avtonomnaya Mongoliya i RSFSR," Zhizn' natsional'nostei, no. 8(14) (1922), pp. 2-5.

-----. "U istokov sovetsko-mongol'skoi druzhby," Narody Azii i Afriki, no. 2 (1968), pp. 131-36.

Binsteed, G.C. "Life in a Khalkha Steppe Monastery," Journal of the Royal Asiatic Society, vol.XXIII,2 (1914), pp. 847-900.

-----. "Some Topographical Notes of a Journey Through Barga and North-east Mongolia," The Geographical Journal, vol.XLIV,6 (December 1914), pp. 571-77.

Bobrik, P.A. Mongoliya. Vladivostok, 1914.

Bogolepov, M.I. and M.N. Sobolev. Ocherki Russko-mongol'skoi torgovli. Tomsk, 1911.

Boloban. A. "Kolonizatsionnyya problemy Kitaya v Manchzhurii i Mongolii," Vestnik Azii, no. 3 (January 1910), pp. 85-127.

-----. Mongoliya v eye sovremennom torgovo-ekonomicheskom otnoshenii. Petrograd, 1914.

Bonch-Osmolovskii, A. "Vneshnyaya torgovlya dal'nego vostoka za vremya voiny i revolyutsii," Novyi vostok, no. 5 (1924).

Boorman, Howard L, ed. Biographical Dictionary of Republican China. 4 vols., London, 1964.

Brandt, Conrad. Stalin's Failure in China, 1924-1927. Cambridge, Mass., 1958.

Brezhnev, V.I. and A.N. Kislov, I.Ya. Smirnov. "Cherez sorok let," Narody brat'ya, pp. 12-30.

Brown, William A. and Urgunge Onon, trans. History of the Mongolian People's Republic. Cambridge,

Mass., 1976.
Brunnert, I.S. and V.V. Hagelstrom. Present Day Political Organization of China, Shanghai, 1912.
Bügd nairamdakh Mongol ard ulsyn tüükh *(History of the Mongolian People's Republic)*. 3 vols., Ulan Bator, 1966-69.
Bulstrode, Beatrix. A Tour in Mongolia, London, 1920.
Burdukov, A.V. V staroi i novoi Mongolii. Moscow, 1969.
-----. "V zapadnoi Mongolii v 1921 godu," in Narody brat'ya, pp. 36-44.
Buyan-Bator. "Mezhdunarodnyi imperializm i osvobozhennaya Mongoliya," Narody dal'nego vostoka, no. 5 (1921), pp. 603-12.
Cahen, Gaston. Histoire des Relations de la Russie avec la Chine sous Pierre le Grand (1689-1730), Paris, 1912, repr. Peking, 1940.
Carr, Edward H. The Bolshevik Revolution, 1917-1923. 3 vols., London, 1960.
Carruthers, Douglas. Unknown Mongolia. 2 vols., London, 1913.
Chang Chung-fu. Chung-hua min-kuo wai-chiao shih *(Diplomatic History of the Republic of China)*. 2nd. ed., Taipei, 1957.
-----. "Hsieh-tsai 'tsai-lun Wai-meng ch'e-chih' ti hou-mien" *(A note to the background of "Once again on the abolition of autonomy")*, Tu-li p'ing-lun, no. 209 (July 12, 1936), pp. 4-15.
-----. "Ta Hsu Tao-lin hsien-sheng kuan-yü 'Wai-meng wen-t'i hui-ku i-wen" *(A reply to Mr. Hsu Tao-lin's article, "Doubts regarding the 'Reexamination of the Outer Mongolian question'")*, Tu-li p'ing-lun, no. 204 (June 7, 1936), pp. 3-12).
-----. "Wai-meng wen-t'i ti hui-ku" *(A reexamination of the Outer Mongolian question)*, Tu-li p'ing-lun, no. 198 (April 26, 1936), pp. 3-8.
Chang Hsing-t'ang. Pien-chiang cheng-chih *(Frontier administration)*. Taipei, 1962.
Chang Mu. Meng-ku yu-mu chi *(Records of Mongolian pastures)*. Peking, 1859, repr. Taipei, 1965.
Chang P'eng-yuan, comp. "Min-kuo chih-kuan nien-piao ch'u kao (1912-16)" *(A preliminary study of offices and their occupants during the Republican period, 1912-16)*, Chung-yang yen-chiu yuan, Chin-tai shih yen-chiu so chi-k'an, vol. 3,2 (1972), pp. 1-122.
Chao Erh-hsun, ed. et al. Ch'ing-shih kao *(A draft*

*history of the Ch'ing)*. Peking, 1927-28, repr. Hong Kong, n.d.

Ch'en Ch'ung-tsu. Wai meng-ku chin-shih shih *(A modern history of Outer Mongolia)*. Shanghai, 1926, repr. Taipei, 1965.

Ch'en Ch'ing-lung. "Ch'ing-tai t'ien-shan nan-pei ti mao-i" *(Trade to the north and south of the T'ien-shan during the Ch'ing)*, Shih-huo yueh-k'an, vol. VI,3 (June 1976), pp. 85-94.

Chen, Jerome. Yuan Shih-k'ai, 1859-1916. London, 1961.

Ch'en Lu. Chih-shih pi-chi *(Diary of Ch'en Lu)*. Shanghai, 1919.

Ch'en Po-wen. Chung-O wai-chiao shih *(A diplomatic history of Sino-Russian relations)*. Shanghai, 1929.

Chen,Vincent. Sino-Russian Relations in the Seventeenth Century. The Hague, 1966.

Ch'eng Teh-shou. Pien-chiang she-wai kuan-hsi *(The foreign relations of the Chinese frontier)*. Taipei, 1962.

Cheng Tien-fang. A History of Sino-Russian Relations. Washington, 1957.

Chi, Madeleine. China Diplomacy, 1914-1918. Cambridge, Mass., 1970.

Ch'i Yun-shih, comp. Huang-ch'ao fan-pu yao-lueh *(Essential information on the tribes in the Ch'ing empire)*. 1845, repr. 2 vols., Taipei, n.d.

The China Yearbook. H.G.W. Woodhead, ed., London, 1916-21, Tientsin, 1921-28.

Choibalsan, Kh., and D. Losol, D. Demid. Mongolyn ardyn ündesnii khuv'sgal ankh üüsej baiguulagdsan tovch tüükh *(A brief history of the origins of the Mongolian people's national revolution)*. 2 vols., Ulan Bator, 1934.

Choibalsan, Kh. "Sükhbaatar bol mongol ardyn khuv'sgalt namyn joloodogch bögööd tüünii zokhion baiguulagch mön" *(Sükhbaatar, leader and founder of the MPRP)*, in Kh. Choibalsan. Iltgel ba ügüüllüüd, Ulan Bator, vol. 3 (1953), pp. 373-90.

Chou K'un-t'ien. Pien-chiang cheng-ts'e *(Administrative policy for the frontier)*. Taipei, 1962.

Chow Tse-tsung. The May Fourth Movement. Stanford, 1969.

Chung-O kuan-hsi shih-liao *(Historical sources on Sino-Russian relations)*:

———: Chung-tung t'ieh-lu yü O cheng-pien *(The Chinese*

*Eastern Railway and the Russian revolution)*. Wang Yü-chün and T'ao Ying-hui, eds., Taipei, 1974.

-----: I-pan chiao-she (1920) *(General relations, 1920)*. Kuo T'ing-i and Wang Yü-chün, eds., Taipei, 1975.

-----: I-pan chiao-she (1921) *(General relations, 1921)*. Wang Yü-chün and T'ao Ying-hui, eds., Taipei, 1973.

-----: O cheng-pien (1920) *(The Russian revolution, 1920)*. Kuo T'ing-i and Wang Yü-chün, eds., Taipei, 1968.

-----: O cheng-pien yü i-pan chiao-she (1917-1919) *(The Russian revolution and general relations, 1917-19)*. 2 vols., Wang Yü-chün, ed., Taipei, 1960.

-----: Tung-pei pien-fang, Wai meng-ku (1921) *(Manchuria frontier defense, Outer Mongolia, 1921)*. Wang Yü-chün and T'ao Ying-hui, eds., Taipei, 1975.

-----: Wai meng-ku (1917-1919) *(Outer Mongolia, 1917-19)*. Li Yü-shu, ed., Taipei, 1959.

Chuo Hung-mou. Meng-ku chien *(Mirror of Mongolia)*. Peking, 1919, repr. 1933.

Clubb, O. Edmund. China & Russia. London, 1971.

-----. Twentieth Century China. New York, 1966.

Courant, Maurice. L'Asie Centrale aux XVII^e et XVIII^e siècles. Paris, 1912.

Dallin, David. The Rise of Russia in Asia. New Haven, 1949.

-----. Soviet Russia and the Far East. New Haven, 1948.

Damdinsüren, Ts., ed. Övgön Jambalyn yaria *(Tales of old Jalbal)*. Ulan Bator, 1959.

Darevskaya, E.M. "Aleksei Vasil'evich Burdukov," in Ocherki po istorii russkogo vostokovedeniya, vol. 6 (Moscow, 1963), pp. 187-217.

-----. "Russkie revolyutsionery v Mongolii," Proceedings of the 2nd Mongolist Congress, Ulan Bator, 1970, vol. 1, pp. 160-65.

-----. "Stepan Ivanovich Popov v Mongolii (1913-1920 gg.)," Sibirskii istoricheskii sbornik no. 2 (Irkutsk, 1974), pp. 84-100.

Dash, D. Ardyn khuv'sgalyn manlai khüchin *(Vanguard of the people's revolution)*. Ulan Bator, 1972.

-----. "Janjin Sükhbaataryn juramt tsergüüd" *(Partisans of Commander Sükhbaatar)*, MAKhN-yn tüükhiin asuudal, no. 8 (Ulan Bator, 1973), pp. 91-112.

-----. Mongol tümnii tölöö zütgesen and nökhöd (1921 ony ardyn khuv'sgald oroltsson Orosyn khuv'sgalchad zoriulav) *(Comrades who served the Mongolian people: Russian revolutionaries who participated in the Mongolian revolution)*. Ulan Bator, 1967.

Dashdavaa, Ch. "D. Sükhbaataryn namtryg sudlan bolovsruulj baigaa n'"*(Researching Sükhbaatar's biography)*, Shinjlekh ukhaan am'dral, no. 2 (1974), pp. 51-54.

Dashjamts, D. "Nachalo rasprostraneniya idei Marksizma-Leninizma v Mongolii (1917-1921)," Problemy dal'nego vostoka, no. 1 (1977), pp.102-13.

Dendev, L. Mongolyn tovch tüükh *(A short history of Mongolia)*. Ulan Bator, 1934.

Dillon, E.J. "Chinese Pale of Settlement," English Review, (January, 1913), pp. 283-300.

-----. "Secession of Mongolia from China," Contemporary Review, (April 1912), pp. 579-84.

Dilowa Hutukhtu. "The Narobanchin Monastery in Outer Mongolia," Proceedings of the American Philosophical Society, vol. 96,5 (October 1952), pp. 587-98.

Diplomaticheskii slovar'. A.A. Gromyko, ed., Moscow, 1971-73.

Dogsom (Doksom), D. "Istoricheskie uroki 15 let revolyutsii," Tikhii okean, no. 3(9) (July-September 1936), pp. 63-94.

Dokumenty vneshnei politikii SSSR. Moscow, 1957-.

Dügersüren, L. "Khatanbaatar Magsarjav Uliastai khotyg tsagaantnaas chölöölsön n'" *(The liberation of Uliastai from the Whites by Khatanbaatar Magsarjav)*, Tüükhiin sudlal, vol. VIII,1-12, pp. 199-211.

Dunn, Edward. The Truth About Outer Mongolia. Shanghai, 1935.

E.S. "Khronologiya vazhneishikh sobytii v istorii vneshnei Mongolii i Mongol'skoi Narodnoi Respubliki," Sovremennaya Mongoliya, no. 3(6) (May-June 1934), pp. 96-105.

Eudin, Xenia J. and Robert C. North. Soviet Russia and the Far East, 1920-1927. Stanford, 1957.

Ewing, Thomas E. "Chinese and Russian Policies in Outer Mongolia, 1911-1921," Ph.D. Thesis, Indiana University, 1977.

-----. "Revolution on the Chinese Frontier: Outer Mongolia in 1911," Journal of Asian History, vol. 12,2 (1978), pp. 101-119.

Fairbank, J.K., ed. The Chinese World Order. Cambridge, Mass., 1968.

-----. "A Preliminary Framework," in Fairbank, The Chinese World Order, pp. 1-19.

Farquhar, David M. "The Ch'ing Administration of Mongolia up to the Nineteenth Century," Ph.D. Thesis, Harvard University, 1960.

-----. "The Origins of the Manchus' Mongolian Policy," in Fairbank, *The Chinese World Order*, pp. 198-205.

-----. "Some Technical Terms in Ch'ing Dynasty Chinese Documents Relating to the Mongols," in L. Ligeti, ed., *Mongolian Studies*, Budapest, 1970.

Fletcher, Joseph F. "China and Central Asia, 1368-1884," in Fairbank, *The Chinese World Order*, pp. 206-24.

Forbath, Ladislaus, ed. *Die Neue Mongolei*, Berlin, 1937.

Friters, Gerard M. *Outer Mongolia and Its International Position*. Baltimore, 1949.

-----. "The Prelude to Outer Mongolian Independence," *Pacific Affairs*, vol. X,2 (June 1937), pp. 168-89.

Galsan, S. "Sükhbaataryn Galsangiin durdatgal" *(Galsan's recollections of Sükhbaatar)*, *MAKhN-yn tüükhiin asuudal*, no. 8 (1973), pp. 150-64.

Gataullina, Lidiya M. *Mongol'skaya Narodnaya Respublika v sotsialisticheskom sodruzhestve*. Moscow, 1964.

Galsanpuntsag, D. "D. Sükhbaataryn üil am'drald kholbogdokh nom züin toim" *(A bibliographical essay on the life of D. Sükhbaatar)*, *MAKhN-yn tüükhiin asuudal*, no. 8 (1973), pp. 178-84.

Genkin, I. "Konets Ungerna i nachalo novoi Mongolii," *Severnaya Aziya*, no. 2 (1928), pp. 75-90.

Gilmour, James. *Among the Mongols*. Repr. New York, 1970.

Gol'man, M.I. *Problemy noveishei istorii Mongol'skoi Narodnoi Respubliki v burzhuaznoi istoriografii SShA*. Moscow, 1970.

-----. "Tsennyi istochnik po noveishei istorii MNR," *Kratkie soobshcheniya Instituta narodov Azii*, no. 76 (1965), pp. 191-94.

-----, and G. I. Slesarchuk. "Russkie arkhivnye materialy o vzaimootnosheniakh Rossii i Mongolii v 30-50-x godakh XVII v.," *Kratkie soobshchenya Instituta narodov Azii*, no. 76 (1965), pp. 166-81.

Gongor, D. *Khalkh tovchoon* *(A short history of Khalkha)*. Ulan Bator, 1970.

-----. "MAKhN-yn tüükhiin uugan negen survaljiin

uchir" *(One original source for the history of the MPRP)*. Tüükhiin sudlal, vol. IX,1-12 (1971), pp. 39-69.
-----. "Oktyabriin khuv'sgalyn nölöögöör örnösön ündesnii erkh chölöönii khödölgöön ba khuv'sgalt nüüts bülgüüd" *(The national-liberation movement which developed under the influence of the October Revolution and the secret revolutionary groups)*, Tüükhiin sudlal, vol. VIII,14 (1970), pp. 17-30.
Gorokhova, G.S. "Sovetskaya memuarnaya literatura o Mongolii," Narody Azii i Afriki, vol. 3 (1971), pp. 165-69.
Grumm-Grzhimailo, G.E. Zapadnaya Mongoliya i uriankhaiskii krai. 3 vols., St. Petersburg, 1914, Leningrad, 1926-30.
Gur'ev, B. "Mongoliya i Kitai i ikh politicheskie vzaimootnosheniya," Vestnik Azii, no. 11-12 (May 1912), pp. 21-40.
-----. Politicheskie otnosheniya Rossii k Mongolii. St. Petersburg, 1911.
Gurevich, B.P. "Vzaimootnosheniya sovetskikh respublik s provintsiei Sin'tszyan v 1918-1921 godakh," Sovetskoe kitaevedenie, no. 2 (1958), pp. 96-105.
Haithcox, John P. "The Roy-Lenin Debate on Colonial Policy: a New Interpretation," The Journal of Asian Studies, vol. XXIII,1 (November 1963), pp. 93-101.
Hammond, Thomas T, ed. The Anatomy of Communist Takeovers. New Haven, 1974.
-----. "The Communist Takeover of Outer Mongolia: Model for Eastern Europe?," in Hammond, The Anatomy of Communist Takeovers, pp. 107-44.
-----. "The History of Communist Takeovers," in Hammond, The Anatomy of Communist Takeovers, pp. 1-45.
Hangin, John C. Köke Sudur (The Blue Chronicle). Wiesbaden, 1973.
Harrison, Marguerite. Red Bear or Yellow Dragon. London, 1924.
Haslung, Henning. Men and Gods in Mongolia. London, 1935.
-----. Tents in Mongolia. London, 1934.
Heissig, Walther. Geschichte der mongolischen Literatur. 2 vols., Wiesbaden, 1972.
-----. "Mongolischen Literatur," in Handbuch der Orientalistik, vol. 52, Mongolistik, Leiden,

1964, pp. 227-74.
Hertslet, Godfrey, E.P., ed. Treaties, &c., Between Great Britain and China; and Between China and Foreign Powers. 2 vols., 3rd. ed., London, 1908.
Ho Ch'iu-t'ao. Shuo-fang pei-sheng *(Records of the northern region)*. 1858, repr. Taipei, 1964.
Houn, Franklin W. Central Government of China, 1912-1928. Madison, 1959.
Hsiao I-shan. Ch'ing-tai t'ung-shih *(A comprehensive history of the Ch'ing)*. 5 vols., Taipei, 1962-63.
Hsieh Hsiao-chung. Kuo-fang yü wai-chiao *(National defense and diplomacy)*. Repr. Taipei, 1967.
Hsieh Pin. Meng-ku wen-t'i *(The Mongolian question)*. Shanghai, 1935.
Hsiung Hsi-ling. "Tui-yü Chung-O t'iao-yueh chih t'ung-yen" *(Bitter thoughts on Sino-Russian treaties)*, in Wu Hsiang-hsiang, ed., Min-kuo ching-shih wen-pien, vol. 3, pp. 667-68.
Hsu, Immanuel C.Y. The Rise of Modern China. New York, 1970.
Hsu Nai-lin. Ch'ou-pien ch'u-yen *(Preliminary remarks on planning the frontier)*. Repr. Taipei, 1969.
Hsu Shu-cheng pi shih *(A secret history of Hsu Shu-cheng)*. Peking, 1921.
Hsü Shu-hsi. China and her Political Entity. New York, 1926.
Hsu Tao-lin. Hsu Shu-cheng hsien-sheng wen-chi nien-p'u ho-k'an *(Mr. Hsu Shu-cheng, his writings and biographical chronology)*. Taipei, 1962.
-----. "Tsai-lun Wai-meng ch'e-chih" *(Once again on the abolition of Outer Mongolian autonomy)*, Tu-li p'ing-lun, no. 209 (July 12, 1936), pp. 5-14.
-----. "'Wai-meng wen-t'i hui-ku' ti i-wen" *(Doubts regarding the article "A reexamination of the Outer Mongolian question)*, Tu-li p'ing-lun, no. 203 (May 31, 1936), pp. 10-18.
Hsueh Chung-san, and Ou-yang Yi. A Sino-Western Calendar for Two Thousand Years, 1-2000. Changsha, 1940.
Hu Ch'iu-yuan. O-ti ch'in-Hua shih-kang *(A brief history of Tsarist agreession against China)*. 2 vols., Taipei, 1962.
Huang Fen-sheng. Meng-Tsang hsin-chih *(A new history of Mongolia and Tibet)*. 2 vols., Canton, 1938.
Huc, E.R. Souvenirs d'un voyage dans la Tartarie et le Thibet. 2 vols., Paris, 1868.

Hummel, Arthur W. Emminent Chinese of the Ch'ing Period (1644-1912). Washington, D.C., 1944.
Iezuitov, V.M. Ot Tuvy feodal'noi k Tuve sotsialisticheskoi. Kyzyl, 1956.
Imshenetskii, B.I. Mongoliya. Petrograd, 1915.
Inchinnorov, S. "Ikh udirdagchiin dotnyn khan'" *(The dear friend of the great leader)*. Shinjlekh ukhaan am'dral, no. 1 (1973) pp. 5-8.
-----. "Tüükhen barimt todruulakhad" *(Clarifying historical facts)*, Shinjlekh ukhaan am'dral, (1973), pp. 27-31.
Die Internationale Beziehungen im Zeitalter des Imperialismus,14 vols., M.N. Pokrovskii ed., Berlin, 1931-40.
Internatsionalch nairamdlyn üilsed khüchin zütgegsed. *(Memoirs of those who rendered service to international friendship)*. D. Dash, ed., Ulan Bator, 1970.
Isono, F. "The Bogro's Letter to the Japanese Emperor and a Japanese Called Kodama," Proceedings of the 2nd Mongolist Congress, Ulan Bator, 1970, vol. 1, pp. 214-16.
-----. "The Mongolian Revolution of 1921," Modern Asian Studies, vol. 10,3 (1976), pp. 375-94.
Istoricheskii opyt bratskogo sodruzhestva KPSS i MPRP v bor'be za sotsializm. Moscow, 1971.
Istoriya diplomatii. 3 vols., Moscow, 1959-65.
Istoriya Mongol'skoi Narodnoi Respubliki. 2nd. ed., Moscow, 1967.
Istoriya Sibiri. 5 vols., Leningrad, 1968-69.
Istoriya Tuvy. 2 vols., Moscow, 1964.
Jagchid, S. Meng-ku chih chin-hsi *(Old and new Mongolia)*. 2 vols., Taipei, 1955.
-----. "Wai Meng-ku ti 'tu-li,''tzu-chih,' ho 'ch'e-chih'" *(Outer Mongolia, its independence, autonomy, and abolition of autonomy)*, in Wu Hsiang-hsiang, Chung-kuo hsien-tai shih ts'ung-k'an, vol. 4, Hong Kong, 1962.
Jamsran, L. "Manj tsin uls 'shine bodlogo' gegchee Mongold kheregjüülekh gesen n'" *(Measures taken by the Ch'ing to implement its New Administration in Mongolia)*. Tüükhiin sudlal, vol. X (1974), pp.86-101.
Jansen, Marius B. The Japanese and Sun Yat-sen. Stanford, 1970.
Jügder, Ch. "Iz istorii obshchestvenno-politicheskoi i filosofskoi mysli v Mongolii v XIX veke," Proceedings of the 2nd Mongolist Congress, vol.

1, pp. 195-99.

Kahn, Harold L. Monarchy in the Emperor's Eyes. Cambridge, Mass., 1971.

Kalabashkin, A.I. "Nekotorye novye yavleniya v ekonomike Mongolii vtoroi poloviny XIX-nachala XX v.," Kratkie soobshcheniya Instituta narodov Azii, no. 76 (1965), pp. 182-90.

Kallinikov, A. "Aratskoe revolyutsionnoe dvizhenie v doavtonomnoi Mongolii," Revolyutsionnyi vostok, pt. 1: no. 5 (1934), pp. 137-56; pt. 2: no. 6 (1934), pp. 43-64.

-----. "U istokov mongol'skoi revolyutsii (Materialy k istorii revolyutsii 1921 g. i MNRP)," Khozyaistvo Mongolii, pt. 1: no. 2(9) (March-April 1928), pp. 59-82; pt. 2: no. 3(10) (1928), pp. 58-69.

-----. Natsional'no-revolyutsionnoe dvizhenie v Mongolii. Moscow-Leningrad, 1926.

-----. Revolyutsionnaya Mongoliya. Moscow, 1925.

-----. "Vooruzhennaya bor'ba za osvobozhdenie Mongolii (Materialy k istorii revolyutsii 1921 goda i MNRP)," Khozyaistvo Mongolii, no. 1(14) (January-February, 1929), pp. 86-100.

Kapitsa, M. Sovetsko-kitaiskie otnosheniya. Moscow, 1958.

-----. and V.I. Ivanenko. Druzhba, zavoevannaya v bor'be. Moscow, 1965.

Kapur, Harish. Soviet Russia and Asia, 1917-1927. Geneva, 1966.

Kara, Dzh. "Mongol ardyn khuv'sgalyn üyeiin khoyor mongol bichmel barimtyn tukhai," Proceedings of the 2nd Mongolist Congress, vol. 1, pp. 221-24.

Kartunova, A.I. and E.N. Shakhnazarova. "Komintern i mongol'skaya narodno-revolyutsionnaya partiya," Problemy dal'nego vostoka, no. 2 (1974), pp.174-85.

Kashintsev, D. "Chuiskii trakt v Mongoliyu," Novyi vostok, no. 8-9 (1925), pp. 133-43.

Kendall, Elizabeth. A Wayfarer in China. London, 1913.

Kennan, George F. Soviet-American Relations, 1917-1920. 2 vols., New York, 1967.

Kent, A.S. Old Tatar Trails. Shanghai, 1919.

Kheifets. A.N. Sovetskaya diplomatiya i narody vostoka, 1921-1927. Moscow, 1968.

-----. Sovetskaya Rossiya i sopredel'nye strany vostoka, 1918-1920. Moscow, 1964.

King, Frank H.H. Money and Monetary Policy in China,

1845-1895. Cambridge, Mass., 1965.
Kislov, A.N. Razgrom Ungerna. Moscow, 1964.
Knutson, Jeanne. Outer Mongolia: A Study of Soviet Colonialism, Hong Kong, 1959.
Knyazev, N. Legendarnyi baron. Harbin, 1942.
Kolarz, Walter. The Peoples of the Soviet Far East. New York, 1954.
Komintern i vostok. P.A. Ul'yanovskii, gen. ed., et al., Moscow, 1969.
Korostovetz, Iwan J. Von Cinggis Khan zur Sowjetrepublik. Berlin, 1926.
Kotlyarevskii, S. "K voprosu o zheleznodorozhnom stroitel'stve v Mongolii," Novyi vostok, no. 2 (1922), pp. 429-33.
Kotvich, V. Kratkii obzor istorii sovremennago politicheskago polozheniya Mongolii. St. Petersburg, 1914.
Kuang Lu, et al. Meng-ku yen-chiu *(Studies on Mongolia)*, Taipei, 1968.
Kungurov, G., and I. Sorokovikov. Aratskaya Revolyutsiya. Irkutsk, 1957.
Kurts, B. "Problemy vostochnoi torgovli SSSR," Novyi vostok, no. 10-11 (1926), pp. 138-51.
Kushelev, Yu. Mongoliya i mongol'skii vopros. St. Petersburg, 1912.
Larson, Frans. Larson, Duke of Mongolia. Boston, 1930.
Lattimore, Owen. High Tartary, Boston, 1930.
-----. The Mongols of Manchuria, New York, 1934.
-----. Mongol Journeys. London, 1941.
-----. Nationalism and Revolution in Mongolia. Leiden, 1955.
-----. Nomads and Commissars. New York, 1962.
-----. "Prince, Priest, and Herdsman in Mongolia," Pacific Affairs, vol. 8,1 (March 1935), pp.35-47.
-----. "Religion and Revolution in Mongolia," Modern Asian Studies, vol. 1,1 (1967), pp. 81-94.
-----. Studies in Frontier History. London, 1962.
Lazarev, K.I. "Tri poseshcheniya Mongolii," Narody brat'ya, pp. 45-50.
Lazitch, Branko, and Milorad M. Drachkovitch. Lenin and the Comintern. 2 vols., Stanford, 1972.
Lee, Robert H.G. The Manchurian Frontier in Ch'ing History. Cambridge, Mass., 1970.
Lenin, V.I. Polnoe sobranie sochinenii, 55 vols., 5th ed., Moscow, 1960-65.

Leong, Sow-theng. Sino-Soviet Diplomatic Relations, 1917-1926. Honolulu, 1976.

Li Chien-min. "Yen Hui-ch'ing yü t'ing-chih chiu-O shih-ling tai-yü" *(Yen Hui-ch'ing and the suspension of diplomatic recognition of Tsarist diplomats in China)*, Chung-yang yen-chiu yuan, Chin-tai shih yen-chiu so chi-k'an, vol. 6 (June 1977), pp. 123-44.

Li Chien-nung. The Political History of China, 1840-1928. J. Ingalls and S.Y. Teng, trans, Princeton, 1956.

Li Yü-shu. Wai-meng cheng-chiao chih-tu k'ao. *(The political and religious system of Outer Mongolia)*. Taipei, 1962.

-----.Wai Meng-ku ch'e-chih wen-t'i *(On the question of the abolition of Outer Mongolian autonomy)*. Taipei, 1961.

Ligüü, B. "Mongol-Orosyn soelyn khariltsaa" *(Mongolian-Russian cultural relations in the 19th century)*, Shinjlekh ukhaan akademiin medee, no. 1 (1971), pp. 5-15.

Lin Wei-kang. "O-Meng chiao-she shih-mo" *(A complete history of Russo-Mongolian negotiations)*, in Wu Hsiang-hsiang, Min-kuo ching-shih wen-pien, 1914, repr. Taipei, 1962.

Liu Hsu-chuan, ed. Meng-ku shih-liao hui-pien *(Collected historical sources for Mongolia)*. Taipei, 1976.

Liu Shou-lin. Hsin-hai i-hou shih-ch'i nien chih-kuan nien-piao *(Offices of the Republican government and their occupants, 1912-1928. Chronological tables)*. Peking, 1966.

Lobanov-Rostovsky, A. Russia and Asia. New York, 1933, repr. Ann Arbor, 1965.

Luvsandorj, P. BNMAU-yn dotood zakh zeeliin assudal *(The question of the internal market of the MPR)*. Ulan Bator, 1970.

L'vov, A.K. "Sovremennyi Uryankhai," Novyi vostok, no. 6 (1924), pp. 161-72.

Ma Ho-t'ien. Chinese Agent in Mongolia. John De Francis, trans., Baltimore, 1949.

MacMurray, John V.A., comp. Treaties and Agreements With and Concerning China, 1894-1919. 2 vols., New York, 1921.

Maiskii, Ivan. "Mongoliya," Novyi vostok, no. 1 (1922), pp. 154-83.

-----. Mongoliya nakanune revolyutsii, 2nd. ed., Moscow, 1959.

Malozemoff, Andrew. *Russian Far Eastern Policy, 1881-1904*. Berkeley, 1958.

Mancall, Mark. "The Ch'ing Tribute System: An Interpretative Essay," in Fairbank, *The Chinese World Order*, pp. 63-89.

-----. *Russia and China. Their Diplomatic Relations to 1728*. Cambridge, Mass., 1971.

Masato, Matsui. "The Russo-Japanese Agreement of 1907: Its Causes and the Progress of Negotiations," *Modern Asian Studies*, vol. 6,1 (1972), pp. 33-48.

McCormack, Gavan. *Chang Tso-lin in Northeast China, 1911-1928*. Stanford, 1977.

Mehra, Parshotam. "Mongol-Tibetan Treaty of January 11, 1913," *Journal of Asian History*, vol. 3,1 (1969), pp. 1-22.

Meijer, Jan M, ed. *The Trotsky Papers, 1917-1922*. 2 vols., The Hague, 1971.

Meng Ssu-ming. *The Tsungli Yamen*. Cambridge, Mass., 1962.

*Mezhdunarodnye otnosheniya na dal'nem vostoke*. 2 vols., Moscow, 1973.

Michael, Franz. *The Origin of Manchu Rule in China*. Baltimore, 1942.

Mirovitskaya, R.A. *Dvizhenie v Kitae za priznanie sovetskoi Rossii (1920-1924)*. Moscow, 1962.

*Mongol ardyn armiin 50 jil* (50 years of the Mongolian people's army). Ulan Bator, 1971.

*Mongol ardyn juramt tsergiin durdatgaluud* (Memoirs of the Mongolian people's partisans). L. Dügersüren and G. Tserendorj, eds., Ulan Bator, 1969.

*Mongol ardyn khuv'sgalt namyn negdügeer ikh khural (Undsen barimt bichgüüd)* (First congress of the MPRP, basic sources). Ulan Bator, 1971.

*Mongol ardyn khuv'sgalt namyn tüükhend kholbogdokh barimt bichgüüd* (Documents on the history of the MPRP). 3 vols., Ulan Bator, 1966-70.

*Mongol ardyn namyn guravdugaar ikh khural* (The third congress of the MPRP, 1924). Ulan Bator, 1966.

*Mongolia, Yesterday and Today*. Tientsin, n.d.

*Mongolyn sonin bichig* (News of Mongolia). No. 151 (July 11/24, 1915), and no. 135 (March 5/18, 1915), repr. by The Mongolia Society, Bloomington, 1968.

*Mongol'skaya Narodnaya Respublika*. Moscow, 1971.

Morley, James W. *The Japanese Thrust into Siberia, 1918*. New York, 1957.

Moses, Larry W. "Inner Asia in International Relations: The Role of Mongolia in Russo-Chinese Relations," The Mongolia Society Bulletin, vol. XI,2 (Fall 1971), pp. 55-75.

-----. "Revolutionary Mongolia Chooses a Faith: Lamaism or Leninism," Ph.D. Thesis, Indiana University, 1972.

Moskovskaya torgovaya ekspeditsiya v Mongoliyu. Moscow, 1912.

Murphy, George G.S. Soviet Mongolia. Berkeley, 1966.

Narimanov, N. "Lenin i vostok," Novyi vostok, no. 5 (1924), pp. 9-13.

Narody brat'ya. S.M. Budennyi, ed., Moscow, 1965.

Nasanbaljir, Ts. "Jibzandamba khutagtyn san" *(The treasury of the Jebtsundamba Khutukhtu)*, Tüükhiin sudlal, vol. VIII,22 (1970), pp. 143-53.

-----, comp. Revolyutsionnye meropriyatiya narodnogo pravitel'stva Mongolii v 1921-1924 gg. Moscow, 1960.

Nathan, Andrew J. Peking Politics, 1918-1923. London, 1976.

Natsagdorj, Sh. Ar Mongold garsan ardyn khödölgöön *(The people's movement in Outer Mongolia during the Ch'ing)*. Ulan Bator, 1956.

-----. Manjiin erkhsheeld baisan üyeiin Khalkhyn khurangui tüükh *(A brief history of Khalkha during the Ch'ing)*. Ulan Bator, 1963.

Navaannamjil, G. Övgön bicheechiin ügüülel *(Memoirs of an old clerk)*. Ulan Bator, 1956.

Norton, Henry K. The Far Eastern Republic of Siberia. London, 1923.

Obruchev, V.V. "Bol'she vnimaniya chuiskomu traktu," Novyi vostok, no. 8-9 (1925), pp. 125-32.

-----. Ot Kyakhty do Kul'dzhi. 2nd. ed., Moscow, 1950.

Ocherki istorii mongol'skoi narodno-revolyutsionnoi partii. Trans. from the Mongolian, Moscow, 1971.

Oglaev, Yu. O., ed. S internatsional'noi missiei. Elista, 1970.

Proceedings of the 2nd Mongolist Conference. 2 vols., Ulan Bator, 1972-73.

"On toollyn khelkhee (1912-1930)" *(A Mongolian lunar-solar calendar)*, Tüükhiin sudlal, vol. VII,1-4 (1968), pp. 213-35.

Oni vstrechalis' s Sukhe-Batorom. R.F. Tugutov, ed., Ulan-Ude, 1967.

Onon, Urgunge, trans. Mongolian Heroes of the Twentieth Century. New York, 1976.
Ossendowski, Ferdinand. Beasts, Men and Gods. New York, 1922.
-----. "With Baron Ungern at Urga," Asia, vol. XXII (August 1922), pp. 614-18.
Otter-Barry, R.B. "Mongolia. Its Economic and Political Aspect," Journal of the Royal Central Asian Society, vol. 1,3 (April 1, 1914), pp. 3-19.
Outer Mongolia. Treaties and Agreements. Washington D.C., 1921.
Pai Mei-ch'u. Wai Meng-ku shih-mo chi-yao *(A concise history of Outer Mongolia)*. Peiping, 1929.
Parlett, Sir Harold. A Brief Account of Diplomatic Events in Manchuria. London, 1929.
Pasvolsky, Leo. Russia in the Far East. New York, 1922.
Pavlovich, M. "Lenin i narody vostoka," Novyi vostok, no. 5 (1924), pp. 3-8.
Pavlovsky, Michel N. Chinese-Russian Relations. New York, 1949.
Penskii, N. "Ekonomicheskie vzaimootnosheniya SSSR s Mongoliei," Novyi vostok, no. 10-11 (1926), pp. 163-72.
Perry-Ayscough, H.C.C., and R.B. Otter-Barry. With the Russians in Mongolia. London, 1914.
Persits, M.A. Dal'nevostochnaya respublika i Kitai. Moscow, 1962.
-----. "Vostochnye internatsionalisty v Rossii i nekotorye voprosy natsional'no-osvoboditel'nogo dvizheniya (1918-yul' 1920)," Komintern i vostok, pp. 52-109.
Petech, L. China and Tibet in the Early 18th Century. Leiden, 1950.
Phillips, G.D.R. Russia, Japan, and Mongolia. London, 1942.
Pi Kuei-fang. Wai-meng chiao-she shih-mo chi *(A complete record of Outer Mongolian negotiations)*. Shanghai, 1928, repr. Taipei, 1968.
Piassetsky, P. Russian Travellers in Mongolia and China. 2 vols., London, 1884.
Pien-chiang lun-wen chi *(Collected articles on the frontier)*. 2 vols., Taipei, 1964.
P-ii (Pestovskii), B.A. Sovremennaya Mongoliya. Petrograd, 1915.
Pipes, Richard E. "Domestic Politics and Foreign

Affairs," in Ivo. J. Lederer, ed. Russian Foreign Policy, New Haven and London, 1962, pp. 145-69.
Pollard, Robert T. China's Foreign Relations, 1917-1931. New York, 1933.
Popov, A. "Tsarskaya Rossiya i Mongoliya v 1913-1914 gg.," Krasnyi arkhiv, vol. 6(37) (1927), pp. 3-68.
Poppe, N.N. "Mongol'skaya Narodnaya Respublika," Vestnik Instituta po izucheniyu istorii i kultury SSSR, no. 4(11) (1954), pp. 7-23.
Pozdneyev, A.M. Mongolia and the Mongols. 2 vols., Bloomington, 1971-77.
-----. Ocherki byta buddiiskikh monastyrei i buddiiskago dukhovenstva v Mongolii. St.Petersburg, 1887.
Przheval'skii, N.M. Mongoliya i strana tangutov. Repr. Moscow, 1946.
Price, Don G. Russia and the Roots of the Chinese Revolution, 1896-1911. Cambridge, Mass., 1974.
Price, M. Philips. Siberia. London, 1914.
Puntsagnorov, Ts. Mongolyn avtonomit üyeiin tüükh, 1911-1919 *(History of the Mongolian autonomous period, 1911-1919)*. Ulan Bator, 1955.
Pürev, O. "D. Sükhbaataryn üil am'drald kholbogdoltoi dursgalt gazruud" *(Places connected with the life of D. Sükhbaatar)*, MAKhN-yn tüükhiin asuudal, no. 8, 1973, pp. 113-37.
Pye, Lucien W. Warlord Politics. London, 1971.
Quested, R.K.K. The Expansion of Russia in East Asia, 1857-1860. Kuala Lumpur, 1968.
Rahul, R. "The Role of Lamas in Central Asian Politics," Central Asiatic Journal, vol. XII (1968-69), pp. 209-27.
Rasidondug, Sh., trans. Petitions of Grievances Submitted by the People (18th-beginning of 20th Century). Wiesbaden, 1975.
Rhoads, Edward J. China's Republican Revolution. Cambridge, Mass., 1975.
Richardson, H.E. A Short History of Tibet. New York, 1962.
Rinchen, B. Üüriin tuyaa *(The dawn's ray)*. Ulan Bator, 1971,
Rish, A. "Mongoliya po strazhe svoei nezavisimosti," Tikhii okean, no. 4(6) (1935), pp. 98-112.
Rokossovskii, K.K. "My vsegda vmeste," Narody brat'ya, pp. 5-11.
Rossabi, Morris. China and Inner Asia,from 1368 to

*the Present Day*. London, 1975.

Rupen, Robert. "The Buryat Intelligentsia," *Far Eastern Quarterly*, vol. 15,3 (May 1956), pp.383-98.

-----. "Mongolian Nationalism," *Journal of the Royal Central Asian Society*, pt. 1: vol. 45,2 (April 1958), pp. 157-78; pt. 2: vol. 45,3 (October 1958), pp. 245-68.

-----. *Mongols of the Twentieth Century*. 2 vols., Bloomington, 1964.

-----. "Outer Mongolian Nationalism, 1900-1919," Ph.D. Thesis, University of Washington, 1954.

*Russko-kitaiskie otnosheniya v XVII veke*. N.F. Demidova and V.S. Myasnikov, comps., 2 vols., Moscow, 1969-72.

Sagaster, Klaus. "Herrschaftsideologie und Friedensgedanke bei den Mongolen," *Central Asiatic Journal*, vol. XVII,2-4 (1973), pp. 223-42.

Salomon, Hilel. "The Anfu Clique and China's Abrogation of Outer Mongolian Autonomy," *The Mongolia Society Bulletin*, vol. X,1 (Spring 1971), pp. 67-86.

-----. "China's Policy Toward Outer Mongolia, 1912-1920," Ph.D. Thesis, Columbia University, 1969.

-----. "Sino-Mongolian 'Cooperation' in Urianghai, 1919," *The Mongolia Society Bulletin*, vol. X,2 (Fall 1971), pp. 42-51.

Sandag, Sh. "Avtonomit yum uu, tusgaar togtnol yum uu?" *(Autonomy or independence)*, *Shinjlekh ukhaan akademiin medee*, no. 1 (1971), pp. 19-24.

-----. *Mongolyn uls töriin gadaad khariltsaa* *(The foreign relations of Mongolia, 1850-1919)*. Ulan Bator, 1971.

-----. "Politicheskoe i ekonomicheskoe polozhenie vneshnei Mongolii v kontse XIX-nachale XX v.," *Mongol'skii sbornik*, Moscow, 1959, pp. 126-38.

Sanjdorj, M. *Khalkhad Khyatadyn möngö khüülegch khudaldaa nevterech khögjsön n' (XVIII zuun)* *(The penetration of Chinese usurious capital into Mongolia in the 18th century)*. Ulan Bator, 1963.

-----. "Olnoo örgögdsön arvan negdügeer ond gazraas irsen ba medüülen yavuulan tushaasan bichgüüdiin ödriin temdgiin tukhai" *(The diary of documents sent and received by the Mongolian revolutionary government in 1921)*. *Tüükhiin sudlal*, vol. 9,1-12 (1971), pp. 127-34.

Savvin, V.P. Vzaimootnosheniya tsarskoi Rossii i SSSR s Kitaem. Moscow-Leningrad, 1930.

Sbornik diplomaticheskikh dokumentov po mongol'skomu voprosu (23 avgusta 1912 g.-2 noyabrya 1913 g.). St. Petersburg, 1914.

Schapiro, Leonard. The Communist Party of the Soviet Union. 2nd. ed., New York, 1971.

Schrecker, John E. Imperialism and Chinese Nationalism. Cambridge, Mass., 1971.

Schwartz, Benjamin. Chinese Communism and the Rise of Mao. 3rd. ed., Cambridge, Mass., 1958.

Schwartz, Harry. Tsars, Mandarins and Commissars. New York, 1964.

Seifullin, Kh.M. K istorii inostrannoi voennoi interventsii i grazhdanskoi voiny v Tuve (1918-1922 gg.). Kyzyl, 1956.

Serebrennikov, I.I. Velikii otkhod. Harbin, 1923.

Serruys, Henry. "Additional Note on the Origin of Lamaism in Mongolia," Oriens Extremus, vol. 13, (December 1966), pp. 165-73.

-----. "Early Lamaism in Mongolia," Oriens Extremus, vol. 10,2 (October 1963), pp. 181-216.

Shastina, N.P. Russko-mongol'skie posol'skie otnosheniya XVII v. Moscow 1958.

-----. Shara tudzhi. Mongol'skaya letopis XVII veka. Moscow and Leningrad, 1957.

Shereshevskii, B.M. Razgrom semenovshchiny. Novosibirsk, 1966.

-----. Zabaikal'e v period dal'nevostochnoi respubliki, 1920-1922. Chita, 1920.

Sheridan, James E. China in Disintegration. New York, 1975.

-----. Chinese Warlord. The Career of Feng Yü-hsiang. Stanford, 1966.

Shirendev (Shirendyb), B. Istoriya mongol'skoi narodnoi revolyutsii 1921 goda. Moscow, 1971.

-----. Khicheengüi said Tserendorj (1868-1928). Ulan Bator, 1965.

-----. Mongoliya na rubezhe XIX-XX vekov. Ulan Bator, 1963.

-----. Narodnaya revolyutsiya v Mongoliya i obrazovanie MNR 1921-1924. Moscow, 1956.

-----. "1921 ony ardyn khuv'sgalyn ach kholbogdol, Mongolyn tüükhend tüümnii ezlekh bair" *(The significance of the 1921 people's revolution and its place in Mongolian history)*, Proceedings of the 2nd

Mongolist Congress, vol. 1, pp. 5-14.

Shoizhelov, Siren (Natsov). "Avtonomicheskoe dvizhenie Mongolii i tsarskaya Rossiya," Novyi vostok, no. 13-14 (1926), pp. 351-63.

-----. "Lamaizm v Mongolii," Novyi vostok, no. 25 (1926), pp. 378-81.

-----. "Mongoliya i tsarskaya Rossiya," Novyi vostok, no. 13-14 (1926), pp. 351-63.

-----. "Mongoliya i yaponskii imperializm," Novyi vostok, no. 8-9 (1925), pp. 199-205.

-----. "Natsional'no-osvoboditel'noe dvizhenie Mongolii," Novyi vostok, no. 6 (1924), pp. 245-54.

-----. Tuvinskaya narodnaya respublika. Moscow, 1930.

-----."Zapadnaya Mongoliya," Novyi vostok, no. 4 (1923), pp. 151-61.

Shumyatskii, B. and Ch. Partijin (Partisan?). Mongolyn khuv'sgalyn üüssen shaltgaan *(The origins of the Mongolian revolution)*. Ulan Bator, 1934.

Sibirskii revolyutsionnyi komitet (Sibrevkom). Novosibirsk, 1959.

S-kii (Speranskii), A.F. "Materialy k istorii interventsii," Novyi vostok, no. 2 (1922), pp. 591-603.

Slusser, Robert M. and Jan F. Triska. A Calendar of Soviet Treaties, 1917-1957. Stanford, 1959.

Slusser, Robert M. "The Role of the Foreign Ministry," in Ivo. J. Lederer, ed. Russian Foreign Policy, London, 1962, pp. 197-239.

Smirnov, I.Ya. "Boi 1921 goda," Narody brat'ya, pp. 31-35.

Sovetsko-kitaiskie otnosheniya, 1917-1957. Moscow, 1959.

Sovetsko-mongol'skie otnosheniya, 1921-1966. Moscow, 1966.

Sovetsko-mongol'skie otnosheniya, 1921-1974. Vol. 1, Moscow, 1975.

Strasser, Roland. The Mongolian Horde. London, 1930.

Strong, Anna Louise. China's Millions. 2 vols., New York, 1928.

Stulov, E. "Osnovnye voprosy politicheskoi istorii vneshnei Mongolii," Sovremennaya Mongoliya, no. 1(4) (1934), pp. 3-29.

D. Sükhbaatar. Barimt bichgiin tüüver (1915-1925) *(D. Sükhbaatar, documents 1915-25)*. B. Shirendev and

Sh. Natsagdorj, eds., Ulan Bator, 1971.
D. Sükhbaataryn tukhai durdatgaluud *(Reminiscences of D. Sükhbaatar)*. D. Gongor and Ts. Dolgorsüren, eds., Ulan Bator, 1965.
D. Sükhbaataryn üil am'draltai kholbogdokh barimt materialyn emkhetgel *(Collection of source material on the life of D. Sükhbaatar)*. G. Pürvee and Ts. Sonomdagva, eds., Ulan Bator, 1964.
Sun Fu-k'un. Meng-ku chien-shih hsin-pien *(A new history of Mongolia)*. Hong Kong, 1951.
Sürenkhorloo, Ts. "MAKhN-yn ankhny möriin khötölbör" *(The first program of the MPRP)*. Tüükhiin sudlal, vol. VI,4 (1966), pp. 5-15.
Svechnikov, A.P. Russkie v Mongolii. St. Petersburg, 1912.
-----. "Russkie v Mongolii," Vestnik Azii, no. 3 (January 1910), pp. 158-73.
Ta-ch'ing Hsuan-t'ung cheng-chi shih-lu *(Veritable records of the reign of Hsuan-t'ung, 1908-11)*. 2 vols., repr. Taipei, 1964.
Tan, Tennyson. The Political Status of Mongolia. Shanghai, 1932.
Tang, Peter S.H. Russian and Soviet Policy in Manchuria and Outer Mongolia, 1911-1931. Durham, N.C., 1959.
T'ao Chü-yin. Pei-yang chün-fa t'ung-chih shih-ch'i shih-huo *(History of the period of Pei-yang warlord rule)*. 6 vols., Peking, 1957-61.
-----. Tu-chün-t'uan chuan *(History of the warlords)*. Shanghai, 1948.
Teng, S.Y. The Taiping Rebellion and the Western Powers. Oxford, 1971.
Tomilin, V. Mongoliya i ee sovremennoe znachenie. Moscow, 1913.
Treadgold, Donald W. "Russia and the Far East," in Ivo. J. Lederer, ed., Russian Foreign Policy, London, 1962, pp. 531-74.
Tseden, B. Mongol-zövlöltiin nairamdal ba MAKhN (1920-1940) *(Mongolian-Soviet friendship and the MPRP, 1920-40)*. Ulan Bator, 1967.
-----. "D. Sükhbaatar bol Mongol, zövlöltiin evdershgüi nairamdlyn tölöö tsogtoi temtsegch" *(D. Sükhbaatar, fighter for unbreakable Mongolian-Soviet friendship)*. MAKhN-yn tüükhiin asuudal, no.8 (1973), pp. 52-77.
Tsedev, D. "Damdingiin Sükhbaatar bol tsergiin

garamgai janjin" *(D. Sükhbaatar, outstanding military commander)*. MAKhN-yn tüükhiin asuudal, no. 8 (1973), pp. 16-39.

-----. Ikh shav' *(Ikh Shav')*. Ulan Bator, 1964.

-----. "Mongol ardyn armiin tüükhiin zarim asuudal" *(Some questions of the history of the Mongolian people's army)*, Tüükhiin sudlal, vol. IX,1-12 (1971), pp. 147-60.

-----. "Mongol ardyn armiin daichin zamnalyn khuudasnaas" *(From the pages of the militant path of the Mongolian people's army)*, Tüükhiin sudlal, vol. IX, 13-25 (1973), pp. 35-51.

Tsedevsüren, D. "Khuv'sgalt ukhuulgyn khuudasnaas" *(From the pages of revolutionary agitation)*, Shinjlekh ukhaan am'dral, no. 4 (1970), pp. 10-13.

Tserendorj, G. Niislel khüreenii mongol khudaldaany toim *(The history of Mongolian commerce in Urga)*. Ulan Bator, 1961.

-----, and B. Tseden, eds. Mongol-zövlöltiin ard tümnii gan bat nairamdal *(The firm friendship of the Mongolian and Soviet peoples)*. Ulan Bator, 1967.

Tsibikov, B. Razgrom ungernovshchiny. Ulan-Ude, 1947.

"Tsogt khuv'sgalch, tuushtai internatsionalch" *(Fiery revolutionary, thorough-going internationalist)*, Namyn am'dral, no. 1 (1975), pp. 55-58.

Tucci,Giuseppe, and Walther Heissig. Die Religionen Tibets und der Mongolei. Stuttgart, 1970.

Tudev, L. Za polyarnoi zvezdoi. Moscow, 1968.

"Ulsyn arkhiv" *(State archives)*, Shinjlekh ukhaan am'dral, no. 4 (1970), p. 16.

Valliant, Robert B. "Japanese Involvement in Mongol Independence Movements, 1912-1919," The Mongolia Society Bulletin, vol. XI,2 (1972), pp. 1-32.

Veit, Veronika. Arad-un Qatan Bagatur Magsurjab (1878-1927). Bonn, 1974.

-----. "Sendegijn Zagd, Reminiscences of a Mongol Soldier," Zentralasiatische Studien, vol. 5 (1971), pp. 199-224.

"Velikii syn mongol'skogo naroda (K 80-letiyu so dnya rozhdeniya Sukhe-Batora)," Problemy dal'nego vostoka, no. 1 (1973), pp. 199-203.

"Vospominaniya o Mongolii," in D.D. Lubsanov, gen. ed., Issledovaniya i materialy po Mongolii, Ulan-Ude, 1974, pp. 217-29.

Weale, B.L. The Fight for the Republic of China.

London, 1918.

Weigh, Ken Shen. *Russo-Chinese Diplomacy, 1689-1924.* Shanghai, 1928.

Wen Kung-chih. *Tsui-chin sa-nien Chung-kuo chün-shih shih* (A military history of China for the last thirty years). 2 vols., Shanghai, 1930, repr. Taipei, 1962.

Whiting, Allen S. "Soviet Offer to China," *Far Eastern Quarterly*, vol. X,4 (1951), pp. 355-64.

-----. *Soviet Policies in China, 1917-1924.* Stanford, 1966.

Wright, Mary C., ed. *China in Revolution: The First Phase, 1900-1913.* New Haven and London, 1971.

Wu, Aitchen K. *China and the Soviet Union.* New York, 1950.

Wu Hsiang-hsiang. *O-ti ch'in-lueh Chung-kuo shih* (A history of Tsarist aggression against China). 3rd. ed., Taipei, 1959.

Yakhontoff, Victor. *Russia and the Soviet Union in the Far East.* New York, 1931.

Yano Jin'ichi. *Kindai Mōkoshi kenkyū* (Studies on the modern history of Mongolia). 6th. ed., Tokyo, 1940.

Yao Hsi-kuang. *Ch'ou-Meng ch'u-i* (Preliminary remarks on planning for Mongolia). 1908, repr. Taipei, 1965.

Yao Ming-hui. *Meng-ku chih* (Notes on Mongolia). Shanghai, 1907, repr. Taipei, 1967.

*50 Years of the MPR. Statistical Collection.* Ulan Bator, 1971.

Yü Yuan-an. *Nei Meng-ku li-shih kai-yao* (A survey of the history of Inner Mongolia). Shanghai, 1958.

Yudin, V.I. "U istokov mongol'skoi narodnoi revolyutsii," in A.T. Yakimov, ed., *Mongol'skii sbornik*, Moscow, 1959, pp. 105-25.

Yueh Ch'ien. *Chung-Su kuan-hsi shih-huo* (A history of Sino-Soviet relations). Hong Kong, 1955.

Zlatkin, I.Ya. *Istoriya dzhungarskogo khanstva (1635-1758).* Moscow, 1964.

-----. *MNR. Strana novoi demokratii.* Moscow, 1950.

-----. *Ocherki novoi i noveishei istorii Mongolii.* Moscow, 1957.

Zyryanov, I.I., ed., et al. *Pogranichnye voiska SSSR, 1918-1928.* Moscow, 1973.

www.ingramcontent.com/pod-product-compliance
Lightning Source LLC
LaVergne TN
LVHW040200080826
844660LV00001B/46

* 9 7 8 0 9 3 3 0 7 0 0 6 6 *